Tolerance Is a Wasteland

Tolerance Is a Wasteland

PALESTINE AND THE CULTURE
OF DENIAL

Saree Makdisi

UNIVERSITY OF CALIFORNIA PRESS

University of California Press
Oakland, California

© 2022 by Saree Makdisi

Library of Congress Cataloging-in-Publication Data

Names: Makdisi, Saree, author.
Title: Tolerance is a wasteland : Palestine and the culture of denial /
  Saree Makdisi.
Description: Oakland : University of California Press, [2022] | Includes
  bibliographical references and index.
Identifiers: LCCN 2021045239 (print) | LCCN 2021045240 (ebook) |
  ISBN 9780520346253 (hardback) | ISBN 9780520975798 (ebook)
Subjects: LCSH: Arab-Israeli conflict—1993- | Denial (Psychology) |
  Propaganda, Zionist. | Palestine—History.
Classification: LCC DS119.76 .M3435 2022 (print) | LCC DS119.76 (ebook) |
  DDC 956.05/3—dc23/eng/20211012
LC record available at https://lccn.loc.gov/2021045239
LC ebook record available at https://lccn.loc.gov/2021045240

31 30 29 28 27 26 25 24 23 22
10 9 8 7 6 5 4 3 2 1

For Fareed Armaly

Contents

Preface

On a hilltop on the western flank of Jerusalem stand the most sacred monuments to Zionism. Theodor Herzl, the founder of modern Zionism, is buried there. Nearby Memorial Park includes the graves of various Israeli prime ministers and presidents, including Golda Meir, Yitzhak Rabin, Shimon Peres, and Chaim Herzog. On the northern slope of the same hill is the national military cemetery. And on the western edge is Yad Vashem, the World Holocaust Remembrance Center: the world's definitive Holocaust museum and one of the compulsory stops for visiting foreign leaders, whose tours of the country generally culminate there. Taken as an ensemble, the hilltop complex expresses Israel's understanding of its identity, its claim to the land, the heroism of its leaders and soldiers, and the relationship of all these things to the calamity of the Holocaust. According to Israel's narrative of itself, never again letting such a tragedy unfold fundamentally requires a bold and pioneering state committed not only to its own self-defense but to the defense of the Jewish people at large. As expressed by the language of these commemorative sites, then, the values that Israel seeks to project—the values that it has worked assiduously to identify with itself—include loss, remembrance, anguish, community, moral obligation, tolerance, democracy, renewal, protection, rescue, redemption, vigilance, heroism, righteousness, and strength.

Visitors to Yad Vashem are encouraged to take advantage of the museum's outdoor areas with their views of the surrounding landscape, into which the institution's campus is carefully and deliberately integrated—a claim to the land itself being, after all, an integral part of the project the complex aims to represent. Directly across from and a bit below the museum—many of its outdoor areas directly overlook it—is a forest of recently planted pine trees running up the slope from the valley opposite the museum, atop which slope stand the ugly regimented concrete blocks of an Israeli hilltop town, Giv'at Shaul. Between and behind the trees, visitors to Yad Vashem can (if they wish) clearly distinguish older houses made of stone, mixed in with trees other than the homogenous rows of thickly planted pines constituting the new forest: carobs, almonds, the stumps of olive trees. These houses are the remains of the village of Deir Yassin: the site of one of the most terrible massacres of Palestinian civilians by Zionist militants that took place during the ethnic cleansing of Palestine in 1948 and, for Palestinians, a byword for the Nakba itself.[1]

Needless to say, no mention is made of Deir Yassin in the commemorative complex overlooking it. What remains of the village has carefully been made to disappear into the forest or among the concrete slabs of Giv'at Shaul. A few of its surviving houses have been renovated and integrated into the Kfar Shaul Mental Health Center (that the site of a massacre has been converted into a psychiatric hospital is indicative, perhaps, of a wider psycho-political malady). The crumbling graves of Deir Yassin's cemetery are buried under garbage and debris from the road running above it. The brochure describing Jerusalem Forest, planted on the town's lands by the Jewish National Fund shortly after the calamity of 1948, makes no mention of it; instead, it draws attention to the Nations Grove, located at the very heart of the forest planted on the site of the massacre, where, after visiting Yad Vashem, "heads of state from all over the world are invited to plant trees symbolizing peace, cooperation and brotherhood."[2]

Deir Yassin does not appear on any Israeli map. It has carefully and almost surgically been made to disappear. When, in 2006, Neta Shoshani, an Israeli arts student, tried to access the Israeli government archival holdings on Deir Yassin, she was barred from the more "sensitive" material, even though Israel's extraordinary fifty-year ban on accessing such materials (most countries allow thirty years for such archives) had expired eight years earlier, in 1998. Even without the missing archival evidence, Shoshani produced a documentary film about the massacre, featuring interviews with witnesses to the event and its aftermath. One of her interviewees was Professor Mordechai Gichon, a lieutenant colonel in the Israeli army reserves, who had been an intelligence officer in the Haganah—one of the army's paramilitary precursors—at the time of the massacre. "To me it looked a bit like a pogrom," said Gichon, who died in 2016. "If you're occupying an army position—it's not a pogrom, even if a hundred people are killed. But if you are coming into a civilian locale and dead people are scattered around in it—then it looks like a pogrom. When the Cossacks burst into Jewish neighborhoods, then that should have looked something like this."[3] After Shoshani's appeal, a secretive government ministerial committee retroactively extended the ban on the Deir Yassin archive to 2012. Following years of judicial procedures, Shoshani, joined by that time by the newspaper *Ha'aretz*, petitioned all the way to the Israeli High Court. After viewing the documentary evidence in private, the High Court judges extended the ban on public access to the archive indefinitely.[4]

The juxtaposition of Yad Vashem with Deir Yassin captures in a nutshell the argument that this book unfolds. Part of what is at stake here is the extent to which the affirmation of the one site is directly related to the denial and repression of the other. Palestinians, of course, commemorate Deir Yassin and other sites that have similarly been strategically folded and disappeared into a new Israeli landscape. But the memory, the traces, the archives, even the very *site* of Deir Yassin have been expunged and covered over materially, figuratively, legally, and discursively by the Israeli state. Deir Yassin has been removed from all records and maps. No signs lead the way to it; there are no commemorative markers or plaques or memorials dedicated to the victims of the massacre. It has been covered over in every imaginable way by a forest planted over its ruins, by the incorporation of what remains of its homes into a new Israeli town with an altogether different name. It and its traumas are literally nowhere to be seen. On the other hand, Yad Vashem, built immediately overlooking Deir Yassin in the years right after the massacre, is in a sense—far more than are the religious sites of Jerusalem—the spiritual home of Israel, capturing simultaneously its source of origin and the mission and destiny and promise to "never for-get" that it never tires of proclaiming to the world.

One site is covered over and denied; the other, essentially built right on top of it, is loudly affirmed; attention is endlessly called to it. Even visiting foreign leaders are conscripted into this dual narrative of simultaneous affirmation and denial—of denial *by* affirmation—when, after visiting Yad Vashem, they plant trees in the name of "peace" and "brotherhood" on the very site of the massacre at Deir Yassin, not to commemorate the victims of the massacre but to claim the space all the more completely for the commemoration of Yad Vashem. The memory of one site is quite literally suppressed by and through the affirmation of the other. One trauma, one set of memories, is to be revered; the other, to be expunged and covered over, partly by drawing so much attention to the former. Denial and affir-mation are not opposites, it turns out, but two sides of the same coin; and the loud affirmation of values such as "tolerance," "diversity," "vigilance," "redemption," and so on helps to enable the transaction of unspeakable—and unspoken-of—crimes.

Acknowledgments

This book could not have been written without the support, encouragement, criticism, and feedback of friends, colleagues, and family members.

Earlier and shorter versions of chapters 2 and 4 appeared as two articles in *Critical Inquiry:* "The Architecture of Erasure" appeared in vol. 36, no. 3 (Spring 2010); and "Apartheid / Apartheid / [<blank>]" appeared in vol. 44, no. 2 (Winter 2018). An earlier version of chapter 1, translated by Elias Khoury, was published in the Arabic edition of the *Journal of Palestine Studies* (Winter 2018).

I presented versions of the arguments elaborated in the following chapters at a number of venues over a period of years. I am indebted to audience questions and feedback and to the generosity of my hosts during talks I presented at the University of California, Los Angeles; the American University of Beirut; University of California, San Diego; Brown University; National Autonomous University of Mexico; Columbia University; the Wits Institute for Social and Economic Research at the University of Johannesburg; the District Six Museum in Cape Town; the University of Westminster; Trinity College; University of Sydney; and the University of Melbourne.

I am especially indebted to Patrick Wolfe, Ghassan Hage, David Theo Goldberg, David Lloyd, David Palumbo-Liu, Claire Moon, Tom Mitchell, Michael Rothberg, Melanie Jackson, Huda Zurayk, Aris Sarafianos, Cesare Casarino, Elias Khoury, Camille Mansour, Peter Beinart, Nikhil Pal Singh, Niels Hooper, and Stephen Sheehi, who read or heard either versions or parts of chapters, or the entire draft of this book and discussed it with me at length. Fady Joudah's poetical insights and the connection to Mahmoud Darwish mean more to the project than he knows. The access to the ravaged geography of Palestine made possible by Adel Manna and especially Nadera Shalhoub-Kevorkian, and their feedback on this project, was indispensable. In his inimitable way, Ackbar Abbas helped me figure out what my argument actually is. My parents and my brothers Ussama and Karim, as well as Christina, Maissa, and Samir either read or heard versions of these arguments over many years, and I am always grateful for their insight and support. My cousin Fareed Armaly was there from the very inception of this project to help me think it through; he patiently read and reread versions of the whole book as it came together over the years and offered his criticism and guidance every step of the way. It is to him that this book, such as it is, is dedicated.

Introduction

The question that this book aims to answer seems simple: how can a violent project of colonial dispossession and racial discrimination be repackaged—via a system of emotional investments, curated perceptions, and carefully staged pedagogical exercises—into something that can be imagined, felt, and profoundly believed in as though it were the exact opposite: the embodiment of ecological regeneration, multicultural tolerance, and democratic idealism? Israel was founded through a process of ethnic cleansing and the subsequent colonization of forcibly occupied land. It maintains and enforces not only a decades-old military occupation but also a stark system of ethnic and racial distinction and separation across all the territory it has seized since 1948. (I should note from the outset that throughout this book I use the terms "race," "racial group," "racism," and the like as they are understood in international law, notably the landmark 1965 International Convention for the Elimination of All Forms of Racial Discrimination [ICERD], which explicitly encompasses any distinction, exclusion, restriction, or preference based on national or ethnic origin, as well as color or descent, as a form of racial discrimination.)[1] It has a system of government characterized by what the instruments of international law specifically identify as apartheid. It systematically demolishes homes belonging to one racial group—Palestinian Arabs, whether they are citizens of the state or not—while equally systematically building homes for another racial group—Israeli Jews—in the service of a stark logic of racial exclusion. Similarly, it selectively restricts health care, access to education, access to water, freedom of movement, and other basic rights—including even access to sufficient nutrition—to one racial group while granting extraordinary privileges to the other. Even as I write this introduction in the spring of 2021, Israel is undertaking a massive COVID-19 vaccination program that has seen its citizens and Jewish settlers in the occupied territories inoculated against a deadly virus, while scrupulously going out of its way to avoid vaccinating the 4 million Palestinians living under its military occupation, for whose welfare it is accountable under international law.

Biomedical apartheid gets no more blatant than that. And yet, far from being condemned for this bleak racialization of medicine, Israel's COVID vaccination program has been celebrated around the world as an example of the state's pioneering spirit in science and technology, its determination to protect its population from all threats, its ability to mobilize public resources for the common good. This cascade of praise fits into a larger pattern. For decades, Israel has been embraced by the most liberal sectors of European and especially American society as the very embodiment of the progressive values of tolerance, plurality, inclusivity, and democracy—and, hence, as a project that can be passionately defended for its lofty ideals despite well-documented evidence to the contrary.

Essential to this miraculous act of political alchemy is a specific form of denial in which the Palestinian presence in and claim to Palestine (as well as Zionism's role in violently attempting to negate that claim) are not simply refused, covered up, or negated outright. Rather, they are occluded in such a way that that act of denial is itself denied by being expressed not in negative terms but through the positive affirmation of various wonderful virtues. Thus, for example, although very few people—and even fewer self-avowed liberals or leftists—would knowingly support and invest emotionally in a state that flaunts its methodical demolition of entire villages after their inhabitants had been driven in terror from their homes, many would happily support a state that plants trees, greens an apparently barren landscape, and loudly claims to make the desert bloom. What, then, if the removal of houses is both materially and figuratively covered up by—in fact, transacted through the process of—planting trees over their ruins in order to occlude the constitutive act of violence? A state that engages in— that announces itself as—a project of greening the landscape, making the desert bloom, inventing clever new forms of irrigation and so forth would (and has, and does still) attract all the necessary ethical, emotional, financial, and political support that it needs from liberal supporters around the world who would never for a moment contemplate endorsing a project of ethnic cleansing and home demolition as such. As the following chapters show, the emphasis of the positive value not only makes it possible to overlook the dark history occluded by the act of joyous affirmation, but also makes the dark history possible in the first place; it nourishes and sustains it over the years.

There is, of course, a strand of Zionism that does not traffic in such forms of denial.[2] It can be seen in, for instance, Yisrael Beiteinu ("Israel Is Our Home"), the tellingly named political party of Israel's former defense minister Avigdor Lieberman. Without beating around the bush, Lieberman—a former nightclub bouncer from Moldova—has bluntly called for the removal of the remaining Palestinians from within Israel and the completion of what the Israeli historian Benny Morris calls the "transfer" (i.e., the expulsion) of Palestinians from their land and homes that began, but did not end, in 1948.[3] "They have no place here," Lieberman said of the country's indigenous Palestinians who are citizens of the Israeli state; "they can take their bundles and get lost."[4] Lieberman's Zionism is unsophisticated and brutal: there is a problem that must be dealt with: the persistence of the Palestinians on their ancestral homeland, land that Zionists claim for an exclusively Jewish state. The only question is what is the best method for dealing with the problem. For Lieberman, expulsion is the obvious answer.

Here is how Benny Morris himself works through this conundrum, albeit at an earlier historical moment than the one addressed by Lieberman today: faced with the overwhelming Palestinian presence in Palestine in the early twentieth century, the Zionist movement, Morris says, could have pursued four paths toward the establishment of a Jewish state in a country that started the twentieth century with a population that was 93 percent non-Jewish. The first option, Morris says, was further Jewish immigration; but this would not have worked because the indigenous Palestinians would have gone on outnumbering the immigrant European Jews. A second option was apartheid—a Jewish minority lording it over a Palestinian majority; but this would have been bad for public relations with the West. A third option was partition; but there was no way to partition Palestine without leaving too many Palestinians behind in the territory of the putative Jewish state.[5] "The last, and let me say obvious and most logical solution to the Zionists' demographic problem lay the way of transfer," Morris concludes, using the euphemism that Zionists have used since the 1920s to signify the forcible expulsion of the Palestinians from their homeland. "You could create a homogeneous Jewish state, or at least a state with an overwhelming Jewish majority, by moving or transferring all or most of the Arabs out of its prospective territory. And this is in fact what happened in 1948."[6]

Morris is perfectly right, of course: a Jewish state could never have been created in Palestine without mass forcible expulsions, massacres, home demolitions, and so on. Which is why, as far as he is concerned, "there are circumstances in history that justify ethnic cleansing."[7] Fine: we can agree, we can disagree—but at least we know, in arguing with Benny Morris, that we are talking about an event that we all know to have taken place; the only question is whether what happened was right or wrong, justified or not. And, as I noted, a considerable strand of Zionist thought approaches the question of Palestine and the fate of the Palestinians from a similar standpoint. The early Zionist pioneer Vladimir Jabotinsky (the forefather of the Likud party) set the tone for this approach in his uncompromising 1923 essay "The Iron Wall," and the tradition continues to this day with people like Morris or the University of Haifa demographer Arnon Sofer, who argues, like Morris, that "a state with an overwhelming majority of Jews," which he supports, fundamentally requires the deployment of endless violence. Therefore, Sofer concludes, "we will have to kill and kill and kill. All day, every day." The "only thing that concerns me," he adds, "is how to ensure that the boys and men who are going to have to do the killing will be able to return home to their families and be normal human beings." But in the end the point of all this is not just killing for the sake of killing. "Unilateral separation doesn't guarantee 'peace,'" Sofer says; "it guarantees a Zionist-Jewish state with an overwhelming majority of

Jews."[8] Again, we can argue about whether this is right or wrong at a moral level, justified or not—but at least, in arguing with Sofer, as with Morris or Lieberman, we are all in agreement that this kind of violence is necessary if you support the creation and maintenance of an exclusively Jewish state in what has historically been (and still is) a culturally and religiously heterogeneous land; the only question is whether one supports or opposes the existence of such a state given these circumstances. Morris, Lieberman, and Sofer all do, and they explain why they do in perfectly rational terms: if mass killing and ethnic cleansing are what is required, then so be it. At least they are honest about it.

But it is difficult for most people to be quite so blunt, quite so strident, quite so uncompromisingly honest in their support for violence, mass murder, and ethnic cleansing essential to Israel's control over the Palestinians, as expressed so bleakly by Arnon Sofer. Most people who support Zionism and Israel—especially in the United States and Europe—are, I assume, decent people motivated by the best intentions and by what they believe to be a just cause. The tragedies of Jewish history and the immense loss of the Holocaust loom large in their minds. I have no doubt that the majority of them would be incapable of voicing—let alone actually consciously supporting—the monstrosities that a Sofer or a Morris has no hesitation in expressing. But, in order for it to be possible at all, their position is founded on the form of denial and repression that this book investigates. I am interested here in a form of denial very different from the one brilliantly elaborated by Stanley Cohen in *States of Denial*: not merely ignorance (readily facilitated in any case by the mainstream media in the United States and Europe); not merely the denial of Palestinian history, Palestinian dispossession, and Palestinian rights; but the denial that they have been denied in the first place, and the concomitant affirmation of a whole range of other values—including but limited to the values projected by the hilltop complex centered on Yad Vashem—that are designed to occlude not merely the Palestinian presence but the fact that it has already been occluded.[9]

In discovering this politico-emotional formation, in fact, we have arrived at a Zionism of a kind different from the one represented by Lieberman. This is the form of contemporary Zionism (still the dominant one in the United States and Europe) founded on the repression or denial of knowledge of the ethnic cleansing of Palestine in 1948. This is the Zionism that, in its more liberal formulations (that of Amos Oz, say), is even happy to talk about Israel relinquishing the territories occupied in 1967, as long as the Nakba, the fate of the refugees of 1948, and the status of Israel's second-class Palestinian citizens—that is, the constitutive racism of Israel as a state (which chapter 2 examines in detail)—are not brought into the discussion; as long as the "good Israel" of 1948 can be redeemed from the "bad Israel" of 1967.

The chapters that follow explore the mechanisms of affirmation and denial—affirmation *as* denial—that are essential to such a position. I explore a range of venues, from the haunted landscapes of the thickly planted forests covering over the ruins of hundreds of Palestinian villages forcibly depopulated in 1948 and subsequently reduced to rubble, to the theater of "pinkwashing," in which Israel presents itself to the world as a gay-friendly haven of cultural inclusion despite its long-standing repression of cultural minorities, its hardwired constitutional commitment to violently homophobic religious structures, and its increasingly explicit forms of racism. The centerpiece of the book is a reading of the site of the so-called Museum of Tolerance presently being built on top of the ruins of a Muslim cemetery in Jerusalem: a site that was methodically desecrated in order to clear space for the construction of a monument supposedly devoted—without a trace of irony—to "tolerance."

From a Palestinian perspective, it is all too tempting to see such efforts and projects as merely hypocritical: Israel loudly proclaims its commitment to afforestation, for example, but it meanwhile uproots and destroys hundreds of thousands of olive trees planted by Palestinian farmers and tended over the generations. (Israeli troops or settlers have uprooted an estimated 2.5 million trees just in the parts of Palestine occupied since 1967, a third of them olive trees, not to mention the obliteration of olive orchards and citrus groves in the territories occupied since 1948.[10]) What is at stake, however, is far more than hypocrisy. Hypocrisy, like lying, necessarily involves a kind of self-knowledge: I say *this*, but I knowingly do *that*.[11] That is not what is happening here. The *this* and the *that*—the affirmation and the denial—are simultaneously necessary to each other *and* split from each other in Zionist discourse and practice. Thus, someone who passionately emphasizes one side of the coin (the affirmative, positive value) can be totally oblivious to the presence and even the existence of the other side (the act of denial). And yet the act of denial simply could not take place without the affirmation of the positive value.

This is an act of denial so complete, so comprehensive, that it cannot recognize itself as an act of denial in the first place: it erases its own traces in the very process of being transacted. That is why it is not merely hypocrisy but something more interesting, more troubling, more problematic— and infinitely more difficult to challenge.[12] The hypocrite, called out for her hypocrisy, might well blush in shame. Someone engaging in this form of denial, however, will go to his grave denying that he ever denied, because of the specific structure of the form of denial he practices, which allows him not merely to see but to focus obsessively on the value he is upholding while remaining blissfully ignorant of the presence, the people, the history he is helping to stamp out and obliterate—not, in this specific form of Zionism, by invoking a hardened discourse of colonial superiority or rigid racial separation (to which other forms of Zionism resort), but, on the contrary, through the very affirmation of classic liberal values.[13]

This split between affirmation and denial stems in part from the rhetorical structure of Zionism itself, going back to its origins in late-nineteenth-century Europe. Edward Said pointed out more than four decades ago that there was from the beginning a structural bifurcation in the Zionist program. Zionism, Said argues, is a system simultaneously of accumulation (of power, land, and above all legitimacy) and of displacement (of other people, other ideas, other and prior forms of legitimacy).[14] While acquiring for itself a long unchallenged hegemony in the most liberal sectors of US and European society, "Zionism has hidden, or caused to disappear, the literal historical ground of its growth, its political cost to the native inhabitants of Palestine, and its militantly oppressive discrimination between Jews and non-Jews."[15] Zionism's ability to conceal its own ongoing history allows people who might vehemently oppose US or South African racism, for instance, to nevertheless support Zionist racial discrimination against non-Jews in Palestine without fully recognizing that that is what they are doing.[16] In the United States, this has produced the remarkable phenomenon of PEP people: those who are Progressive Except Palestine—the environmentally conscious vegan, for example, who can reconcile in herself outraged opposition to racial or gender discrimination and social and ecological violence in the United States, on the one hand, with passionate support for Israel, on the other. In the United Kingdom, the concealment produces phenomena like the contemporary Labour party, which leans left on most issues with the singular and glaring exception of the question of Palestine. "I support Zionism without qualification," declared Kier Starmer, the current leader of the party, during a leadership campaign in which the question of Zionism featured prominently.[17] I have personal friends on the left who in their younger days spent time on a kibbutz in Israel because that was the kind of thing young leftists did at a certain moment in Euro-American cultural history.

As Said noted long ago, such a contradiction is made possible by the bifurcation in Zionism. The Zionist program always had two sides: what it meant for Jews (as well as for non-Jewish Europeans and Americans anxious to atone for the violent history of Western anti-semitism up to and including the Holocaust), and what it meant for Palestinians. "One was a careful determination to implement Jewish self-betterment," Said points out. "About this, of course, the world heard a great deal. Great steps were taken in providing Jews with a new sense of identity, in defending and giving them rights as citizens, in reviving a national 'home' language. Yet," he continues, "the other, dialectically opposite component in Zionism, existing as its inferior where it was never seen (even though directly experienced by Palestinians), was an equally firm and intelligent boundary between benefits for Jews and none (later, punishment) for non-Jews in Palestine."[18] In Said's account, this bifurcation enabled a certain kind of blindness. The tragic history of the Jewish people in Europe—and, for that matter, the resurgence of certain forms of anti-semitism in the contemporary world—enable an emotional as much as a political investment in the Zionist project, which becomes a source of pride for what it has meant for Jews, the revival of Hebrew, and Israel's many achievements in science, technology, medicine, and so on. Said's point is that one can be completely on board with this side of Zionism without ever taking into account, or even being aware of, Zionism from the standpoint of its victims, to use his memorable phrase.

Said pushes this bifurcation in Zionism perhaps a bit too far, however. Although he refers to it as a dialectic, he is not really developing a dialectical argument. The two sides of his coin function separately from each other rather than depending on each other: there is Zionism for Jews over here, and Zionism for Palestinians over there. My argument is that these two aspects of Zionism are actively bound up with and need each other. At least through the first part of its existence and until the 2000s, the Zionist project in Palestine fundamentally depended on the support and sustenance of the most (otherwise) progressive and liberal sectors of US and European society, including Jewish communities that have historically been associated with progressive and liberal causes and that have, for example, deep affinities with the civil rights struggle in the United States. Indeed, even some of the most prominent Black intellectual giants— including W. E. B. Du Bois, Martin Luther King, and James Baldwin—at one time or another expressed their sympathy for the Zionist cause (Malcolm X was a notable exception). In the United States, in fact, support for Israel has historically been more of a Democratic than a Republican issue. Only in recent years have Republicans joined in enthusiastically, driven by a resurgence of right-wing populism, racism, and so-called Christian Zionism in the GOP heartland—very different values than those that drew liberals to the Zionist cause as dressed up by people like Amos Oz in the dreamy heyday of the 1960s and 1970s. A similar dynamic obtains in Britain with Labour support for Zionism (and indeed the recent party purge of Labour figures critical of Israeli policy, including Jeremy Corbyn, Ken Livingstone, and Ken Loach, only reinforces this alignment). In France, many of the leading intellectuals of the left, including Jean-Paul Sartre, Michel Foucault, and Jacques Derrida (not to mention the contemporary self-styled philosopher Bernard-Henri Lévy) were or have been sympathetic to Israel; Gilles Deleuze and Jean Genet were notable exceptions. There is simply no way that Zionism could have attracted and maintained the support of these left-leaning sectors of society without the forms of denial that this book aims to explore. And, in turn, there is no way that the Zionist project in Palestine could have sustained the level of damage it has inflicted on Palestinians—everything from ethnic cleansing to home demolition, torture, land expropriation, and outright bombardment—without European and American support in general, and the support of progressives and liberals in particular.

Yet it is very difficult, in a liberal Western society, and as a liberal Western subject, to knowingly—self-knowingly above all—endorse a contemporary project of ethnic cleansing. It is difficult in particular to construct an ethical sense of self, to sustain a sense of liberal identity, while simultaneously endorsing a project of ethnic cleansing. It is difficult to reconcile your strong commitment to democracy and civil rights with your support for a state that practices apartheid and negates civil rights, not to mention other political rights and even fundamental human rights. It is difficult to balance your vigilant support for the separation of church and state (especially if you benefit from such a separation in your own country) with your support for a state in which government and religion are as institutionally inseparable as they are in Iran or Saudi Arabia: states that you despise *precisely because* of their repressive conflation of religion and politics. It is difficult to coordinate your endorsement of civil marriage or married women's rights with your support for a state that has no institution of civil marriage and that officially empowers only the Orthodox rabbinate to transact matters of personal status for Jews, policies that severely restrict the rights of married women and in certain respects (such as divorce) binds them to the will of their husbands—even if there are unofficial workarounds for these matters. It is difficult to square your support for principles of inclusivity and tolerance with your support for a state founded on the premise of exclusion and intolerance.

But ignoring, looking aside, refusing to recognize: these are difficult to sustain on their own, and provide no basis for the construction of a liberal and ethical sense of self. What is needed in addition is a set of values to *affirm* in a positive sense. Or, better yet, a set of values to affirm, the very affirmation of which transacts denial, in such a way that the act of denial is doubly or even triply invisible: first because you deny it; second because your act of denial is so sweeping and comprehensive that it is itself denied (I call this the denial of denial, a notion to which I return in the chapters to follow); and finally because the act of affirming some other value is so hyperbolic, so loudly exaggerated, so theatrically overstated and overperformed that it completely occludes the act of denial that it simultaneously expresses.

Occlusion is a key notion here, and even the dictionary definition helps us think through what is at stake in the political sense of the word. Most simply, to occlude is to obstruct or close, to cover or hide; but, beyond those verbs, to occlude also encourages us to think of the ways in which something might be carefully placed in the way of something else, "to exclude or render obscure, as if by a blockage; to overshadow," as the Oxford English Dictionary explains the term.[19] Under the right circumstances, that which occludes can attract so much attention to itself that its performance of occlusion—let alone that which is occluded—is rendered invisible: the act of occlusion is itself occluded.

In this case, I am especially interested in acts of affirmation that occlude acts of denial. More specifically, I'm interested in acts of affirmation that, in the very process of being affirmed, also occlude an act of denial in which they participate, knowingly or otherwise. In this case the act of occlusion is so effective that it erases the very trace of denial even as it transacts it. "To occlude is an act that hides and conceals, creates blockage, and closes off," Ann Stoler argues; "that which occludes and that which is occluded have different sources, sites of intractability, forms of appearance, and temporal effects. They derive from geopolitical locations as much as they do from conceptual grammars that render different objects observable."[20] From a certain carefully managed geopolitical point of view, only *that which occludes* is there to be seen; *that which is occluded* disappears, together—and this is hugely significant—with the ability to recognize the act of occlusion itself as an *act* or a *process*: although it is carefully staged and even engineered, it is reified, naturalized, faded into the background, rendered permanent, unremarkable, and hence taken for granted as having always already been in place.

In this book I am interested in four particular moments of affirmation-denial—affirmation *as* denial—which I believe are fundamental to understanding not only the history and nature of Zionism's conflict with the Palestinians, but also the extent to which this conflict has endured *because* of the ways it has been nourished and sustained by the support of outside implicated subjects (to use Michael Rothberg's insightful term).[21] Indeed, the ongoing support of these implicated subjects is absolutely predicated on the maintenance of these (and other) acts of occlusion and denial, without which their support would be untenable for the reasons to which I have alluded.

The first chapter of this book explores the transformation of the landscape of Palestine in the aftermath of the ethnic cleansing of 1948. After the Zionist militias that would eventually coalesce into the Israeli army completed their expulsion of hundreds of thousands of Palestinians from Palestine, the terrain left behind was an eerie landscape of empty houses, very often intact and undamaged, complete with all the contents of Palestinian domestic life from the urbane (books, family photographs, silverware, furniture, paintings, clothes, mementos) to the humble and rustic. This landscape had to be remade in the image of the new Jewish state, and the first step (which actually took many years and remains incomplete, especially in and near the larger cities) was the demolition of Palestinian homes, mosques, churches, and cemeteries as well as the methodical extirpation of the cultivated landscape of citrus and olive groves and prickly pear cacti to which those homes and other spaces once corresponded. No sooner had Palestinian villages been demolished (bulldozed, dynamited, bombed from the air) than the agencies and auxiliaries of the new state—in particular the Jewish National Fund—started planting forests over their ruins. Unlike the demolition of family homes, which was done as quietly as possible, the project of tree planting over the ruins of these now unmentioned, disappeared, erased-from-all-maps villages was, and still is, carried out with much fanfare and under the banner of grand proclamations. People—particularly Jewish people—are invited to "plant a tree in Israel," to donate funds for afforestation, to make the desert bloom, and to visit ceremonial tree-planting sites where they can actively participate in this quite literally *wonderful* endeavor.

As though by magic, then, a project of ethnic cleansing has been transformed into one of family-centered tree planting, and by virtue of that transformation it has secured the support it needs from implicated subjects who would never knowingly lend their support to a process of mass eviction and home demolition, but *do* lend their support as long as it is disavowed and almost literally un-known, turned into something positive and affirmative, such as greening the landscape. The deliberate and systematically worked-through occlusion of the Palestinian presence in (and hence claim to) the land has thus itself been occluded by a transformative act of affirmation to which hyperbolic levels of acclaim and attention are drawn.

Who, after all, could possibly be against such an innocent exercise as the planting of trees? And who, for that matter, could be against democracy? Against, especially, what we are often told is "the only democracy in the Middle East?" What could possibly be wrong with the affirmation of the value of a "Jewish and democratic state?" That is the question addressed in the second chapter, which opens with a discussion of the often repeated mantra in support of a "Jewish and democratic state," which is frequently recited by liberal supporters of Israel in the United States as a justification for their support for that state. The repetition of the mantra—its obviously self-contradictory, even oxymoronic, status apparently invisible to its proponents (a state cannot be simultaneously for a particular group *and* for everyone)—occludes a far more complex politics of systematic racial segregation inside pre-1967 Israel as well as (even more starkly) the territories occupied in 1967. In fact, as the chapter shows, a point-by-point comparison with both international legal instruments (notably the UN's Convention on the Elimination of All Forms of Racial Discrimination as well as the Apartheid Convention, which builds on it) and with Apartheid-era South Africa shows that Israel is, in a clinical (not merely a rhetorical) sense, an apartheid state, as a series of recently published reports (by a UN agency, by the Israeli human rights organization B'tselem, and, most recently, by Human Rights Watch) confirms. Merely raising this claim in the United States *still* leads to outbursts of anger and outrage, however—and to recapitulations of the exculpatory mantra of the "Jewish and democratic state."

Here, then, we can see occlusion at work in a structure similar to that explored in chapter 1: the repeated invocation of the apparently magic phrase "Jewish and democratic state" occludes the harsh reality of an apartheid regime, so that Israel's status as an apartheid state is denied by affirming its status as a democracy. Again, affirmation and denial are two sides of the same coin. A form of fetishism in the psychoanalytic sense is also in play here. That is, the affirmation of the fetish, namely, the positive value (Jewish democracy), displaces and occludes not only the denial of those Palestinians expelled from their homes in 1948 and denied the right of return (i.e., the condition of possibility of the foundation of Israel as a Jewish state[22]), but also the civil and political rights of those Palestinians who survived the Nakba and are now second-class citizens of Israel, subject to an array of discriminatory laws in a profoundly racial state (i.e., the condition of possibility of maintaining Israel as a Jewish state). As the following chapters show, what is clear is that no self-identified liberal subject would knowingly endorse driving people of the "wrong" ethnicity from their homes, barring their return, stripping them of rights, penning them in open-air prisons like Gaza. Affirming the fetish of "democracy," reciting the mantra of the "Jewish and democratic state," allows liberal supporters of Israel to occlude their endorsement of those historical and ongoing material circumstances, to dis-regard them while focusing their emotional attention on the fetish, to persist in the misreading of a situation of violent dispossession. This is probably the most extreme version of what David Theo Goldberg has identified as "postracialism," a wiping away of "the very conditions out of which guilt could arise." In such a situation there is no guilt, Goldberg adds, "because there is nothing recognizable to be guilty about, least of all the guilt itself."[23] Far from feeling guilty, indeed, Israel's liberal overseas supporters are proud of their support for that state precisely as an affirmation of their liberal principles.

Chapter 3 explores the sudden proliferation of new forms of denial following the same pattern I have already identified (that is, denial through affirmation of a positive value). This renewed activity took place in the context of a global deterioration of Israel's perceived status around the world, stemming from its ever more ruthless forms of punishment of Palestinians (notably the widely televised bombardments of Gaza in 2008–9 and 2014), as well as its embrace of an ever more explicit language of colonial racism. Even as more attention was being drawn to its repression of Palestinian rights, Israel suddenly emerged as a global icon of gay rights. Almost literally out of the blue, Israel was being marketed as a gay vacation destination and Tel Aviv as a hub of global gay culture rivaling Berlin and San Francisco, as a site for heavily promoted gay porn shoots, and (inevitably) as the obvious location for the Eurovision Song Contest, a Europhilic celebration of camp. Even the Israeli army was rebranded as a stalwart champion of gay rights. Although there has long been a gay scene in Tel Aviv, there was, of course, nothing organic about its sudden rise to prominence on a global scale. What queer Palestinian and other international activists quickly identified as a project of "pinkwashing" was a carefully engineered development in public relations undertaken explicitly in order to provide cover for Israel's ongoing suppression of Palestinian rights. How, after all, could a country so open and tolerant of gay rights possibly be repressive? That was one message to be propagated; the other was that Palestinian culture is itself repressive and homophobic, and hence undeserving of global solidarity, especially from those invested in discourses of rights, equality, diversity, inclusivity, and so on. What is most interesting about Israel's pinkwashing experiment, however, is that it amounted to a nearly total failure. And what that failure revealed is that the political logic which this book explores is not nearly as stable as it once was.

The final chapter, which forms both the origin and the culmination of this book, centers on an almost unbelievable moment in the history of specifically American Zionist emotional and political investment in Israel. In 2004, the Museum of Tolerance in Los Angeles—an institution deeply involved in the transformative repackaging, for an American audience, of Zionist settler colonialism as a humanitarian endeavor, a "natural" response to the calamity of the Holocaust[24]—announced that it was planning to open a branch in Jerusalem. The museum hired the noted LA-based architect Frank Gehry to design its Jerusalem building, and developed interior designs for the display spaces, which, despite the museum's name, were to have nothing to do with "tolerance" in the ordinary English-language understanding of that term, but rather with the history of Zionism. The edifice, in other words, was actually a museum of Zionism packaged as a museum of "tolerance"; and, as the chapter shows, all the obsessive and narcissistic forms of self-regard at the expense of the other that I touch on in this introduction were articulated in the plans for the display spaces.

But then everything took a strange twist, in which I myself played a minor role. For it turned out that the museum was being built on the site of the largest and most important Muslim cemetery in Jerusalem, in active use until the mid-twentieth century. I personally know people with family members buried there. (I say "it turned out," by the way, but of course Muslim authorities and institutions had been protesting this all along—and were utterly ignored both by Israeli municipal officials and by the Museum of Tolerance in LA). When the building's planners found out that workers were indeed excavating bones and other human remains, they surrounded the site with hoarding, hired only Jewish excavators, and pressed ahead. Inevitably, despite all the attempts at a cover-up, the scandal blew into the open: "Israel Plans to Build 'Museum of Tolerance' on Muslim Graves," read the headline in the *Independent*.[25] They were building a "museum of tolerance" on another people's graveyard, from which human remains were hastily being disinterred and unceremoniously discarded in unmarked cardboard boxes!

It is extraordinary, is it not? But the most extraordinary thing yet is that the Museum of Tolerance adamantly refused—and still refuses—to see what is wrong. It insisted on pushing ahead with the project. This is where I played my own minor role in this story. I published an essay about this grotesque project in the journal *Critical Inquiry*, and the editors invited Frank Gehry himself to reply to my article. That he did, very angrily, and he defended his project while denouncing me (he also got the museum directors and their Israeli advisors to reply to me as well, even more unpleasantly). This was in the spring of 2010. Just as our debate was about to be published by the journal, Gehry suddenly announced that he was withdrawing his services from the museum project. Over that summer, I received repeated messages from his office asking to schedule a meeting. When I finally replied (I really had no interest in meeting him, assuming that our encounter in person would be as unpleasant as it had been in print, if not more so), we arranged a meeting for September 2010. In that meeting, he explained to me that my article had helped clarify the situation and had helped lead to his withdrawal from the project.

My role in this sordid episode, and even Gehry's role, is not, however, the focus of chapter 4, which is instead interested in the question of what it means that a museum of "tolerance" could be forcibly implanted on the hastily excavated remains of a Muslim cemetery in such a way that, despite all the negative publicity and protests (by some Israeli Jews as well as Palestinian Muslims, incidentally), those responsible—and their backers, not coincidentally heavily connected to Los Angeles and to Hollywood in particular (George Clooney among others has ties to the institution)—simply could not see what was wrong with their endeavor. In fact, they have persisted with the project ever since, having hired an Israeli architecture firm after Gehry's withdrawal, and yet another firm after they had a falling out with the first one (apparently over financial arrangements). The chapter on the museum works through all these narrative layers and offers a meditation on the larger symbolic and political meanings of the project, tying it to the broader patterns of denial with which this book is ultimately concerned.

The museum episode offers an encapsulated version of the overall argument of the book. In this case, the Palestinian claim to a cemetery space is being denied; that denial is then occluded first by the attempt to literally cover it up and then by other layers of denial, but mostly by the hyperbolic and absurdly theatricalized investment in a discourse of "tolerance." For Zionism, we are told, is a mission of tolerance; to question or oppose it is therefore to engage in "intolerance." The chapter argues that this militarized deployment of a discourse of "tolerance" expresses a broader set of patterns of affirming positive values (in this case "tolerance," in the previous chapters greener landscapes or "democracy" etc.) as a means of occluding not only the denial of the Palestinian presence in and claim to Palestine, but also that occlusion, the denial of the denial: the affirmation of a positive value as an act of denial that renders itself illegible as such to its affirmers. Only a profound form of denial could enable the placement of a monument to Zionism-as-tolerance on an ethnically cleansed graveyard. After all, not many people would knowingly endorse the desecration of a cemetery; but who would not want to support tolerance? This monument to "tolerance," however, occupies a site of destruction and usurpation, a site of the erasure of memory and the effacement of belonging, a site of racial violence and catastrophic injustice. "Tolerance," it turns out—this kind of tolerance, at least—is nothing but a wasteland.

1 Sustainability

My absence is entirely trees.

— Mahmoud Darwish

So, having grown up in the Bay Area, I fondly remember those Jewish national fund boxes that we would use to collect donations to plant trees for Israel. Years later when I visited Israel for the first time, I saw the fruits of that effort and the Israeli ingenuity that has truly made a desert bloom.

— Kamala Harris

When Said, the narrator of Emile Habibi's darkly satirical 1972 novel, *The Pessoptimist*—which is set during and immediately after the ethnic cleansing of Palestine in 1948—returns from over the border in Lebanon, he takes shelter in the courtyard of the Jazzar mosque in Acre and is besieged by people asking him if he happened to have come across people from their villages, which were occupied and destroyed by Zionist militias, their people driven from their homes:

> "We are from Kwaykat, which was demolished and its people scattered; did you meet anyone from Kwaykat?"
> I found the repetition of the "k" in Kwaykat amusing. But my suppressed laughter was thankfully preempted by the voice of a woman from behind the sundial: "The girl is not sleeping, o Shukriyya; she's dead, o Shukriyya."
> A stifled cry came to our ears, and everyone caught their breath until the cry died away. Then they returned to their questions. I said "no."
> "I am from Manshiyya. Not a stone remains standing there, other than the tombstones. Do you know anyone from Manshiyya?"
> "No."

"We here are from Amqa. They obliterated it completely. Do you know anyone from Amqa?"

"No."

"We here are from Berweh. They threw us out and demolished it. Do you know anyone from Berweh?"

"Actually, I know one woman who was hiding with her child among the sesame stalks."

I heard many voices trying to figure out who this woman was, naming more than twenty mothers, until someone shouted, "Stop! She is mother Berweh, and her fate is our fate too." So they stopped.

But then the voices resumed, even more insistently, naming one village after another, which I understood had to have been destroyed by Zionist troops:

"We are from al-Ruweis."

"We are from al-Hadtha."

"We are from al-Damoun."

"We are from al-Mazraa."

"We are from Shaab."

"We are from Mi'ar."

"We are from Waarat al-Sarris."

"We are from al-Zib."

"We are from al-Bassa."

"We are from al-Kabri."

"We are from Iqrit."[1]

Iqrit, al-Kabri, al-Bassa, al-Damoun, al-Ruweis, Berweh, Manshiyya, and the other villages mentioned here are all actual places, only a few of the hundreds of Palestinian villages forcibly depopulated during what was for Palestinians the catastrophe of 1948.[2] During this calamitous event, explains Constantine Zurayq in the book in which he coined the term "Nakba" to describe what happened, hundreds of thousands of Palestinians "are forced to flee pell-mell from their homes. They have their wealth and property stripped from them and wander like madmen in what is left of Palestine and in the other Arab countries. They do not know what fate has in store for them, nor what means of livelihood they should seek."[3] Almost all—87 percent—of the Palestinian towns and villages in what would become the state of Israel were emptied of their people as 800,000 Palestinians were driven from their homes.[4] Their subsequent return to their homes was (and remains to this day) blocked, first by gangs of Zionist militants and later by the Israeli army (into which those gangs eventually coalesced), despite their moral and legal right of return, as recognized by the United Nations.[5]

The Nakba is most productively thought of, however, not as a single episode that took place in 1948 but as an ongoing process. "Invasion is a structure, not an event," as the historian Patrick Wolfe once put it.[6] That is to say, the Nakba began but did not end in 1948. The refugees of that original moment of displacement have yet to be allowed to return; the Palestinians who survived the ethnic cleansing of their homeland in 1948, who now constitute a fifth of the population of Israel within its pre-1967 borders, remain second-class citizens of a state that legally and institutionally privileges Jews over non-Jews. Palestinian homes continue to be demolished, not only in the occupied West Bank and East Jerusalem but also—on an astonishing scale—within Israel itself. And Palestinians continue to be removed from their homes, denied entry to their country, stripped of residency rights, and expelled from Jerusalem. The Nakba continues, in other words; but, put somewhat differently, it's also not over, not complete, not a done deal: it continues to be contested and resisted by Palestinians. Indeed, for all its capacity for sheer destruction, it remains clearer than ever that the Zionist settler-colonial project in Palestine remains a fraught affair. The structure that emerged in 1948 is yet incomplete; it has not ended—but neither has it been entirely successful. This duality of extreme violence coupled with profound insecurity plays a major role in the ongoing conflict.

After the guns had fallen silent and the last shuffling echoes of the banished families' footsteps had faded into an eerie silence, the new Israeli state controlled a desolated terrain: a Palestinian Arab landscape of (now) empty and partially ruined villages, tens of thousands of acres of rich olive and citrus groves, and a surrounding and connecting texture of scrubland. The mixture of cultural and natural processes over time had rendered the eastern Mediterranean landscape of Palestine both a natural and a cultural heritage, according to Jala Makhzoumi. "As a repository of what remains of the native Mediterranean forest," she argues, "the rural landscape is a *natural heritage*, its diverse fabric combines woodlands and valuable maquis scrubland, a habitat for the region's exceptional biodiversity." But she adds that "traditional rural landscapes are a *cultural heritage*, a place of identity and a repository of vernacular use, management practices and traditional socio-cultural values and perceptions."[7] That is, the Palestinian landscape that fell into Israeli hands was a hybrid of social and natural processes—as much the result of culture as of nature in a raw sense—that had coevolved over centuries.

From the beginning—from even before the actual desolation of Palestine—the Zionist plan was to claim this landscape and turn it into something else, alienating it both materially and symbolically from its indigenous people, most of whom had been "transferred" across the armistice lines into the neighboring Arab countries. "Transfer" is the Zionist euphemism for the forcible expulsion of the Palestinian population, which was widely discussed and planned long before the actual outbreak of hostilities in 1948, it being understood from a Zionist standpoint that, as Josef Weitz put it in 1940, "there is no way but to transfer the Arabs [i.e., Palestinians] from here to the neighboring countries, to transfer all of them, perhaps with the exception of Bethlehem, Nazareth and the old Jerusalem. Not one village must be left."[8] In late 1948, Weitz himself established the Transfer Committee, whose intention was, as he put it, "preventing the Arabs [i.e., Palestinians] from returning to their places [through] the destruction of villages as much as possible during military operations . . . [and through] preventing of any cultivation of land by them, including reaping, collection [of crops], picking [of olives] and so on."[9]

Despite the excessive use of force designed to cause as much damage as possible to Palestinian homes in order to render them uninhabitable during the fighting, entire villages survived the war intact. As Nur Masalha points out, Israel's methodical demolition of Palestinian villages continued long after the war, into the 1950s and 1960s.[10] It was only in the spring of 1965—almost twenty years after the Nakba—"that a clear policy was established to 'level' the abandoned villages with the aim of 'clearing' the country, to quote the official term used at the time."[11] This would stop tourists from raising, as one Foreign Ministry official put it, "superfluous questions" about the ghostly landscape of ruins inhabited by Israelis.[12] The plan "was to 'level' an area stretching from the Galilee panhandle southward; to include every hill, mound, and hut, so that the land would be 'clean.' As one interviewee said, this would prevent Arab [i.e., Palestinian] villagers from claiming one day: 'That is my tree. This was my village.'"[13] Neither tree nor village would be left: the idea was that the erasure of the landscape would erase with it the political rights and claims based on belonging.

An integral part of this process of destruction and erasure was rewriting, both in the material sense and at the level of symbols. Arabic place-names were erased and replaced with Hebrew ones, reclaiming the topography in and through language, much as had been done in other settler-colonial endeavors—only in this case not in the fifteenth century or the seventeenth, but in the televisual glow of the twentieth century. The Naming Committee was established to produce a new Hebrew topography on the new maps that corresponded to the creation of a new landscape. After 1948, as Meron Benvenisti points out, "the country had become a blank slate upon which the committee could inscribe names as it wished," and the result was a mixture of either vaguely authentic or wholly invented biblical or pseudo-biblical place-names.[14] Hundreds of Palestinian villages were erased from the maps—their very names wiped clear or "transferred," so to speak, into new, Hebrew place-names—as they were being wiped off the surface of the earth.

One intention here was to produce a seemingly peaceful pastoral landscape complete with biblical place-names, as though the modern Jewish viewer of the land could somehow be transported back in time to the moment of the Bible itself. "The gaze that sees a 'pastoral, Biblical landscape' does not register what it does not want to see; it is a visual exclusion that seeks a physical exclusion," Rafi Segal and Eyal Weizman argue. "Like a theatrical set, the panorama can be seen as an edited landscape put together by invisible stage hands that must step off the set as the lights come on." This kind of landscape, they point out, does not simply signify power relations: it functions as a mechanism of domination and control.[15] And its main intention was to rewrite the territory and landscape of Palestine, to eliminate the indigenous Palestinian presence in order to secure a more purely Jewish vision of the land. "It is precisely in order not to see the Palestinian that they [Jewish settlers] are obliged to form a vision that conceals him," Uri Eisenzweig notes; "in short, *emptied of all otherness, the dreamed-of space is necessarily seen as Self.*"[16] This attempt to claim the space by eliminating all traces of the other has a dual structure: on the one hand, it seeks to deny the Palestinian presence and hence the Palestinian claim to the land; on the other hand, by creating a carefully managed, putatively Jewish landscape—Segal and Weizman's theatrical set—it also affirms a contrary bundle of values. At its most powerful, then, this landscape structure denies its own denial of the Palestinian presence in the very process of affirming its contrary, allowing the viewer to bask in the emptied-out stage set as though it were always already empty and waiting to be fulfilled: a land without a people for a people without a land, to use the notorious Zionist catchphrase.

This attempt to erase the indigenous landscape and the Palestinian presence remains starkly incomplete, however. Israel within its pre-1967 delineations is saturated with the ruins of Palestinian homes. The intact ruins of the village of Lifta, for example, still stand at the very entrance to Jerusalem on the main highway leading up from Tel Aviv: the ghostly ruins of an entire Palestinian village announcing the visitor's arrival in the city that Israel claims to be its capital. The paradox is that that very claim is both premised on the denial of the Palestinian presence—which led to the desolation of Lifta and the expulsion of its people—and utterly given the lie by the continuing presence of these haunted houses on the foothills of the holy city, and, of course, by those same people, who may have been banished from their now ruined homes but remain steadfast in demanding their rights, including above all the right of return to their land.

And throughout the rest of the country the ruins of Palestinian homes—or for that matter reclaimed Palestinian homes whose inhabitants were driven away so that new "owners" could live in them—are everywhere. Sometimes they provide the eerie silent backdrops to the contemporary Jewish presence. Sometimes they stand in the background of children's play areas. Sometimes they mark a strange absence on a busy city street, as in much of Jaffa, where the graceful arches and bricked-up windows of Palestinian homes, with trees growing out of their roofs, beg the viewer to ask what most viewers presumably suppress from their thought: Whose houses are these? Where are their owners? Sometimes they constitute a whole part of a city: the wadi al-Salib district of Haifa, for instance, is a veritable ghost town of derelict Palestinian homes, an entire neighborhood without the inconvenient presence of neighbors. As their homes stand derelict and empty or boarded up, those "neighbors" themselves languish in refugee camps, barred from returning to their own houses. The interesting thing about this landscape of haunted ruins is that it exists in

Ruins of a Palestinian home, Galilee. Photo by author.

Ruins of a Palestinian home, Jaffa. Photo by author.

Ruins of Palestinian homes, Haifa. Photo by author.

the background, as it were, of everyday Israeli life without seeming to attract much interest or attention. The questions that ought to be asked are not.

More often than not, however, a herculean effort was (and is still being) made to cover up the ruins of Palestinian homes and entire villages. And the primary mechanism for this covering over is afforestation—planting trees and even entire forests over the ruins of demolished Palestinian villages to make them disappear into a new, Europeanized landscape. Although the typical colonial project has been one of *de*forestation, the Zionist project in Palestine set itself to the task of planting new forests.[17] In fact, the previously built-up areas of almost half of the depopulated villages documented by Walid Khalidi in his classic *All That Remains*—the authoritative encyclopedia of the Nakba—have been planted over with forests and are now included in tourist and recreational sites, national parks, or nature reserves.[18] One of the officials responsible for putting up the signs in these parks admits quite bluntly that a large portion of Israel's parks "are on lands where Palestinian villages used to stand, and the

Saffourieh in the 1930s. Photo courtesy of the Institute for Palestine Studies.

forests are intended to camouflage this."[19] One of the clearest examples is the forest planted on the ruins of the town of Saffourieh, whose original inhabitants languish in refugee camps in Lebanon, or as what the Israeli authorities call "present absentees" in Nazareth and other towns in the Galilee. The densely planted pine trees clustered together on a hilltop look suspiciously and unnaturally out of place because they are—they are covering up the ruins of an entire town.

Biriya Forest is the largest in the Galilee, to take another example. According to the institution in charge of it, it "boasts a variety of fascinating sites—groves, springs, an ancient synagogue, a lime pit, revered tombs, diverse flora, hiking trails and scenic lookouts."[20] Indeed, while the tourist brochure on the forest goes on at great length about all the wonders one can encounter there, it studiously avoids any mention of the Palestinian villages of Biriyya, Alma, Dishon, Qaddita, Ayn Zaytun,

and Amqa (the latter mentioned in the passage from *The Pessoptimist* with which this chapter opens), the stones of whose smashed homes are still scattered among its trees.[21] Canada Park "is rich in natural woodland scenery, planted forests and especially fruit trees, which can be seen throughout the area," we are told by its brochure.[22] What we are not told is that it was planted on the ruins of Imwas, Yalu, and Beit Nuba.[23] Lavie/South Africa Forest is planted on the ruins of the village of Lubya.[24] And so on and on for hundreds of villages. There is no such thing as wilderness in Palestine; only depopulation.[25] That searing line by Mahmoud Darwish—"My absence is entirely trees"—captures this perfectly.

The forests do more than simply cover up the Palestinian absence: they provide a different set of values to attract the viewer (and donor). As I note earlier, there is a duality in play here: both the denial of the Palestinian

Forest planted over the ruins of Saffourieh. Photo by author.

صفــوريـــة

Saffourieh before and after its destruction. Photo by Jason Bechtel, Interfaith Peace-Builders.

Forest planted over al-Ghabsiyya. Photo courtesy of Institute for Palestine Studies.

claim to the land and the affirmation of another value, the exaggerated emphasis of which plays a key role in concealing the Palestinian presence. This dual structure allows Zionists to deny the Palestinian claim to the land in a displaced way, by affirming a set of values (in this case, "natural" scenery and the "miracle" of tree planting, "making the desert bloom," etc.). The denial of Palestinian rights is thus carefully mediated rather than drawing attention to itself; one can express it without actually acknowledging its full significance. I come back to this point shortly, but I wish to note here that this structure of displacement allows otherwise liberal people to endorse ethnic cleansing without having to come to terms with the fact that that is what they are doing: they are admiring a beautiful forest, after all—not ethnic cleansing. Thus, as Heidi Grunebaum points out, the forests are structures enabling complicity literally by displacing the material ground on which they stand.[26]

When the Israeli fire watcher who is the main character of A. B. Yehoshua's short story "Facing the Forests" wanders through the forest

Picnic tables among the ruins of Kafr Bir'im. Photo by author.

over which he is keeping watch, he is pleased by the play of light and shadows filtering through the trees. But he also has a sense that there is something eerie about the forest. "This isn't a rustling forest but a very still one, like a graveyard. A forest of solitudes. The pines stand erect, slim, serious; like a company of new recruits awaiting their commander." It turns out that chiseled stones are scattered among the trees, outlining buildings; that, as he discovers, the forest is "growing over, well, over a ruined village."[27] The militaristic language Yehoshua uses to describe the trees (as recruits awaiting their commander) speaks to the militarization of trees throughout the Zionist project in Palestine. The irrepressible Josef Weitz, as usual, put it most bluntly: "If we are to conquer the soil—only the forest, only the tree will lead us to our goal."[28] From the beginning, in other words, the Zionist obsession with planting trees has had less to do with a concern for "nature" or a pristine landscape (which the Israeli forests certainly are not in any case) than with a drive to control the land. "Every Jew that moves to Israel will need to go immediately to the work of afforestation," David Ben-Gurion, the country's first prime minister,

Trees planted over the ruins of Palestinian homes, Kafr Bir'im. Photo by author.

declared, making tree planting an integral component of the settler-colonial project.[29]

Trees were thus militarized not merely in Israeli fiction but in historical fact, drafted into a Jewish "militia," providing "not only proxy Jewish bodies but a proxy Jewish land police."[30] As Allon Tal points out, "Forests communicated permanence, prosperity, and control," and thus afforestation didn't just cover up the remains of the Palestinian presence (a question that Tal is not particularly interested in) but also conveyed a claim to the permanence of the new colonial settlement. And the deployment of trees was thought of exactly as a military exercise in a war of occupation—a "mechanized assault," Tal calls it. First, fires were set to the native ecosystem to eradicate existing vegetation; then bulldozers (the same ones the Israeli army routinely and systematically uses to demolish Palestinian family homes to this day) were brought in for brush elimination. Then "herbicides joined the arsenal wielded to suppress native trees and shrubs."[31] This ecocidal violence was intended to ensure that when the new plantings went in—and Israeli forests are overwhelmingly monocultural—

nothing else would survive. (But, of course, native species did survive—a point I return to shortly).

The standards for tree planting in these new Israeli forests were designed to maximize the trees' coverage and density as well as the speed of their growth, in order to secure the territory and blanket it as quickly and efficiently as possible. Trees were planted never more than two meters apart.[32] Species that grew aggressively were the most favored. Eucalyptus trees were brought from Australia, partly because they grow very quickly (they can reach a height of 11 meters in just seven years), and partly because they overwhelm competitor species by blocking sunlight and rendering the soil more acidic, destroying native species and preventing other plants from germinating or growing. Deploying Eucalyptus, in other words, is the arboreal equivalent of deploying a chemical weapon: it clears the terrain quickly and leaves few native survivors. Following Eucalyptus, the emphasis shifted to pine, identified as a "pioneer species" for similar reason, as it constructs "a noncompetitive environment: its needles enhance the acidity of the soil and prevent the growth of most other forms of vegetation."[33] As a result, by the 1990s, the new Israeli forests were overwhelmingly made up of one species at a time: they may have seemed "magical" and "mystical," "natural" and "wonderful," to quote from the various national park brochures, but they were—in stark contrast to the indigenous landscape of maquis scrubland that had developed slowly and adaptively over time in combination with human activity—extraordinarily fragile, poorly adapted to the local climate, water-intensive; in short, zones of ecological catastrophe. In claiming to demarcate a zone of "nature" different from culture, they turned the logic of the indigenous landscape (in which nature and culture were coextensive and symbiotic) on its head.

While parts of the territories militarily occupied by Israel in 1967 (notably the West Bank) were landscaped to suggest a kind of quasi-biblical pastoral to enhance Jewish settlers' sense that they were returning to an ancient homeland, the landscaping in much of the parts of Palestine occupied in 1948 was explicitly intended to Europeanize the land, to reclaim it from what seemed the unproductive disorder of the native landscape. This Europeanization of the indigenous terrain was a matter of explicit policy.[34] "Pine trees construct a distinctly Eastern European landscape," Irus Braverman points out. "The pines therefore mediate between what the ex-European eye longs for and what it is visible to it."[35] This is often made explicit; Carmel National Park, planted over the ruins of the Palestinian village of al-Tira, is nicknamed "Little Switzerland" because of its forced resemblance to an alpine vista.[36] This Europeanized landscape was visually at odds with the indigenous terrain, and it remains so to this day: it's clear at a glance to anyone with even a passing familiarity with the indigenous landscape that the dense alpine forests blanketing the land very clearly do not belong. And this was a matter of intention. "The newly planted, orderly pine plantations stood in stark contrast to the chaotic, natural maquis scrublands with their gnarly oaks and impenetrable assorted shrubs," writes Tal. "For Weitz, these natural woodlands were not only devoid of value but almost an affront to civilization."[37] The colonial logic of all this is clear: settlement brings order, system, and modernity to a backward, chaotic, unproductive, unsettled indigenous landscape of barren "neglect," to use Weitz's term. The native cultural logic, in other words, is one of barrenness; the settler-colonial logic is one of improvement and order, of which massive and uniformly distributed pine plantations—every tree the soldier of a figurative battalion—seemed to be living proof.

   This claim to have transformed barrenness into green fertility, which emerged from Zionist settler-colonial discourse, is still made by the Jewish National Fund (JNF), the agency charged by the state for planting and maintaining Israel's forests. "Israel is one of only two countries in the world that entered the 21st century with a net gain in its number of trees," proclaims the JNF on its website. "But Israel was not blessed with natural forests; its forests are all hand-planted. When the pioneers of the State arrived, they were greeted by barren land." The JNF claims to have "planted more than 240 million trees all over the State of Israel, providing luscious belts of green covering more than 250,000 acres. JNF national forest development work creates 'green lungs' around congested towns and cities, and provides recreation and respite for all Israelis."[38] I return later in this chapter to the JNF's claims about how wonderful it is, but first it must be noted that although this organization is empowered by the state to help manage state lands (93 percent of the land within the state, the overwhelming majority of it violently usurped from its rightful Palestinian

owners after the ethnic cleansing in 1948, as Gary Fields points out[39]),
and although its website boasts that it serves "all Israelis," its mission is
actually much more specific. After all, it elsewhere proudly boasts that it
"is the caretaker of the land of Israel, on behalf of its owners—Jewish people everywhere."[40] That's a very different claim from serving "all Israelis,"
one in five of whom is a Muslim or Christian Palestinian.

As is made clear by its slogan about the land belonging to "Jewish people everywhere" rather than, say, to the citizens of the state (never mind
the Palestinians whose land it actually is), the Jewish National Fund plays
a pivotal role in the maintenance of Israel's system of institutionalized
apartheid. Nowhere, in fact, is the extent and institutionalization of this
kind of discrimination—"ethnocracy" is the term used by Oren Yiftachel
in his scholarship on land planning in Israel[41]—more glaringly obvious
than in the legal pronouncements of the JNF. Empowered by the state for
its role in managing state land, this institution at once acknowledges and
adamantly justifies its long-established record of discriminating against
Palestinian citizens by pointing out that it "is not a public body which acts
on behalf of all the citizens of the state. Its loyalty is to the Jewish people
and its responsibility is to it [the Jewish people] alone. As the owner of
JNF land, the JNF does not have to act with equality towards all citizens
of the state." Moreover, it points out, "Israel's Knesset [parliament] and
Israeli society have expressed their view that the distinction between Jews
and non-Jews that is the basis for the Zionist vision is a distinction that is
permitted" and, indeed, that its allocation of land to Jews alone "is in complete accord with the founding principles of the state of Israel as a Jewish
state and that the value of equality, even if it applies to JNF lands, would
retreat before this principle."[42] There is little one needs to add to this
candid confession of rank racial discrimination by one of the key organs
of the Zionist state—except that it is buried in legalistic Hebrew in a
tedious court document that was never intended to be seen by liberal
Western eyes.

What, then, does the JNF intend for liberal Western eyes to see? The
answer is simple: all the stuff about planting trees in a barren landscape
and making the desert green, which glowing Western liberals like Kamala
Harris would later regurgitate without question. This is not simply a hypocritical ruse: the affirmation of the ecological value of redeeming a "bar-

ren" Palestine to make it a wonderful green Israel is absolutely integral to the JNF's role in denying and erasing—by trying to plant over as much of the evidence as possible—the Palestinian presence in and claim to the land. The act of affirming the positive value of greening the land is inextricably bound up with the negative reality of ethnic cleansing and ecocidal disappearance in such a way that emphasizing the former makes the latter fade away into a carefully managed void: the absence *is* the trees, to touch on Darwish again.

In short, as Nur Masalha puts it, the JNF is involved in a campaign of greenwashing ethnic cleansing. For if, as JNF propaganda makes clear, tree planting is an integral part of the settler-colonial process of reclaiming a primitive and unproductive native landscape and making it progressive, tree planting is . . . tree planting. What could be more innocent than planting trees? What could be more evocative of a claim to be nurturing and developing the land? "Planting a tree confirms the undeniable ethical value of Israel (and by extension the West's project in the East)," Masalha points out.[43] This claim of ethical superiority overrides the hidden question of what (and who) was there before the trees were planted, rendering it superfluous. Thus, although the earliest JNF officials, like Josef Weitz, were unabashed proponents of premeditated ethnic cleansing, and although the JNF was (and is) an integral component of the Zionist settler-colonial and apartheid project in Palestine, after 1948 and especially into the 1960s and on to our own time, it successfully repackaged itself as an environmental organization involved in greening the planet and saving us all from global warming.

"The true mission of the JNF," writes Ilan Pappe, "has been to conceal these visible remnants of Palestine not only by the trees it has planted over them, but also by the narratives it has created to deny their existence."[44] Discussing the JNF's role in what he calls memoricide, Pappe argues that in its forests "Nakba denial is so pervasive, and has been achieved so effectively, that they have become a main arena of struggle for Palestinian refugees wishing to commemorate the villages that lie buried beneath them. They are up against an organization—the JNF—which claims that there is only barren land under the pine and cypress trees it has planted there."[45] Pappe is right, of course, but we need to be attentive to the ways in which this memoricide (or greenwashing, to use Masalha's term) is articulated in such a way that the recto of the enthusiastic affirmation of tree planting covers up the verso of the denial of the Palestinian presence so effectively that it becomes unavailable even (perhaps especially) to those engaging in it.

In other words, what is at stake in JNF tree planting is an act of seduction so powerful that it encompasses and seduces the seducers themselves. But it is by no means limited to the seducers: the JNF continues to prioritize tree planting as one of the principal ways in which it both raises funds and, more important, drafts non-Israeli Jewish (and other) communities into the endorsement and support of its programs. As Heidi Grunebaum points out, "Tree-planting in JNF forests by non-Israeli Jewish communities has conscripted transnational complicity with the excision of Palestinians from their homes and lands where the forests have been cultivated upon destroyed villages."[46] "Get back to your roots," the JNF website exhorts American Jews; "Jewish National Fund invites you to plant a tree with your own hands in the soil of Israel at the Harvey Hertz–JNF Ceremonial Tree Planting Center at Neot Kedumim, the world's only biblical landscape reserve. Located just ten minutes from Ben-Gurion Airport and 20 minutes from Jerusalem, the Ceremonial Tree Planting Center offers visitors the opportunity to plant saplings that will later be transferred to sites throughout Israel."[47] The website adds that each planter will be given a special prayer and a commemorative certificate. Thus are implicated subjects walked through a scripted space to participate in the JNF's project to occlude the ethnic cleansing of Palestine (most of its forests are planted over the ruins of Palestinian villages).[48]

The sociologist Norman Klein has developed the notion of what he calls scripted spaces to express the ways in which a viewing subject can be placed in an immersive multimedia environment where he or she seems to enjoy autonomy and freedom of movement but where in fact every step of the way is thoroughly planned in advance.[49] Klein is especially interested in more contained scripted spaces—shopping malls and casinos are among the examples he works through—but much of what he suggests applies to the situation in which implicated subjects can be located within occluding narratives in Israel. Scripted spaces are a mode of perception, a way of seeing, he argues. "Scripted spaces are a walk-through or click-through environment (a mall, a church, a casino, a theme park, a computer game)," he writes. "They are designed to *emphasize* the viewer's journey—the space between—rather than the gimmicks on the wall. The audience walks *into* the story. What's more, this walk should respond to each viewer's whims, even though each step along the way is prescripted (or should I say preordained?). It is gentle repression posing as free will," he adds; "from front to back, the choices are defined; yet somehow the walk is supposed to feel open."[50] Again, Klein mostly has in mind relatively small-scale spaces like malls or casinos. But what he says works on a larger scale as well. The point of his scripted spaces, after all, is not simply that they seem to involve freedom of choice whereas they are actually monitored, engineered, and limited in various ways, but above all that they are designed as environments intended to locate the viewer in a narrative in which he or she can be almost literally immersed—a fiction, as he puts it, navigated by the audience as a fact.[51] The ceremonial tree-planting exercises in which American, and especially Jewish American, implicated subjects are invited to participate are perfect examples of Klein's notion.

This elaborate scripting is what Grunebaum herself experienced as a young Jewish South African who participated in the collection of money for JNF tree planting and then went with her family to Israel to see "South Africa Forest," which their funds had enabled. Years later, she discovered to her horror that "South Africa Forest" was planted over the ruins of the Palestinian village of Lubya, and intended precisely to occlude it. She recounts both the cultural practice of JNF planting and its scripted spaces, and her rediscovery of the occluded materialities in her documentary film *The Village under the Forest.* The point is that the people who contribute funds to tree planting, or who go out of their way to plant trees at one of the centers the JNF makes available to foreign visitors, have no idea that they are participating in a program of ethnic cleansing. They're just helping to plant trees; what could be more innocent than that?

Here we must add another corrective to the claims made by the JNF that Israel is a country committed to afforestation and planting. For the program of tree-planting was preceded by—and to this day operates alongside—an equally methodical and single-minded program of tree uprooting and destruction. As the dust settled on what remained of Palestine in 1948, one of the first tasks the pioneers of the new state undertook was to start uprooting and bulldozing fruit and olive trees planted by Palestinians and tended by them over countless generations. Tens of thousands of acres of citrus groves—including most of Jaffa's famous orange orchards, which survive today only in such oblique references to them as McVitie's Jaffa Cakes, introduced in 1927[52]—were destroyed because the new settlers found citrus too labor-intensive and not as efficient or as amenable to modern agricultural practices as field crops.[53] And olives were seen by the new settlers as even less efficient than citrus. Moreover, "the olive was identified with 'enemy' Arab agriculture, seen as primitive and conservative, and was thus marginalized in Israel, which sought to develop advanced, modern agriculture."[54] Thus, as with the people, so with the trees they had once cared for—and forty thousand acres of fertile olive trees were uprooted and destroyed in the years after 1948.

Nor was the destruction of Palestinian olive and fruit orchards accomplished simply through the act of brute bulldozing. Wherever possible, wherever Palestinian communities that had survived the Nakba remained, JNF planters installed their dense coniferous forests right up to the doors of the Palestinian towns (most of whose land was also expropriated for this purpose and for Jewish development in general). And the tall conifer trees were planted up to the edges of whatever Palestinian orchards had survived. Muhammad Abu Hayja tells the story of what happens to the orchards of the long-unrecognized Palestinian village of Ayn Hawd al-Jadida. The original town of Ayn Hawd was sealed off to its former residents—who remained nearby during the ethnic cleansing of Palestine, "present absentees" in Israel's tortured legal parlance—and was eventually handed over to Jewish immigrants connected with the Dada movement who turned it into an artists' colony, despite the Palestinian residents' appeals to return to their intact houses.[55] The "present absentees" ended up seeking shelter and constructing new houses in what had been their fields, which were promptly encircled by JNF forests. "At the same time they put up the barbed wire, they planted cypress trees among our olive and fruit trees, which had been planted in the 1920s," Abu Hayja says. "Cypresses grow very fast, and soon they reached fifteen meters high, overshadowing and suffocating the shorter olive trees, blocking out the sun. Gradually, the olive trees stopped producing olives and died. Naturally, we could no longer plant where they had planted. All our fig trees, our apple and plum trees, all died off." He adds, "To this day I hate cypress trees, because they killed our fruit trees and were planted right in front of our houses to close us in, to shut out the air, to block the view of the sea."[56] Of course, the cypresses were planted not just to kill off the fruit trees and block the Palestinians' view of the sea but also—indeed, first and foremost—to block the outside view of the Palestinians themselves.

Nor did the destruction of Palestinian olive trees end in the immediate aftermath of 1948. To this day, olive groves throughout the West Bank are subject to regular—weekly, sometimes even daily—attack, either by armed Jewish settlers (under the protection of the Israeli army) or by the army or the state itself, on the pretext of building roads, clearing "closed military areas," or constructing yet another Jewish settlement on Palestinian land. The attacks by settlers are usually on a small scale: a dozen trees burned down here, fifty cut down there. Army demolitions take place on a larger scale and can destroy hundreds of trees at a time. But even small numbers add up. All in all, since 1967, Israel has overseen the destruction of 800,000 olive trees in the territories occupied that year.[57]

Nor is the olive the only species systematically targeted for destruction. Another species eradicated by Israelis is the prickly pear cactus, tradition-ally planted by Palestinian communities at the entrances to towns, or to demarcate a border between the fields of one village and those of another, with the prickly pears themselves (a delicious fruit) a kind of bonus byproduct. The cacti were bulldozed or uprooted along with the villages with which they had developed in a symbiotic relationship over centuries. It's a curious feature of the prickly pear, however, that it is almost impos-sible to completely eradicate; as long as even a tiny rhizome remains in the soil, the plant will come back. And so, wherever one goes in Israel's artifi-cial forests, or wherever one wanders outside the forests, one consistently comes across prickly pear bushes erupting from the earth or bursting out from between the pine or eucalyptus trees planted over them. And, inevi-tably, close by, one encounters the ruins of Palestinian homes.

There are two added points to be made about prickly pears. One is that, despite the systematic attempt to eradicate this species, Israelis born in Israel like to refer to themselves as *sabras*, Hebrew for the Arabic *sabr* (prickly pear). More interestingly, however, although I grew up in Lebanon under the assumption (shared by many) that, given their remarkable

Prickly pear cactus near ruins of Palestinian homes, Galilee. Photo by author.

Prickly pear cactus near ruins of Palestinian homes, Galilee. Photo by author.

proliferation, prickly pears are native to our part of the world, they are not: *Opuntia ficus-indica* is actually native to central Mexico and was brought back by Columbus to Spain, whence it was propagated around the Mediterranean basin to the point that, having been domesticated over the centuries, it has become at home. Here, then, we have two tales of adaptation: on the one hand, a gradual process of incorporating a new species into an existing ecosystem that, as with other species, is in any case a symbiotic fusion between the natural and the cultural; and, on the other hand, an attempt to violently obliterate an existing ecosystem with all of its integrated and coevolved species and to replace it with a transplant that, while adept at destroying everything that stands in the way, actually really does not fit very well itself. For the monocultural forests that have replaced the biodiverse indigenous landscape are drought-intolerant eco-logical disaster zones poorly adapted to the local environment and prone to disease and wildfire. Given that Zionism itself is an attempt to violently impose an ethno-religious monoculture on a land that has through its his-tory always been multicultural, these brittle forests are the perfect embod-iments of Zionism's broader conflict with the Palestinians.

Nor has this attempt to erase and replant yet been abandoned. For dec-ades its main center of gravity was in the Galilee and the north, but in recent years it has shifted to the south and in particular to the Naqab (or Negev) Desert. In the decades following the destruction of Palestine in 1948, the new Israeli state asserted its control over the desert by expelling the majority of the indigenous Bedouin Palestinian population and trying to corral most of those who remained into a tightly restricted area within it, forcing them to abandon their traditional way of life and of course the landscape to which it corresponded.[58] A combination of military rules, forcible relocations, and home demolitions ensured that these measures to impose what Ahmad Amara, Oren Yiftachel, and others have identified as a form of colonial terra nullius were largely successful: most of the desert was emptied of its indigenous population during this period, and kept clear of them while new Jewish settlements were developed. "Like other settler societies that expanded into regions populated by minority groups, the Judaization effort was greatly assisted by a legal formulation that denied most Arabs landownership, possession, or recognition of their localities," Alexandre Kedar, Ahmad Amara, and Oren Yiftachel argue. "Thus a parallel process to Judaization has been the de-Arabization of the Negev land, through eviction, destruction, renaming, legal denial, and coerced urbanization and spatial concentration, which continue to this day."[59]

In recent years, indeed, the pace of development of these new settlements has led the Israeli government to develop new plans to remove those Bedouin Palestinians who had remained outside the so-called concentration zones into which it intended to corral them. Tens of thousands of Bedouin now face renewed home demolition and internal displacement as the state intensifies its drive to Judaize the southern desert. These Bedouin are now Israeli citizens, but of the "wrong" racial status; their towns are to be demolished to make room for new towns exclusively for the use of Jewish residents. The purpose of building these new Jewish communities, according to Yaron Ben Ezra, the director of the settlement division of the World Zionist Organization, is "to prevent the continued *invasion* of state lands by the Bedouin and to prevent the creation of Bedouin or Arab contiguity."[60] Thus the indigenous people are transformed into foreign invaders, and the foreign invader seeks to take their place as "indigenous."

In January 2017, for instance, the Palestinian Bedouin town of Umm el-Hiran was partially demolished to make room for the construction of a new Jewish community to be called Hiran. And Umm el-Hiran was not alone. But of all the Bedouin towns and villages being demolished by the Israelis, one has stood out: the tiny village of Araqib.[61] Araqib was demolished in July 2010, and it would have made simply one more entry in the long list of Palestinian villages destroyed by the Israeli state, except that in this case the villagers—Israeli citizens, mind you—rebuilt their town. And then the state returned and redemolished it. And then the people rebuilt it. And then it was redemolished. And so on and on over the weary years. By my last count (early 2021), Araqib has been demolished 184 times so far.[62] There's not much left of it now—"rebuilding" is more a symbolic act than anything else (though, of course, so is the repeated demolition)—and the town has already lost all of its fruit trees and other plantings to Israeli bulldozers. On the same land, the JNF is developing yet another forest, Ambassadors Forest, with which it intends to showcase wonderful new techniques for halting desertification and combating global warming.

Israel's repeated—insistent, even pathological—demolitions of Araqib are evidence of a larger collective psychosocial structure. Israel digs away at the Palestinian presence like a man scratching a persistent itch, trying to make it go away. Little else could explain a modern state so persistently going after a harmless, repeatedly demolished hamlet in the middle of the desert, one now made up of little more than timber planks and tarpaulins, only to redemolish it again. This persistence speaks to a significant difference between the Zionist project in Palestine and other, now more mature settler-colonial enterprises. The most obvious comparable cases, the United States and Australia, no longer feel so urgent a need to obliterate or deny the presence of the indigenous peoples whose land they stole in the course of genocidal campaigns of violence that left only a fraction of the original population intact. The white societies there have settled enough that they can relax and call it a day; native resistance still occurs and, when it does, faces disproportionately ugly repression (as recent events in South Dakota remind us), but, no matter how strong the spirit of the indigenous peoples of the Americas or Australia, it is difficult to imagine reversing the conquests of those territories.

The Zionist conquest of Palestine, by contrast, is anything but irreversible. The sheer steadfastness of the Palestinian people, their stubborn refusal to give up and go away, and above all the fact that the indigenous population of Palestine, unlike that in Australia or the United States, to this day still outnumbers the settler population makes the Zionist project, for all its undoubted capacity for sheer violence, that much more insecure. And the insecurity is deeply felt, registered in all kinds of domains. For example, Israel's plaintive insistence that its "right to exist" be recognized, its petulant demand that its identity as a Jewish state be acknowledged, is evidence of this profound insecurity. This is not a physical or military insecurity: no regional power, let alone the largely disarmed Palestinian people, poses even a vaguely serious threat to Israel's existence. Why, then, does it feel insecure? Because at some fundamental level it knows that the Palestinians are still there, they haven't gone away, they haven't given up, they still maintain the right to their land and the will to resist its usurpation. Israel's petulant demand that its "right to exist" be recognized has no equivalent in other settler-colonial regimes: the United States does not demand that its right to exist be recognized by Native Americans, or insist that they acknowledge in writing that it is a white state—because the United States feels no such need to make such demands; it is confident of its own status and power and has confidence in its conquest of the land. Such a demand, in other words, is an indicator of the profound anxiety underlying it. You don't need to ask for acknowledgment of something you know to be true; it's only on a question that you are not confident about that you seek reassurance.

And so Israel goes on making the demand—just as it goes on trying to erase and cover up the Palestinian presence on and claim to the land. At the same time, it cannot bring itself to acknowledge its responsibility for the displacement and continued alienation of the Palestinians; it cannot accept its role in the making of its own history or its agency in the history of ethnic cleansing, which it continues to deny even took place. Thus it continues to demolish Palestinian homes and to cover up their ruins with forests. And not just that: it has passed a law making it all but illegal for Palestinians to commemorate the Nakba of 1948.[63] It violently suppresses Palestinian marches and protests in memory of the destroyed villages. And it deploys hugely disproportionate armed force in overseeing the demolition and destruction of its Palestinian citizens' homes (to say nothing of home demolitions in the territories occupied in 1967). That Israel's denial of the Palestinians is then itself also denied, covered up in further layers of mystification and obscuration, and repackaged in the affirmation of alternative values such as greenscaping or tolerance, is simply part of the larger complex at work here. The memoricide of the Nakba and the denial of the Palestinian presence are ongoing, in other words, not matters of the past; and they are fiercely contested by the Palestinians, who refuse to forget and move on.

All of this, again, speaks to the brittle fragility of the Zionist project. That sense of fragility is expressed in various other ways as well. It is what drives the narrative of A. B. Yehoshua's short story "Facing the Forests," for example; the awareness that Israeli forests invariably contain the ruins of Palestinian villages, and the fear that those forests might burn down and reveal those ruins—the naked truth—for all the world to see, is palpable in that story. The fear of the Palestinian narrative is given form, too, in the way in which Yehoshua silences his Palestinian character quite literally by denying him a tongue: there's an awareness, in other words, but also the awareness that that awareness can't really be spoken, at least not in the voice of those supposedly banished and disappeared.

Patrick Wolfe points out the contradictory nature of settler society's anxiety about the persistence of the native, especially in a case of botched or incomplete settlement as in Palestine. Negatively, Wolfe observes, the settler society strives for the dissolution of native societies. Positively, however, "the ongoing requirement to eliminate the Native alternative continues to shape the colonial society that settlers construct on their expropriated land base. In this positive sense, the logic of elimination marks a return whereby the Native repressed continues to structure settler-colonial society."[64] In other words, Israel's ongoing denial of the Palestinian presence actively shapes its settler culture: the negative attempt to absent, to negate, the Palestinians continually reappears in positive terms as the affirmation of something else. The more the Palestinians are repressed, the more the affirmation of other values gets expressed; and the more loudly those other values are expressed, the more the Palestinian presence gets denied, erased, and covered over.

As noted earlier, the Nakba began but did not end in 1948; the Zionist invasion of Palestine is a structure, not an event. As Elizabeth Strakosch and Alissa Macoun have observed, however, "The flipside of invasion being a structure not an event is that [settler] sovereignty is a constant performance claiming to be an essence."[65] Hence the need to go on denying and trying to uproot the Palestinian presence; hence the need to carefully rewrite and curate the landscape as either biblical or Alpine—essentially Jewish or European, or both, but certainly not Arab and Palestinian, certainly not the product of centuries of cultural and social processes weaving the natural and the human into a common fabric of belonging. On this point, too, Wolfe's insights bring clarity. "So far as conquest remains incomplete, the settler state rests—or, more to the point, fails to rest—on incomplete foundations," he argues.[66] And nowhere is this failure to rest more obvious than in the constantly recurated and replanted monocultural forests planted over the ruins of Palestinian villages.

I would emphasize one point before closing this chapter. These Israeli landscapes—like the state project to which they correspond—are incredibly fragile affairs. They have almost no elasticity and are incapable of much adjustment or recalibration: as soon as their brittle frameworks are pushed or pulled apart a little, the outside light comes rushing in, as it were. Materially, for instance, for all the forms of occlusion incorporated into the Israeli psycho-geography of denial, there are all kinds of exceptions to be seen, not only once the viewer adjusts his or her point of view a little, looking to one side or another—noticing the ruined home, the rusting Arabic sign, the moss-covered Muslim grave, the Christian shrine poking out from the treetops attempting to envelop it, the native prickly pear cactus creeping out from under the foreign trees of a seemingly Alpine forest—but also in moments of active disruption of the carefully manipulated stage set designed to conceal it. For example, a fire that burned down JNF forests near Haifa a few years ago revealed the blackened ruins of bulldozed Palestinian villages in between the charred tree trunks; the fire that burned west of Jerusalem in the summer of 2021 revealed the underlying Palestinian landscape of terraced hillsides. And the figurative space through which outside subjects attempt to navigate and view the desolate landscape of racial segregation and violence is just as fragile: it is not impervious to interruption or interdiction. It is, however—or it has been— deeply embedded in liberal culture, where it has been succored and nourished, emotionally invested in, to the point that its removal can be traumatic to the forms of ethical liberal subjectivity implicated in it. There is no doubt, however, that it needs yet more interruption, however traumatic to those who have spent decades congratulating themselves on their ethical subjectivity while aiding and abetting—through their sheer denial— the attempt to run roughshod over an entire people.

2 Democracy

Will we, as Americans and as Israelis, stay true to the shared
democratic values that have always been at the heart of our
relationship? We are both nations built by immigrants and
exiles seeking to live and worship in freedom, nations built
on principles of equality, tolerance and pluralism.

— Hillary Clinton

Israel's Supreme Court is a beautiful monument to a government founded on the highest of human ideals. The
beauty of the architecture and spirit of design left a lasting
impression—the straight lines in the building represent the
immutable nature of truth, while the curved glass and walls
were built to represent the fluid nature of finding justice.

— Kamala Harris

On the question of Israeli democracy there is still little debate across most
of the mainstream political spectrum in the United States. The odd US
politician may occasionally propose in passing that Israel might perhaps
consider showing a little more restraint in arresting children, demolishing
homes, or bombing Gaza, but that it is fundamentally a democracy, and
indeed "the only democracy in the Middle East," is still generally taken for
granted (though cracks in this consensus are finally beginning to appear,
a point I return to in the conclusion). The 2020 presidential election was
anomalous for a number of reasons, and the question of Palestine did not
feature prominently in a discussion dominated by the pandemic of that
year and the egotistical narcissism of Donald Trump. But rewind to any
previous election cycle, and you'll find a familiar narrative playing out.

Consider the previous election, in 2016. "It is imperative that the U.S. stands with Israel, our closest ally and the sole democracy in the region," Marco Rubio said during his presidential campaign in 2016. "I will be on Israel's side every single day, because they [*sic*] are the only pro-American, free-enterprise democracy in the entire Middle East."[1] Israel, according to Rubio's rival Ted Cruz, "is a liberal democracy that shares our values."[2] John Kasich, another rival, was quick to demonstrate his own fealty: "Israel is the only democracy in the Middle East, [and] has in turn been a faithful and dependable friends [*sic*]," he announced.[3] Although not in the running for the presidency, Republican Senate leader Mitch McConnell chimed in: "Today, tomorrow and always Israel's beacon of democracy will continue to shine through the darkness and America will be right there standing proudly alongside our friends," he insisted.[4] Hillary Clinton, the 2016 Democratic party candidate for president, was not to be outdone. "Israel is a vibrant democracy in a region dominated by autoc-racy," she wrote in a letter to donors that year; "the Jewish state is a mod-ern day miracle, a vibrant bloom in the middle of a desert. We must nur-ture and protect it."[5] Even from the more liberal wing of the Democratic party there was (apart from Bernie Sanders's occasional reminders that Palestinians also have rights) little dissent. "Israel lives in a very dangerous part of the world, and a part of the world where there aren't many liberal democracies and democracies that are controlled by the rule of law," said Elizabeth Warren, defending Israel's bombardment of Gaza in 2014; "and we very much need an ally in that part of the world."[6] Nor is this a matter merely of interest and alliance, according to liberal Democrats. "I stand with Israel because of our shared values which are so fundamental to the founding of both our nations," said then California senator Kamala Harris, who would go on to win as vice president in the 2020 elections. "I believe the bonds between the United States and Israel are unbreakable, and we can never let anyone drive a wedge between us." She added that she believed "we should not isolate Israel, the only democracy in the region."[7]

On one hand, of course, it could be said that all that this amounts to is a set of venal politicians pandering to what they imagine to be a certain constituency. On the other hand, the sheer uniformity of opinion across the spectrum of American politics—a startling uniformity of opinion that does not exist for any other topic or question (except perhaps for the related question of "terrorism")—is impressive and suggests a deeper, harder-wired set of beliefs than mere pandering. In particular, the repeated affirmation of the belief that Israel is not only a democracy, and not simply the only democracy in the Middle East, but a Jewish and democratic state does crucial ideological work. Consider, again, the uniformity of this repetition across the spectrum: Palestinians, says reactionary Florida congresswoman Ileana Ros-Lehtinen, must "recognize Israel's right to exist as a free, democratic, Jewish state."[8] We must safeguard, according to Republican senator Bob Menendez, "a secure, peaceful, and democratic Jewish state."[9] Lasting peace, says the liberal Kamala Harris, requires that we "protect Israel's identity, ensure security for all people and include the recognition of Israel's right to exist as a Jewish state."[10] Hillary Clinton says we must safeguard "the Zionist vision of a Jewish and democratic state."[11] Referring to "Israel's proud character, Jewish, democratic and secure," Nancy Pelosi says we must work to "maintain Israel as a secure Jewish and democratic state."[12] Barack Obama says we need to safeguard "the dream of a Jewish and democratic state."[13] John Kerry, his secretary of state, echoes his words precisely, affirming "the dream of a Jewish democratic state of Israel."[14] And so on. In running for president in 2020, Joe Biden and the other major Democratic candidates reaffirmed, again and again and again, their support for what Biden— characteristically jumbling the script a little (though all the right words were there in roughly the right order)—called "Israel's right to have a secure democratic Jewish state in the Middle East."[15]

The repetitions apparently come easily—so easily that they seem not to require any thought because they are repeated so often. But let's slow down and think this through a little: what does it mean to express a concrete political situation in terms of a "dream" or a "vision," a "miracle," and so on—terms that come up consistently in these accounts of Israel? After all, in the most famous political reference to a dream, Martin Luther King Jr.'s "I have a dream" speech, the dream of racial equality is most certainly a vision of a future, not a present. Most references to the "dream" of a Jewish and democratic state, however, point to a present condition, albeit one that seems—like a dream or a vision—not really to be present; that's why it's a *dream*, after all. But, to continue, what does it mean to refer to a *dream* over and over and over again? What kind of work does that affirmation, in itself, do? Does the repetition work the way certain magic spells are said to work: the more you repeat the incantation, the more real the repeated wish seems to be? Or does the mere act of repetition perform the kind of work that one of those hand-cranked emergency lights does: it glows for as long as you crank the handle, but starts to fade as soon as you slow down or stop? Is repetition itself necessary for the work of affirmation it intends?

For, not coincidentally, the sheer repetition of the affirmation of the "Jewish and democratic state" is, as an act, itself startling once you notice and start to track it: a repetition not only across the political spectrum but also within particular speeches. At the very least, it's a kind of *script* that, as in any Hollywood movie, helps us willingly to suspend our disbelief. Consider Nancy Pelosi's speech at the Zionist lobbying group AIPAC's convention in 2017, for instance: "This is the way to continue Israel's proud character, Jewish, democratic and secure . . . a peace agreement that recognizes Israel's right to exist as a democratic Jewish state . . . maintain Israel as a secure Jewish and democratic state . . . a one-state outcome risks destroying Israel's Jewish and democratic character, the spirit of strong support for a Jewish secure and democratic Israel." Almost every other sentence at a certain point of the speech involves the repetition of some variation of the phrase "Jewish and democratic."[16] Or consider Hillary Clinton's 2016 AIPAC speech: "taking our alliance to the next level depends on electing a president with a deep, personal commitment to Israel's future as a secure, democratic Jewish state . . . unwavering, unshakable commitment to our alliance and to Israel's future as a secure and democratic homeland for the Jewish people . . . peace with security is possible and . . . is the only way to guarantee Israel's long-term survival as a strong Jewish and democratic state."[17] Here, too, the distinction between future and present is being glossed over, as though the speaker is describing a present that does not yet really exist or that has not yet happened. And the repetition seems to bridge the gap between the real and the unreal: the more you repeat these magic words, the more the unreal becomes—or seems to become—real. Certainly, the more you repeat it, the more it becomes believable, the more you can believe it.

On the other hand, you have to keep repeating the mantra in order to believe it! For this proposition of a Jewish-and-democratic-state becomes believable only when it is affirmed over and over again: the very act of affirmation generates and sustains the dreamlike state of belief like a kind of trance. The many references to "secure" and "right to exist" that invariably accompany the repetition—"Israel's right to exist as a Jewish and democratic state" (how many times have we heard that plaintive demand?)—suddenly assume new meaning. Materially, militarily, speaking, Israel is about as secure as any state can be: it is a nuclear power equipped with the most advanced conventional weapons available to any state in the world; none of its neighbors pose even the vaguest threat to it in military terms. Why, then, the constant desperate invocations of its need for "security," the endless petulant repetitions of its "right to exist," the invocation of "forever" and "eternal" and "permanent" and so on that almost always accompanies the affirmation of Israel's status as a Jewish-and-democratic-state? No other state that I know of constantly invokes the eternal in this extraordinary way. The answer is that all the sheer military force in the world doesn't make up for a very different kind of insecurity— an immaterial one that we can locate in the realm of the imaginary.

What I propose in this chapter is that the constant repetition of the phrase "Jewish and democratic state" performs a certain kind of imaginary work. First and foremost, as I suggest in this chapter's opening, the affirmation sustains and makes possible a belief in Israel as a democracy that wouldn't be possible without the sheer fact of constant affirmation. The very fact that the incantation is repeated over and again despite the glaring contradiction at its heart (a state can't be both democratic, that is, open to the general will, *and* have a specific religious identity, that is, closed, limited to a particular identity) makes clear that sheer repetition is necessary to sustain the belief being expressed: just like a magic spell, without constant repetition, it would cease to be "true." At the same time, the repetition of the faith (and *faith* really is what we are talking about here) in Israel as a Jewish-and-democratic-state occludes, covers up, denies, the reality that it is in fact legally, technically, constitutionally—not simply rhetorically—an apartheid state. I turn to the details shortly, but just consider what happens when the inverse of the incantation of the Jewish-and-democratic-state mantra comes out into the open.

When, for instance, Jimmy Carter published his book *Palestine: Peace Not Apartheid* in 2006, the reaction pretty much across the entire American political spectrum was instantaneous denial. "We stand with

Israel now and we stand with Israel forever. The Jewish people know what it means to be oppressed, discriminated against, and even condemned to death because of their religion," said Nancy Pelosi, Speaker of the US House of Representatives, in an attempt to contest the primary assertion of Carter's book (which even explicitly exempted Israel within its pre-1967 borders from its analysis, restricting itself to the territories occupied in 1967). "They have been leaders in the fight for human rights in the United States and throughout the world," continued Pelosi. "It is wrong to suggest that the Jewish people would support a government in Israel or anywhere else that institutionalizes ethnically based oppression, and Democrats reject that allegation vigorously."[18] Pelosi's conflation of the Jewish people and the state of Israel is remarkable; even more so is her assertion that Jews, by virtue of being Jews, are incapable of discrimination.

Nor are such forms of denial restricted to politicians. Here, for example, is the *Washington Post* columnist Richard Cohen:

> The Israel of today and the South Africa of yesterday have almost nothing in common. In South Africa, the minority white population harshly ruled the majority black population. Nonwhites were denied civil rights, and in 1958, they were even deprived of citizenship. In contrast, Israeli Arabs [i.e., Palestinians], about one-fifth of the country, have the same civil and political rights as do Israeli Jews. Arabs [i.e., Palestinians] sit in the Knesset and serve in the military, although most are exempt from the draft. Whatever this is—and it looks suspiciously like a liberal democracy—it cannot be apartheid.[19]

Alan Dershowitz, in one of his many furious attempts to rebut Carter's argument, asserts that

> apartheid means pervasive racial segregation laws, media censorship, banning of political parties, torture and murder of human rights activists in detention, indoctrination of children with racial ideology, removal of voting rights, and use of the death penalty for political crimes [all of which are routine Israeli policies, of course]. But in Israel, Muslim and Christian citizens (of which [*sic*] there are more than a million) have the right to vote and regularly elect members of the Knesset [i.e., parliament], some of whom even oppose Israel's right to exist [that's actually against Israeli law: you cannot enter an election without affirming the state's status as Jewish].

There is an Arab [i.e., Palestinian] member of the Supreme Court, and have been Arab [i.e., Palestinian] members of the cabinet. Numerous Israeli Arabs [i.e., Palestinians] hold important positions in businesses, universities, and the cultural life of the nation. There is complete freedom of dissent in Israel and it is practiced vigorously by Muslims, Christians, and Jews alike. And Israel is a vibrant democracy.[20]

In 2012, when he was running for the presidency, Barack Obama distanced himself from Carter's critique and anything even remotely connected to it. "Injecting a term like apartheid" into the discussion over Israel and Palestine, Obama said, is not productive. "It's emotionally loaded, historically inaccurate, and it's not what I believe," he said.[21] And so on and on. There are countless other examples, but let's mention one more.

When, in 2014, Secretary of State John Kerry—apparently unaware that his words were being recorded—warned that Israel risks becoming an apartheid state if peace talks fail, the uproar across the political spectrum was, again, instantaneous and universal. The Republican House minority leader at the time, Eric Cantor, issued a statement denouncing Kerry and adding that "the use of the word apartheid has routinely been dismissed as both offensive and inaccurate, and Secretary Kerry's use of it makes peace even harder to achieve."[22] Then California senator Barbara Boxer, a Democrat like Kerry, also quickly denounced him. "Israel is the only democracy in the Middle East and any linkage between Israel and apartheid is nonsensical and ridiculous," she lashed out.[23] Amid the furor, Kerry himself quickly retracted his statement. Apartheid is "a word best left out of the debate," Kerry confessed in his recantation; "Israel is a vibrant democracy and I do not believe, nor have I ever stated, publicly or privately, that Israel is an apartheid state or that it intends to become one."[24] So there we are, back to square one: the best way to affirm that Israel is not an apartheid state is to reaffirm that it is a democracy. In other words—and notice the consistency across these quotations—the best way to *deny* that Israel is an apartheid state is to *affirm* that it is a democracy; the more the charge of apartheid comes up, the more often you have to repeat the apparently magic incantation to dispel it. Here, as in the other cases explored in this book, the affirmation (of democracy) *is* the denial (of apartheid); the two are bound up with each other.

I later come back to this question of affirmation and denial, but first it's worth delving a little deeper into the material circumstances of both claim and counterclaim.

. . . . .

In 1986 a group of American Jews established a new community in the Galilee. They called it Eshchar. Nefesh B'Nefesh, an organization that encourages foreign Jews to emigrate to Israel, says that the population of Eshchar aims "to live in an environment of mutual tolerance and togetherness, and provides residents with a wonderful place to reside and raise children."[25] Boasting its many appeals to the potential immigrants it hopes to attract—including a wealth of facilities such as a day care center, post office, youth center, sports complex, artisan workshops, an amphitheater, and even a botanic garden—the town proclaims itself a "model pluralistic community," declaring, "Eshchar is a mixed community of religious, non-religious and traditional Jews from all backgrounds committed to mutual respect, pluralism, and openness, and prides itself on its heterogeneous identity including immigrants, Israelis, Ashkenazim, Sephardim, young and old." It adds that its residents "believe the ideological message of heterogeneous community living is essential for the future success of the State of Israel and the Jewish community worldwide."[26]

Seen from a somewhat more skeptical angle, this claim to extraordinary heterogeneity might seem suspiciously homogeneous; after all, everyone in the community is—*and has to be*—Jewish. "When everything is Jewish," Patrick Wolfe points out in his reading of the Zionist project in Palestine, "difference itself becomes Jewish."[27] Although the town is established on land confiscated from Palestinians, not a single Palestinian lives—or is permitted to live—in Eshchar. Access to Jewish community settlements such as Eshchar, which constitute 84 percent of all rural towns inside pre-1967 Israel,[28] is determined by admissions committees responsible for ensuring that (as an Israeli law recently upheld by the country's High Court puts it, rendering de jure what had been de facto practice[29]) potential entrants to the community fit its "unique characteristics" and "social-cultural fabric" and are otherwise "suitable" for its "social life."

Palestinians, including those who own the land on which these communities are built, are by definition "unsuitable"; none has been freely admitted to live in them.[30] Instead, they live in towns that are overcrowded because the state has confiscated the land surrounding them and, even as it establishes one new community after another for Jews— more than six hundred since the establishment of the state—it adamantly refuses to permit Palestinians to develop a single new town of their own, and indeed bulldozes existing Palestinian towns to make room for new Jewish ones.[31] Palestinians constitute around 20 percent of Israel's citizens, but their towns exercise authority over just more than 2 percent of the local government areas of the state, due to what a number of scholars have identified as the Judaization of the land and the carefully engineered mapping of race onto space—biospatialization, as Yinon Cohen and Neve Gordon put it.[32]

Practically a stone's throw from Eshchar are the Palestinian towns of Arab al-Naim, al-Husseiniya, el Qubsi, and Kammaneh. But even as the Israeli government was fast-tracking the development of new Jewish communities in the Galilee, it refused to recognize the existence of these Palestinian towns; it withheld municipal and state services from them; moreover, it slated their homes for demolition and has partially or in some cases entirely demolished them, claiming that they were built without permits, which, strictly speaking, is true—if only because they predate the existence of the state itself: it wasn't there to give them permits when they were first developed in the nineteenth century or earlier. The development of Eshchar was part of a wave of land confiscations in the Galilee (from Palestinians, for Jews) announced in 1976 in order to—as a memorandum written by the Northern District commissioner of the Ministry of the Interior put it—address "the demographic problem" and "expand and deepen Jewish settlement in areas where the contiguity of the Arab population is prominent," with the effect of "diluting existing Arab population concentrations."[33]

Thus, while the roads to Eshchar and sixty-one other towns the development of which was intended to cement the "Judaization of the Galilee" were being neatly paved and signposted,[34] only rutted dirt tracks without signs led to the entrances of Arab al-Naim, al-Husseiniya, el Qubsi, and Kammaneh (and countless other Palestinian towns like them throughout the parts of Palestine that fell in 1948, never mind the territories occupied in 1967). Eshchar was instantly made visible on Israeli maps; the neighboring unrecognized Palestinian villages were not. Eshchar had from its inception wonderful new facilities; the unrecognized villages did not—nor were they connected to the national power grid, postal system, or water or sewage networks, all of which were immediately extended to Eshchar. The new homes in Eshchar had tiled roofs, irrigation systems, and lush lawns; those in the neighboring villages were made of corrugated tin and fabric and, denied municipal services, lacked running water and were surrounded by garbage; there were no plans to build amphitheaters, sports complexes, or botanic gardens there—or even schools. Recently, one of these villages, Arab al-Naim, was officially recognized. The largest obstacle in getting the regional council to extend municipal services turned out to be the "model pluralistic community" of Eshchar, whose residents—living on land confiscated from the neighboring villages, including Arab al-Naim—said they did not want the impoverished Palestinian residents "living next door to them."[35]

Here, then, we arrive at one of the most important features of the Israeli version of apartheid: not simply the inability or refusal of its practitioners and their overseas supporters to recognize it for what it is, but their adamant insistence that they stand for its exact opposite. Thus, Eshchar is an endeavor of "mutual respect, pluralism, and openness," not hostility toward others; a model of "mutual tolerance and togetherness," not a contemporary experiment in racial segregation; a project in "heterogeneous community living," not an attempt to maintain insular homogeneity against surrounding otherness; in short, a vibrant "pluralistic community," not a colonial settlement implanted on land usurped by force from its ethnically cleansed indigenous owners. Along the same lines but on a larger scale, Israel is reputed to be a bastion of Occidental tolerance and liberal democracy—a "Jewish and democratic state" in a desert of backward, violent, fundamentalist Muslim tyranny.

And here, too, we arrive at one of the most important differences between the South African and Israeli versions of apartheid. One of the most compelling facts about South African Apartheid is that it dared to have a proper name, after all; it insisted on calling attention to itself in its system of explicit signs, labels, markers—on every bus, at every beach, at the entrance to every bathroom. In other words, South African Apartheid continually registered itself in the verbal and visual field of everyday life through endless plaques, signs, words, laws, names, classifications—an endless series of binaries constructed around the ultimate "Blankes/Nie Blankes" (Whites/Not Whites). At the end of the day, then, the South African white, irrespective of her personal beliefs or ideological position, had to look at the sign saying "Blankes/Nie Blankes" and affiliate herself accordingly: an awkwardness the Apartheid Museum in Johannesburg reenacts very effectively at its entrance.

The Jewish Israeli, and the supporter of Israel overseas, is never forced into such a confrontation and its attendant forms of recognition and awareness; he never has to make that choice. Nowhere in Israeli law is the right to equality protected; quite the contrary, in fact: dozens of laws explicitly or implicitly discriminate against Palestinian citizens of the state.[36] But, in general, these laws do not brashly call attention to themselves as did their South African precedents; nowhere is it officially signposted that Jews must live *here* (Eshchar, for example) and Palestinians must live *there* (Arab al-Naim, for example). A powerful system of formal and informal mechanisms ensures that things work precisely in that way: a system of such "extreme residential segregation between Jews and Palestinians," as Cohen and Gordon observe, that 99 percent of the 1,214 residential districts listed by Israel's Central Bureau of Statistics are either exclusively Jewish or exclusively Palestinian.[37] But these things seem to happen in the background, as it were, rather than being so visibly and crudely foregrounded as in South Africa. Thus, unlike the South African white, who was always reminded of the forms of privilege she enjoyed at the expense of Black people, the Jewish Israeli, like his supporters overseas, can ascribe to himself the values of tolerance, pluralism, heterogeneity, and so on, and not have to reckon with the status or even the existence of the Palestinians on whose land he lives.[38] Before exploring these visual and cultural distinctions between the two forms of apartheid further, I first must attend to the details of the two systems and what they have in common.

Every single major South African Apartheid law has a direct equivalent in Israel and the territories occupied in 1967.

First and foremost, just as was the case in Apartheid-era South Africa, there is no universal category of citizenship and nationality in Israel. Thus the Population Registration Act of 1950, which assigned to every South African a racial identity according to which he or she had access to (or was denied) a varying range of rights, has a direct equivalent in the Israeli laws that assign to every citizen of the state a distinct racial identity, on the basis of which various rights are also accessed (or denied).[39] In Israel, the categories of race and nation are collapsed into each other.[40] According to the Israeli state and its juridical apparatuses, there is no such thing as an Israeli nation in a secular or nonracial sense, and hence no such thing as Israeli nationality per se. As the High Court put it in 1972 (in a ruling it reiterated in 2013), "There is no Israeli nation separate from the Jewish People. The Jewish People is composed not only of those residing in Israel but also of Diaspora Jewry."[41] As a result, not only Jewish citizens of the state but all Jews everywhere are considered by the organs of the state, on the basis of their racial identity, to have "Jewish nationality," whereas non-Jews, though they may be citizens of the state, are explicitly not members of the "nation"—that is, Jews all over the world, whether they want to be affiliated with Israel or not, the state of whom Israel claims to be. Thus, from the state's inception, "although state passports designated the citizenship (*ezrahut*, or *jinsiyya* in Arabic) of their holders as 'Israeli,'" Shira Robinson points out, "internal identity cards marked their holders' nationality (*le'om* or *qawm* in Arabic) primarily as 'Jewish' or 'Arab,' the racial groupings built into mandatory law and endorsed by the League of Nations."[42]

Israel's nationality law, the 1950 Law of Return, thus applies only to Jews and provides no mechanism to grant nationality to non-Jews. An entirely different law (the 1952 "Nationality" Law) allows the extension of the lesser category of citizenship, but not nationality, to non-Jews.[43] As Robinson argues, "in its explicit privileging of all Jews in the world at the expense of native non-Jews, the Law of Return became Israel's first legal nail in the coffin against the homecoming of Palestinian refugees, and the cornerstone of racial segregation between Israeli citizens."[44] What really counts for Israeli law, as Mazen Masri observes, is not the question of who is a citizen, but that of "who is a Jew?"[45]

Muslim and Christian Palestinians (or at least those who survived the Zionist ethnic cleansing of their homeland in 1948 and their descendants) had to scramble to adapt themselves to a shifting series of residency requirements that the new state made it as difficult as possible to actually meet, even as it imposed martial law on them—but not Jewish citizens—until 1966.[46] When it was finally framed, the law that ultimately granted them citizenship was careful not to mention Jews or Arabs as such, "instead outlining the two paths to acquire automatic status in seemingly neutral, bureaucratic terms," Robinson notes.[47] "The authorized English translation of the citizenship law was tweaked in another way to conceal its discrimination," she adds. "Although its Hebrew name, *Hok ha-Ezrahut*, translates literally as 'Citizenship Law,' the government called it the Israeli Nationality Law [in English] in order to denote the broadest legal meaning of the term as it is understood in English. This was deceptive."[48] As we shall see, the deception serves a purpose.

Thus, in contrast to Jewish citizens, who are recognized as having a national identity as Jews, Israeli law methodically strips Palestinian citizens of their national identity as Palestinians and reduces them to a mere ethnicity. To this very day, as Cohen and Gordon point out, "the word 'Palestinian' does not appear in Israel's statistical abstracts, while only in 1995 did the word 'Arab' finally emerge after decades in which Palestinians were referred to by their religion or as 'non-Jews.'"[49] At most, then, the state grudgingly refers to its Palestinian citizens as generic Arabs.[50] This stark racialization reaches deep into the state's administrative bowels. Jewish citizens, for example, are classified in the state's population registry according to their and their father's country of birth. If both a citizen and his or her father were born in Israel, that citizen is classified as a Jew of "Israeli origin." Palestinian citizens, by contrast, are unable to attain this "Israeli origin" status. "In fact, they have no origin, only religion," Cohen and Gordon observe. "In other words, according to Israel's official statistics, all Jews ultimately become 'Israeli' within the span of two generations, and no Palestinian can ever become 'Israeli.' This produces a bifurcated racial reality in which Jewishness trumps all other categories of identification, which, in turn, both reflects and helps reproduce the state's mechanisms of control as well as its spatial politics."[51]

Strikingly, the term "Israeli Arab" is never used to refer to the Arab Jews who make up a considerable proportion of Israel's Jewish population—the real Israeli Arabs—because of course, in their case, Israel wants to erase their Arab identity and absorb them as Jews, whereas in the case of Palestinian citizens, the reverse holds true: they can't be absorbed as Jews, so their indigestible Arabness is emphasized.[52] Race, in other words, works in both positive and negative ways in Israel, and the logics of racination and de-racination perform extraordinarily complex ideological work in support of the all-important racial distinction between Jewish nationals (settlers) and non-Jewish nonnationals (natives).[53] The result is a starkly racial state that at every possible turn resorts to linguistic tricks and verbal sleights of hand (e.g., mistranslating "citizenship" as "nationality") to cover up that that is exactly what it is.[54] These same verbal tricks are effortlessly parroted by Israel's many admirers in the United States and elsewhere, which is why, when they want to emphasize how wonderfully democratic Israel is supposed to be, they are quick to point out how many "Arabs" there are in its parliament (see the quotations from politicians and others cited above). Not only do they not refer to "Palestinians" as such: their insistence on referring to them as Arabs helps to erase their specifically Palestinian identity. In other words, *affirming* their Arab ethnicity is part of *denying* their presence as Palestinians.

Stripping Palestinian citizens of their national identity as Palestinians is not only merely degrading, however. For, as Dugard and Reynolds argue, "underpinning Israel's discriminatory policies against the Palestinians—both within Israel and in the occupied Palestinian territory—is a legal system that constructs a notion of 'Jewish nationality' and privileges Jewish nationals over non-Jewish groups under Israeli jurisdiction."[55] Thus, in Israel, various fundamental rights—access to land and housing, for example—are attendant upon racial identity ("nationality") as defined by the state, not the lesser category of mere citizenship. As Dugard and Reynolds point out, Palestinians "are hugely restricted in critical areas such as land use and access to natural resources and key services, excluded by planning laws and institutions, and systematically discriminated against at municipal and national levels in the sphere of economic, social, and cultural rights." Meanwhile, they note, "Jewish nationals, whose exclusive interests are served by parastatal institutions such as the Jewish Agency and the Jewish National Fund, are privy to exclusive access to most of the state's territory and to claim extra-territorial rights and privileges in areas controlled by Israel."[56] Indeed, Jews who are not citizens actually have more rights in some domains, particularly with regard to land, than native

Palestinians.[57] In no other country on earth do racially privileged *nonciti-zens* enjoy greater rights than racially disadvantaged residents of the territory controlled by the state.

South Africa's Group Areas Act of 1950, which assigned different areas of South Africa for the residential use of different racial groups, has a direct equivalent in the system of formal and informal regulations that determine access to land inside Israel (and in the territories occupied in 1967 too, even more blatantly). Palestinian citizens of the state are barred from living on land held by "national institutions" such as the Jewish National Fund (JNF), the overwhelming majority of it Palestinian property violently expropriated by the new state after the ethnic cleansing of Palestine in 1948.[58] Nowhere, in fact, is the extent and institutionalization of racial discrimination more glaringly obvious—for those willing to see it—[59] than in the pronouncements of the JNF, which, officially empowered by the state to manage land, advertises itself as "the caretaker of the land of Israel on behalf of its owners—Jewish people everywhere."[60] Land directly owned by the state as opposed to the JNF (every inch of it expropriated from Palestinian families) may, under certain circumstances, be leased to non-Jews, as Gershon Shafir and Yoav Peled observe, "but in practice such leases are rare, outside the Negev, and are limited to short-term, one- to three-year leases. Long-term leases, of forty-nine years, are made exclusively to Jews, and sub-leasing them to non-Jews is prohibited."[61] In other words, the structures of discrimination and separation that so clearly mark the parts of Palestine captured in 1967 are also played out in the parts of Palestine captured in 1948: the only difference is subtlety.

South Africa's Bantu Education Act of 1953, which created a separate and unequal education system for Black South Africans, has a direct equivalent in the administrative procedures that have created separate and unequal primary and secondary education systems for Jewish and non-Jewish citizens of the state of Israel (and the territories occupied in 1967). "There is total separation in formal education between Jews and Arabs, from kindergarten through secondary school, in all forms and grades," Jacob Landau notes.[62] The systematically segregated Palestinian schools inside the state are short of classrooms and other facilities. This second-class system for second-class citizens "lacks completely, or is seriously underprovided with, related education services such as psychological counseling, truancy officers, health-care services, computers, extra-curricular activities, and so on," Shafir and Peled point out.[63] At one point a government committee estimated that the education system for Palestinian citizens lagged behind the one serving Jewish citizens by twenty to twenty-five years.[64] All told, Israel invests more than three times as much per capita in a Jewish citizen than it does in a non-Jewish (i.e., Palestinian) one.[65] The forms of discrimination practiced by the state's education system are even transcoded into its school textbooks, as a comprehensive study by the Israeli sociologist Nurit Peled-Elhanan shows.[66]

And so the list goes on. South Africa's Prohibition of Mixed Marriages Act of 1949 has its equivalent in the Israeli laws preventing Jews from marrying non-Jews: there is no institution of civil marriage in Israel, and Jews are legally allowed to marry only other Jews in Israel, and then only according to Orthodox religious law, because only the Orthodox rabbinate is empowered to transact matters of personal status for Jewish citizens. (Palestinian citizens transact personal status matters through their own religious institutions, but, unlike Orthodox Judaism, both Christianity and Islam permit their adherents to marry outside their faith communities.)

The Natives (Urban Areas) Consolidation Act of 1945 and the Black (Native) Amendment Act of 1952, which required Black South Africans to carry passes and regulated their access to urban areas, have equivalents in the various Israeli laws regulating and controlling the movement of indigenous Palestinians—but not Jewish settlers—within the occupied territories and between and among the occupied territories, Jerusalem, and Israel.[67] (As I write in spring 2021, the Israeli army has imposed a total ban on Palestinian movement around the West Bank for the week of Passover, as it invariably does every year, closing all checkpoints for the week and sealing Palestinians in their towns and villages for seven days while maintaining freedom of movement for Jews. Thus, Palestinian Muslims are denied access to the great mosques of Jerusalem, and Palestinian Christians from around the West Bank are barred from entering the Church of the Nativity in Bethlehem and the Church of the Holy Sepulchre in Jerusalem on Good Friday and Easter Sunday, but Jews can come and go to their Passover seders just as they please.)

The Public Safety Act of 1953 has an equivalent in the Israeli military regulations permitting the long-term detention without trial of Palestinians

(but not Jewish settlers) in the occupied territories. Indeed, the two populations of the West Bank, Palestinian and Jewish, are subject to two entirely
different legal systems in the same territory: Jewish settlers enjoy the protections of Israeli civil law, which Israel has selectively projected along
racial lines beyond its own borders, while Palestinians are subject to the
much harsher provisions of military law.

The Promotion of Bantu Self-Government Act of 1952, which man-
dated greater official recognition of Bantustans like Transkei, and the
Bantu Homelands Constitution Act of 1971 have an equivalent in the
Oslo Accords' creation of a so-called Palestinian Authority to partially
manage the affairs of Palestinian (but not Jewish) residents of the occupied territories. Indeed, just as South Africa created Transkei, Ciskei, and
Bophuthatswana in order to artificially delete as many Blacks as possible
from South Africa's own population registry, Israel maintains pockets of
the West Bank and all of Gaza as holding pens for the land's non-Jewish
population, while settling the rest of the territory with its own population
in order to be able to have its cake and eat it too: to absorb the land (settling it) but not the people, and to maintain the claim that it is a Jewish
state while keeping to a bare minimum the number of non-Jews who officially live within the state—and hence to perpetuate the fiction that it does
not disenfranchise the majority of the land's population that is Palestinian.
For it is often said that one of the differences between Apartheid-era
South Africa and present-day Israel is that the former involved a minority
oppressing a majority whereas the latter does not.

This is simply not true. Of course Israel disenfranchises the land's
Palestinian majority: there are today approximately 12.5 million
Palestinians and 6 million Israeli Jews.[68] Israel's manipulation of populations and territories, however, obscures as much as possible these material
circumstances: 1.5 million Palestinians are citizens of Israel and have
been linguistically disappeared into the category of "Israeli Arabs," so they
don't count; 7 million Palestinians live in the exile that was violently
forced on them in 1948 by Israel, which continues to deny their legal and
moral right of return, and so they don't count. That leaves the 4 million or
so Palestinians in the occupied territories. At face value, the situation may
not look like a minority oppressing a majority, but that is exactly what is
going on.

A slew of recent reports have elaborated on the nature of Israeli apart-heid. A 2017 report published by the United Nations Economic and Social Commission for Western Asia insists that the different domains—second-class citizenship, occupation, or enforced exile—into which Israel has restricted the Palestinian people "constitute one comprehensive regime developed for the purpose of ensuring the enduring domination over non-Jews in all land exclusively under Israeli control." The report states that "the strategic fragmentation of the Palestinian people is the principal method by which Israel imposes an apartheid regime."[69] In early 2021, the Israeli human rights organization B'tselem published a new position paper on what it called "a regime of Jewish supremacy from the Jordan River to the Mediterranean Sea." In the entire area between the Mediterranean Sea and the Jordan River, the report points out, "the Israeli regime implements laws, practices and state violence designed to cement the supremacy of one group—Jews—over another—Palestinians. A key method in pursuing this goal is engineering space differently for each group." This, B'tselem pointed out, "is apartheid."[70] In the spring of 2021, Human Rights Watch published its own investigation and concluded, similarly, that, in seeking "to maintain the domination by Jewish Israelis over Palestinians," including those who are its citizens, "Israel is commit-ting the crimes of apartheid and persecution against Arabs [i.e., Palestinians] in the occupied territories and Israel itself."[71]

As these new reports remind us, it is vital to take heed of the fact that "apartheid" is not a slang term or an emotional claim: it is a concept clearly articulated in international law, notably the Apartheid Convention of 1973. Article II of the convention specifies the crime of apartheid as constituting "the inhuman acts committed for the purposes of establish-ing and maintaining domination by one racial group of persons over any other racial group of persons and systematically oppressing them."[72] Most of the acts specified in Article II clearly apply to Israel's practices in the territories it has occupied since 1967, leading major international legal scholars and researchers to conclude that—as an exhaustive 2009 study published by the South Africa Human Sciences Research Council states—Israel's practices in the occupied territories "are integrated and comple-mentary elements of an institutionalized and oppressive system of Israeli domination and oppression over Palestinians as a group; that is, a system of apartheid."[73] Dugard and Reynolds, among others, concur in their assessment that Israeli practices in the occupied territories "are in breach of the legal prohibition of apartheid."[74]

Several elements of Article II of the Apartheid Convention are also clearly applicable, however, to the parts of Palestine occupied in 1948, as recent reports now acknowledge. Article II(c) refers to "legislative measures and other measures calculated to prevent a racial group or groups from participation in the political, social, economic and cultural life of the country" by denying to members of a racial group "the right to leave and return to their country, the right to a nationality, the right to freedom of movement and residence, the right to freedom of opinion and expression, and the right to freedom of peaceful assembly and association." Article II(d) refers to "any measures, including legislative measures, designed to divide the population along racial lines by the creation of separate reserves and ghettoes for the members of a racial group or groups, the prohibition of mixed marriages among members of various racial groups, the expropriation of landed property belonging to a racial group or groups or to members thereof." And Article II(e) refers to "persecution of organizations and persons, by depriving them of fundamental rights and freedoms, because they oppose apartheid."

As the preceding argument shows, Israel is in violation of all these stipulations in all the territories over which it rules, not just those it occupied in 1967. This evidence led the Russell Tribunal meeting in Cape Town in 2011 to determine that "Israel's rule over the Palestinian people, wherever they reside, collectively amounts to a single regime of apartheid."[75] And it led the 2017 UN report to conclude that "Israel is guilty of policies and practices that constitute the crime of apartheid as legally defined in instruments of international law," and indeed that "Israel has established an apartheid regime that dominates the Palestinian people as a whole."[76]

There are of course differences between the racial regimes in South Africa and Israel. The system of Apartheid inside South Africa, for all its violence and viciousness, had a different logic than the one that rules in Palestine. The movement of Blacks in South Africa was controlled, not banned altogether, as is the case, for example, with the movement of Palestinians in and out of Gaza, which Israel has largely sealed off from the world for over a decade: an entire generation of children is growing up in Gaza who have never set foot outside the tiny coastal strip. The Apartheid regime in South Africa wanted Blacks to work; killing or starving the labor force—or locking it up in a giant open-air prison like Gaza— would have been unthinkable.

And that of course is the major material difference between South African Apartheid and Israeli apartheid. There is a world of difference between exploitation and expulsion, transfer, elimination, or annihilation; between, as Ghassan Hage puts it, the racism of exploitation and the racism of extermination.[77] In South Africa the system of Apartheid was designed to enable the exploitation of Black labor in houses, offices, and gold mines while denying Black people equal rights. The Israeli system is not, at an ideological level, about exploitation of Palestinian labor. As Gershon Shafir observes, the Zionist settler project in Palestine aimed from its very origins not to *exploit* but to *eliminate* indigenous Palestinian labor.[78]

Of course, there was for years, and there remains to a certain extent even to this day, Israeli exploitation of Palestinian labor in various sectors of the economy (notably construction). But by and large the Zionist project in Palestine aimed whenever possible to replace the native population—to transfer it and reclaim the land. The process that began in 1948 continues to this day every time a Palestinian home is demolished in Jerusalem; every time a Palestinian family is expelled from the ghost town that is central Hebron; every time a Palestinian Jerusalemite is stripped of her residency papers and expelled from the city of her birth; every time a Palestinian family is shattered and broken because of an Israeli law, instituted in 2003, that prevents a Palestinian in Israel or Jerusalem from marrying and living with a spouse from the occupied territories, even though a Jewish Israeli can marry a Jewish colonist from the West Bank and they can live together wherever they please. (When a similar law was proposed at the peak of Apartheid in South Africa in 1980, it was summarily dismissed by that country's high court as an unacceptable violation of Black people's right to family; the Israeli High Court upheld that country's new law in 2006 and has repeatedly upheld it in the years since.)

In a word, as I have put this elsewhere: South African Apartheid was biopolitical in nature, concerned with the management and administration of living Black labor. Israel's is, to borrow the phrase that Achille Mbembe has elaborated so effectively, necropolitical,[79] concerned with the destruction and erasure of Palestinians—something that every Palestinian resists every single day, if only by the sheer act of stubbornly continuing to exist. This necropolitics depends crucially and absolutely, however, on the system of inscrutability and invisibility that allows Israelis and the supporters of Israel to go on practicing or endorsing a violent form of racism without having to reckon with and acknowledge the fact that that is precisely what they are doing. It is unthinkable that most American supporters of Israel—especially in liberal sectors such as the academy—would continue to endorse its racism and apartheid if they saw them for what they are.

·   ·   ·   ·   ·

And this brings us back to the major difference between the racial regimes of South Africa and Israel with which the chapter begins: the legibility of South African Apartheid and the relative illegibility—the inscrutability—of Israeli apartheid. Nowhere in Israel or the occupied territories is there a sign, equivalent to those in South Africa, that baldly says "Jews Only." But there also doesn't need to be: the racism is carried out in practice rather than in language. Whereas South African Apartheid insisted on naming and drawing attention to itself through endless verbal and visual cues, Israeli apartheid seeks whenever possible to elide and cover over the forms of racism that it embodies just as fully. It is a perfect example of what David Theo Goldberg has recently theorized as "racism without racism."[80]

Admirers of Israel can say that it treats all its citizens equally, not so much because they do not realize that discrimination operates at the level of race and "nationality" rather than at the secondary level of citizenship (who can be bothered with such technical subtleties?), but rather because Israelis and their overseas supporters, unlike white South Africans, are spared from being forced to reckon with that realization. They are allowed—and they allow themselves—to see right through it, to parrot the slogans that come easily to the tongue, to indulge in the misrecognition of an ugly reality that is actually staring them in the face, to continuously misrecognize the facts when someone else insists on tabulating, documenting, and presenting them, and to erupt in blind resentful fury if the facts are pushed at them even a little bit too insistently.

What's in play here, then, is a form of denial that cannot bring itself to acknowledge itself for what it is. It is by staring so obsessively at language, not seeing the absent meanings because they are not conveyed in language—"Where does it say 'Jews only'?"—that supporters of Israel allow themselves to avoid recognizing the material reality: there does not have to be a sign explicitly saying "Jews only" in order for Jews only to use a road in the West Bank or to attend a certain school or to live in a certain town in Israel; there doesn't have to be a law saying Jews and non-Jews *cannot marry* for Jews and non-Jews *not to be able to marry* in Israel. Unlike Apartheid in South Africa, where all these kinds of proscriptions were bluntly spelled out, what we see in Israel is racism that avoids language. That doesn't make it any less racist, however.

The biopolitical form of Apartheid in South Africa ended because the white elite there eventually realized (thanks to local resistance and global boycotts and sanctions) that it was ultimately untenable and needed to be dismantled and replaced with a more democratic system of government and representation, and indeed a mechanism of truth and reconciliation was seen to be integral to the process of transition from Apartheid to the system that replaced it. But the very transparency of the system in South Africa ultimately facilitated the white government's own capacity for political calculation. The problem with Israeli apartheid is that it is premised on a lack of transparency, above all to itself; it is positioned out of view; it is unavailable for interrogation, reconsideration, dismantlement. As far as its own practitioners and overseas supporters are concerned, it doesn't even exist in the first place and Israel is a wonderful democratic state: what, then, can there be to reconsider or dismantle? Its necropolitical logic continues to be carried on not in the name of racism but rather, on the contrary, in the name of "mutual respect, pluralism, and openness," "tolerance," and "democracy."

Hence the significance of the denial of apartheid and above all the affirmation of Israel as a democracy with which this chapter opens. Any attempt to question this dual mantra is met with immediate denunciation and reaffirmation, all over again, of the invocation of the democratic-and-Jewish-state. When, in March 2017, the United Nations Economic and Social Commission for Western Asia published the report on Israeli apartheid (quoted from earlier in this chapter), the reaction was instantaneous.

The US ambassador to the United Nations, Nikki Haley, denounced the report as "false" and "defamatory." Israel's other ambassador to the United Nations, Danny Danon, said it was "despicable and constitutes a blatant lie." The new UN secretary general, António Guterres, immediately distanced himself from the report and had it purged from UN websites. At no point was there an attempt to examine the report's careful arguments and evidence (it was authored by two prominent American scholars of international law, Richard Falk and Virginia Tilley, and vetted by three other scholarly readers before publication) or to rebut the argument or to muster counterevidence. Outrage and denial trumped argument and evidence.

Perhaps the most astonishing case of such denial is that of Justice Richard Goldstone, who chaired an international commission investigating Israel's war on Gaza in 2008–9. The Goldstone Report itself was "supportive of a finding of apartheid in the occupied Palestinian territory in respect of Article 2(a) and (c) of the Apartheid Convention," having noted "discrimination and differential treatment" between Palestinians and Israeli Jews in domains including land use, housing, access to natural resources; citizenship, residence and family unification; access to food and water supplies; the use of force against demonstrators; freedom of movement; access to health, education and social services; and freedom of association.[81] But Goldstone himself subsequently published a piece in the *New York Times* insisting, despite all the evidence to the contrary, that the charge of apartheid "is an unfair and inaccurate slander against Israel." It's vital to take note of the language and the forms of elision that I have already touched on here, all of which Goldstone uses in his emotional recantation: "Israeli Arabs [i.e., Palestinians]—20 percent of Israel's population—vote, have political parties and representatives in the Knesset and occupy positions of acclaim, including on its Supreme Court. Arab [i.e., Palestinian] patients lie alongside Jewish patients in Israeli hospitals, receiving identical treatment. To be sure, there is more de facto separation between Jewish and Arab [i.e., Palestinian] populations than Israelis should accept. Much of it is chosen by the communities themselves. Some results from discrimination. But it is not apartheid, which consciously enshrines separation as an ideal. In Israel, equal rights are the law, the aspiration and the ideal; inequities are often successfully challenged in court."[82] As this chapter demonstrates, these claims are not only patently false (there is, for instance, no protection of equality anywhere in Israeli law, and, on the contrary, formal and informal mechanisms of racial discrimination are institutionalized by the state and consistently given the approval of its highest court, beginning with the ways in which it legally classifies and differentiates among citizens) but are couched in the standard Israeli language intended to disappear the Palestinian presence inside the state as part of the overall logic of apartheid. And if a literary scholar like me can figure this out, then so surely can a prominent international jurist; but not, I suppose, a jurist blinded by denial.

And, unsurprisingly, the mantra of the Jewish-and-democratic-state with which this chapter opens is thus crucial to the denial of—and hence the persistence—of this form of apartheid. In affirming Jewish democracy (a positive value), one is simultaneously endorsing a racial state and racial discrimination (a negative reality). What, after all, does it mean to be a Jewish state? As a condition of possibility, it is a state that privileges Jews over non-Jews. What does it mean to be a democracy? It means to be a state that treats all citizens equally without privileging one kind of citizen over another. How, then, can a state both privilege some (Jewish) and be open to all (democracy)? How can a state be both particular and general? The obvious answer is that it cannot be, unless everyone in it fits the limited description, which then makes the proposition itself—Jewish *and* democratic—redundant. Why, then, the endless affirmation of the Jewish-and-democratic-state to describe a state that rules over and structures the daily lives of millions upon millions of non-Jews? What work does this affirmation do? This work: it enables the endorsement of a racial enterprise without acknowledging that that is what it is. As a logical proposition, Israel can genuinely be *both* Jewish *and* democratic if and only if there are no non-Jews left: a condition the state has historically worked as hard as possible to realize by expelling or killing ("We will have to kill and kill and kill . . . all day, every day," as Israel's leading demographic alarmist, Arnon Sofer, once summed up this logic[83]) as many people as it could who did not "fit" the state's definition of itself as Jewish. In the guise of a testament of liberal values, the mantra "Jewish and democratic state" is actually all but a declaration of murderous intent. But the overwhelming majority of those who mindlessly parrot this oxymoronic slogan would never think of themselves as advocates of genocide. And that is precisely the point.

3 Diversity

"In the beating heart of Tel Aviv," the Eurovision website proclaimed effusively, "Habima Square turned orange as the official Opening Ceremony of the 2019 Eurovision Song Contest took place on Sunday 12 May. The lavish affair saw hopefuls from 41 participating countries along with their delegations welcomed to Israel, where in just 5 days, a new Eurovision Song Contest winner will be crowned."[1] Apart from the visiting bands, special guests at the opening ceremony included the transgender Israeli singer Dana International, who had won the song contest in 1998, and Netta Barzilai—"the best ambassador of Israel," according to Benjamin Netanyahu[2]—who had won the contest in Lisbon in 2018, clearing the way for Tel Aviv in 2019. The mayor of Tel Aviv, Ron Huldai, was on stage as well, performing his own version of Barzilai's winning song. After all, the arrival of an event that has come to be regarded as the "gay Olympics" was supposed to be a big win for Tel Aviv, which, in the face of a global cultural boycott, had embarked on a major campaign to market itself as "the gayest city on earth."[3]

For, long before 2019, the Eurovision Song Contest had become all but synonymous with a celebration of European queer camp and pop culture (a point to which I return later in this chapter). Although camp has always had a potentially subversive edge to it, and a historical relationship with various other modes of resistance against power, the Tel Aviv Eurovision contest—an attempt to transfer the celebration of a specifically European queer subculture to the distinctly non-European, militarily occupied, eastern shore of the Mediterranean—represents the ultimate co-optation of whatever liberatory potential the event might still be said to have.[4] Outside the opening ceremony, a small group of activists briefly blocked one of the entrances before being muscled away by police and border guards. "You cannot host a cultural, music event in a place with a racist, apartheid regime," one of them told a local newspaper; "art and culture should be a messenger for change, not for hiding the truth."[5] During their performance, the Icelandic band Hatari furtively flashed a little scarf emblazoned with the Palestinian flag, for which they were duly reprimanded and fined: despite the manifest politicization of the event, rule 2.7 of the competition says it cannot be used for political ends ("the ESC is a non-political event . . . [it] shall in no case be politicized and/or instrumentalized").[6] Even Madonna—who had shrugged off international calls to boycott the event, which she headlined—was chastised when her dancers carried Israeli and Palestinian flags on their costumes: "You cannot mix politics at a cultural event," grumbled the Israeli foreign minister after her performance.[7]

Notwithstanding Eurovision rule 2.7 (the provisions of which the event violated in the most egregious way imaginable), the Tel Aviv contest was, of course, at least as much a political as a cultural carnival, and not only because the visiting participants had crossed an international boycott line to perform there. The event celebrating Israel's claim to inclusion, diversity, and belonging kicked off in the same month that Palestinians commemorate the destruction of Palestine in 1948. Just a half-hour drive away from the Tel Aviv Expo, where Eurovision was held, Palestinians in Gaza had spent the previous year protesting their dispossession and collective imprisonment and demanding their right to return to their land in southwestern Palestine, including the area now occupied by Tel Aviv; over the course of the previous year, Israeli army snipers had killed hundreds of these protesters—including dozens of children—and injured tens of thousands.[8] Closer to the event stage itself, there were more imminent reminders of the ravages of 1948. The Tel Aviv Expo was built on the lands of

al-Sheikh Muwannis, a Palestinian town attacked and forcibly depopulated in the weeks leading up to Israel's declaration of independence in
May 1948.[9] A number of the town's houses remain standing to this day:
not only the Expo but much of the campus of Tel Aviv University was built
on its lands; the university faculty club, for instance, was formerly the Abu
Khalil family home.[10]

Eurovision Tel Aviv is perhaps the most striking example of "pinkwashing," which Ali Abunimah—widely credited with popularizing the term as a
form of critique[11]—has identified as "a rhetorical strategy that deploys
Israel's supposed enlightenment toward LGBTQ issues to deflect criticism
from Israel's abuses and war crimes and to seek to build up support for
Israel among Western liberals and progressives."[12] This form of occlusion
and obfuscation is surely the central element of pinkwashing, but the relationship between Israel's pinkwashing strategy and its structural racism and
war crimes is deeper than merely an act of covering up: as with the other
domains explored in this book, the act of occlusion is inseparable from and
materially coextensive with the act of violence it aims to cover up. Thus,
while Israel's loud affirmation of gay rights certainly does serve to screen its
systematic denial of Palestinian rights ("Look over here, not over there!"),
the affinity is deeper than mere screening. The process of pinkwashing is
made possible by—it returns to, it affirms, it extends and continues—the
violent removal of Palestinians from their land; it makes Palestinians—
including queer Palestinians—disappear. It's not *only* a cover up but *also* an
extension of the same logic of colonial displacement, dis-appearance, and
denial taking place in other sites around Palestine. In exploring the dynamics of Israeli pinkwashing, the main aim of this chapter is to tie its various
manifestations specifically to the broader modes of denial in which this
book is interested; the chapter seeks less to reveal the very existence of pinkwashing (which others have amply documented) than to tie its many forms
and strands together, showing how together they contribute to the larger
mode of denial explored in other chapters: to synthesize discrete elements
and show that the whole is greater than the sum of the parts.

Pinkwashing emerged as one of the key strands of a campaign launched
to restore Israel's image around the world, which had—following years of
Israeli bombardment and abuse of civilian populations in Palestine and in
Lebanon as well—seriously deteriorated by the 2000s. People around the

world generally hold a dim view of Israel, a fact upheld by annual country ratings polls: a 2013 survey conducted for the BBC World Service, for instance, found that while 21 percent of respondents viewed Israel in a favorable light, more than 50 percent saw it negatively, placing it near the bottom of the poll, just barely above North Korea and Iran.[13] A 2009 index of media perceptions of all the countries in the world similarly ranked Israel 192 out of 200, sandwiched between Yemen at 191 and Sudan at 193.[14] What was new, however, was Israel's reputational decline specifically among young and liberal sectors of US and European societies. A group of Jewish marketing specialists with years of experience in advertising and corporate public relations in the United States commissioned a series of surveys and focus groups early in that decade and found to their alarm that perceptions of Israel among young and liberal demographics in the United States was deteriorating at a "devastating" rate.[15] While support for the state remained strong, and was even growing, among conservative, evangelical, older, and white respondents, youthful liberals—the mainstay of European and American Zionism for decades—were abandoning it in droves. And as research was extended over the following years, surveys found that support for Israel even among groups whose support could once be taken for granted was continuing to plummet. Support for Israel among Jewish college students in the United States, for instance, dropped by almost 30 percentage points from 2010 to 2016, while that same constituency's sympathy for Palestinians went the other way.[16]

In fact, the study found that years of grinding Israeli *hasbara* (propaganda and misinformation) may have had an unintended consequence: the more people knew about Israel, it turned out, the less favorably they viewed it.[17] Focus groups found that Israel had come to be associated in their minds with violence, conflict, religious zealotry, concrete landscapes, and "middle-aged ultra-Orthodox men," associations that held little appeal for younger and more liberal demographics.[18] The issues leading the decline were related to human rights, tolerance, and diversity, domains in which Israel was (unsurprisingly) not viewed favorably. One of the authors of the study, Fern Oppenheim, blamed "intersectional" activism on US college campuses for this decline and stressed that these "at-risk" segments of the US population needed to be appealed to, in particular by sidelining explicitly political areas and focusing instead on culture and values. "The future of America no longer believe [*sic*] that Israel shares their values. This is huge! Devastating," she said.[19] If liberal Jewish college students—and similar constituencies—don't perceive a set of shared values tying them to Israel, Oppenheim and her colleagues concluded, the mission of next-wave hasbara is to develop it.

Hence "Brand Israel"—a project undertaken by public relations firms, including Saatchi & Saatchi (remarkably working free of charge[20]) and the Brand Israel Group, a coalition of seven marketing and communications executives, including Oppenheim, "who have volunteered their time over the last two years to research how Israel might improve its image."[21] At meetings convened by the Israeli Ministry of Foreign Affairs and Finance Ministry in coordination with the Prime Minister's Office, "the participants examined specialized research *conducted by American marketing executives* over the last three years. The meeting is the latest manifestation of a growing movement—*begun in America*—to 're-brand' Israel, or to reinvent the country's image in the eyes of both Jews and non-Jews. The driving concept is that Israel will win supporters only if it is seen as relevant and modern rather than only as a place of fighting and religion."[22] The target audience for the effort to rebrand Israel was quickly identified as "liberals" and people aged 16 to 30.[23] And the message to be conveyed through "more positive imaging" was that Israel is "democratic, moral, successful," projected to show Americans (always the main targets) "that there is another Israel beyond the gloomy headlines, an Israel that enjoys and values life like Americans do, and that is highly successful as a productive, vibrant and cutting-edge culture."[24] As far as many Americans are concerned, one of the participating hasbarists points out, Israel is "Gaza and the West Bank and tanks, and they don't see the beautiful culture and the liberal side." "We're hoping," he notes, "to show that Israel is a liberal country, a multicultural, pluralistic country."[25]

The Israeli government took this rebranding project very seriously from the beginning, throwing financial and diplomatic assets at it. The Foreign Ministry allocated $26 million to country branding in 2010, a dramatic increase over previous years.[26] And the effort has encompassed not only the state itself but its many arms and affiliates in other countries, above all the United States. One of the first efforts to bear fruit involved the Foreign Ministry inviting photographers from the magazine *Maxim* to

Israel for photo shoots of scantily clad Israeli models. Many of the shoots (which have continued ever since) are arranged to emphasize militarism as a side dish to sexual appeal, with pictures of an Israeli soldier in a bikini juxtaposed with a shot of her in uniform, or simply showing her posing with a rifle and little else.[27] The Israeli army started accounts on Facebook and Instagram (e.g., @hot_idf_girls) with similar profiles, and shoots featuring male Israeli models in various states of undress soon followed.[28] "All the surveys we have done shows [sic] that the biggest hasbara problem that Israel has is with males from the age of 18–35," claimed David Saranga, consul for media and public affairs at the Israeli Consulate in New York; "Israel does not seem relevant for them, and that is bad for branding."[29] Not one for subtlety, Saranga added that photos of sexy Israeli women constitute what he calls a "Trojan Horse" to lure readers into thinking of Israel as a "modern country with nice beaches and pretty women." The Israeli consul-general, Arye Mekel, also bluntly described the bikini shoots as a branding exercise: "I want people to think about beautiful people in beautiful places when they think of Israel," he said, "as well as [to] see the diversity of Israeli society and culture."[30] Planting such images in people's minds involves a kind of engineering.

Apart from sex appeal, another priority area for Israel's rebranding project was sports. Israel is—remarkably for a non-European entity—a member of the Union of European Football Associations (UEFA), so its teams at least theoretically can qualify for the Europa and Champions leagues as well as the European Championship. In FIFA (Fédération Internationale de Football Association), the global governing body for football, Israel also belongs to Europe rather than Asia (which, apart from politics, makes it far easier for Israel to qualify for the World Cup than it is for countries in Asia, given the way that FIFA privileges European teams through the qualifying rounds). In 2011, despite the UEFA's loud campaign against racism in football, Israel successfully campaigned for the under-twenty-one championship to be played there. In the buildup to the tournament, the English and German football associations (FAs) cooperated closely with the Israeli FA on a variety of "football for all" and other anti-racist messages, and, as Jon Dart points out, "the tournament was promoted by the IFA, UEFA and the Israeli state as an opportunity to bring together diverse groups, to promote mutual respect and tolerance on and off the field, and to portray the Israeli state as a democracy."[31] So much for the UEFA's campaign to "kick racism out of football."[32] Other sporting initiatives have involved bringing winning NFL players to Israel in 2017, though admittedly that fell flat when Michael Bennet, Kenny Stills, Justin Forsett, and others refused to go.[33]

Israel's claims to a high-tech culture have also been brandished as elements in this new branding campaign, not just by the Israeli government but also by that government's many affiliates in the United States. For instance, Israeli hasbarists launched Israel21C, a well-funded advocacy organization that aims to showcase "the country's rich and diverse culture, innovative spirit, wide-ranging contributions to humanity, and democratic civil society."[34] If Israel wants to improve its image around the world, the outfit claims, "it must be seen through the lenses of its humanness, its diversity and all that it contributes through medical advances, technological innovation, art, culture and acts of human kindness.'"[35] As Nada Elia points out, gestures like this under the umbrella of the Brand Israel Group promote "the country's technological accomplishments and its cosmopolitan culture, projecting it as a land of innovation and First World luxury under the blissfully warm Mediterranean sun, and distracting from its problematic image as a battleground for justice and equal rights for all citizens."[36]

Although Israel's claims to high tech and world sports are important, the domain that has received the lion's share of the attention in the Brand Israel campaign is the country's claim to LGBTQ (and, most prominently, gay men's) rights: hence the prominence of pinkwashing. David Saranga, the Israeli consul in New York who helped develop what he called the "Trojan Horse" of scantily clad women to boost appeal for Israel among young heterosexual men in the West, has also been involved in pushing Israel's claim on Western gay identity. Gay culture, according to Saranga, is the entryway to liberal Western culture in general, because of what he terms the "buzz" that culture supposedly enjoys.[37] "Showing young, liberal Americans that Israel also has a gay culture goes a long [way] toward informing them that Israel is a place that respects human rights," Saranga claims. "Israel needs to show this community that it is relevant to them by promoting gay tourism, gay artists and films."[38] Chiming in, a Foreign Ministry official told the *Jerusalem Post* that efforts to let European and

American liberals know about the gay community in Israel "were an important part of its work to highlight this country's support of human rights and to underscore its diversity in a population that tends to judge Israel harshly solely on its treatment of Palestinians."[39] In this image-engineering project, highlighting Israel's support for gay rights amounts to a substitute, a compensation for, its appalling treatment of Palestinians.

Even if Saranga and the Israeli Foreign Ministry aren't offering the most sophisticated cultural analysis, they are on to something. "Within global gay and lesbian organizing circuits," Jasbir Puar points out, "to be gay friendly is to be modern, cosmopolitan, developed, first-world, global north, and, most significantly, democratic."[40] The correlation between a state's claim to gay-friendly status and its claim to sophistication and tolerance extends far beyond global queer constituencies, moreover, and it can be mobilized for a wide range of political purposes. How well a culture supposedly treats its women was once (and indeed still is) used to justify colonial intervention, and, as Puar points out, a new version of that paradigm has emerged in contemporary political culture. "'How well do you treat your women?' became a key measure of the ability of a colonized or developing country to self-govern," Puar argues. "While 'the Woman Question' has hardly disappeared, we can now find its amendment in 'the Homosexual Question,' or 'how well do you treat your homosexuals?' as a current paradigm through which nations, populations and cultures are evaluated in terms of their ability to conform to a universalized notion of civilization."[41] According to this logic, the extent to which a state protects gay rights can be seen as an index of that state's claim to belong to the order of liberal, democratic, open societies—societies privileging rights, diversity, freedom, openness, and tolerance more broadly.

A state that can market itself as supportive of gay rights, then, is a state that can market itself as progressive in general.[42] And a state that presents itself as progressive, liberal, and tolerant also in opposition to neighboring societies that are taken to hold all the opposite characteristics—repression, homophobia, intolerance—gains all the more from the contrast. Thus, from the beginning, Israel's claims to LGBTQ tolerance and diversity have been consistently framed in opposition to supposed Arab and particularly Palestinian intolerance and homophobia. Moreover, the rhetorical opposition between Israel's supposed homophilia and Arab or

Palestinian homophobia has been established in terms that reiterate a much older discourse contrasting Israel's general development, liberalism, tolerance, and advancement with Arab and Palestinian backwardness, degeneration, fanaticism, and so on—itself the manifestation of two centuries of a much broader Orientalist framing of a civilized, sophisticated, rational, productive Western "us" as opposed to a degenerate, irrational, unproductive, and dangerous Eastern "them."[43]

Indeed, from its very inception, modern Zionism has been couched in Orientalist terms intended to emphasize the difference between the Zionists' claim to Occidental superiority and their assumption of the Oriental otherness of the Palestinian Arab. "Between Zionism and the West there was and still is a community of language and ideology," Edward Said points out; "so far as the Arab was concerned, he was not part of this community."[44] The earliest Zionist appeals to European powers (notably the British) were consistently framed in these terms, with the Zionist emphasizing his status as a white European talking to other white Europeans about nonwhite others. "From this distinction all sorts of conclusions follow," Said argues. "Arabs are Oriental, therefore less human and valuable than Europeans and Zionists; they are treacherous, unregenerate, etc." As a result of this binary rhetorical framing, from the beginning, "Zionism and Israel were associated with what 'we' understand and fight for. By contrast, Zionism's enemies were simply a twentieth-century version of an Oriental despotism, sensuality, ignorance, and similar forms of backwardness."[45] Two conclusions follow from this that have been consistent features of Zionist rhetorical strategy ever since: first, Zionism seeks to align itself with white, Western values; second, Zionism's enemies are portrayed also as the enemies of white, Western values—and, moreover, are not to be heard from directly but only via the mediation and representation of Zionists.[46]

Contemporary Zionist exercises in pinkwashing have appropriated and reiterated all of these long-established rhetorical strategies in an attempt to reinforce the vision of Israel not merely as a Western entity in general—which could mean all sorts of things in the age of the so-called War on Terror, which Israel has seized on to busily promote itself as a purveyor of knowledge, strategies, and technologies of death to be deployed against the supposed enemies of the West—but as a *liberal* Western entity in

particular. In this domain, at least when appealing to certain demographics, there is a hyperconscious attempt to sideline Israel as the locus of global Islamophobic militarism (which has enhanced its appeal in recent
years among older and more conservative constituencies while alienating
younger and more liberal ones). Foregrounded instead is Israel as a liberal, LGBTQ-tolerant beach destination, albeit still very much in opposition to an Oriental Other (this time coded specifically as sexually repressive rather than simply religiously extremist in general). To this end, as
Tommaso Milani and Erez Levon point out, a "purported tolerance of
sexual diversity" has been mobilized to reiterate much older ideological
contrasts between East and West. "Articulated in a logic of binary opposition," they note, "Israel is imagined as a 'gay paradise' and set in antonymic
juxtaposition with a supposedly repressive and retrograde Palestine."[47] If,
after all, the Middle East is a region "where women are stoned, gays are
hanged, Christians are persecuted," as Netanyahu loudly claims,[48] Israel
can be curated as an oasis of tolerance and diversity where women,
Christians, and, above all, gay people can feel at home. This carefully
manipulated juxtaposition produces Israel as "the only gay-friendly country in an otherwise hostile region," as Puar notes, and it reiterates the
claim that "Israel is civilized" while Palestinians are "barbaric, homophobic, uncivilized, suicide-bombing fanatics."[49] We are back to the oldest
Orientalist binary, only now rigged up with the addition of a homophilia-
homophobia opposition.

A key part of this pinkwashing strategy is to situate Israel not merely as
an oasis of tolerance in a desert of homophobic extremism but as an active
agent of tolerance at that, ministering to persecuted Palestinian queers. In
other words, a central element of Israeli pinkwashing is the assertion
either that there are no queer Palestinians or that, to the extent that they
exist, they think of Israel as their salvation. You can exist and freely live as
a queer only in Israel, not in Palestine. Thus, Palestinian homosexuals
"seek refuge" in "the only regional territory" that protects gay rights,
according to the liberal Zionist writer Yossi Klein Halevi, for instance. "In
the last few years,' Halevi writes, 'hundreds of gay Palestinians . . . have
slipped into Israel . . . beyond the reach of their families and the P.A.
[Palestinian Authority]."[50] This narrative is widely circulated among agitators for Israel more generally and has been widely disseminated beyond

Israel itself, notably in Western Europe and the United States, where "liberal Zionists, especially queer liberal Zionists, frequently deploy it to represent Israel as 'an oasis of liberal tolerance in a reactionary religious backwater.'"[51] So Israel the oasis of democracy, Israel the oasis of green landscapes, Israel the oasis of high tech is also Israel the oasis of queer freedom in the desert of Islamic religious fanaticism. Such accounts conveniently ignore the fact that no Palestinian, queer or otherwise, is allowed to enter and seek shelter in Israel.

Yet consider how this theme has been accepted at face value by, among others, James Kirchick, a fellow at the Brookings Institution in Washington, DC, and a mainstream advocate of gay rights in the United States. "Israel is light-years ahead of the Palestinians when it comes to gay rights," Kirchick proclaims in a vehement attack on the Palestinian lesbian activist Rauda Marcos, founder of Aswat (Voices), a Palestinian lesbian advocacy organization that is based in Israel (where Marcos lives) but has members and support in the West Bank and Gaza. "If Marcos lived under the auspices of the Palestinian Authority and tried to be the outspoken gay rights advocate that she is in Israel, she could well have ended up with a bullet in her head a very long time ago."[52] One of the recurring claims enfolded within this narrative recapitulated by both Halevi and Kirchick is that Palestinians find freedom—and, by the way, not just sexual freedom but freedom in general—in Israel that they can't even imagine in their own society. Another claim built into this narrative is that Israeli law protects same-sex relations, whereas Palestinian law—or, rather, the law operative in the occupied territories—does not.

I note for the historical record that, in fact, no law in the West Bank bans sexual relations between consenting adults of the same gender. Whereas, as Ali Abunimah points out, the 1936 British Mandate criminal codes, which were absorbed wholesale into Israeli law, made it illegal for men to have sex with women or men in a way that "contravenes natural laws."[53] That specific prohibition remained in effect in Israel until 1977, and laws against sodomy even longer, in contrast to Jordanian law (the basis for the legal system in the West Bank since 1948), in which no such criminalization was imported from classic nineteenth-century European homophobia.[54] This is not to say, of course, that there is no homophobia in the West Bank or elsewhere in the Arab and Muslim world; there is, and it's not impossible that some queer Palestinians have left their repressive family or community environments to find a kind of anonymous freedom living on the margins of Tel Aviv. But homophobia and the sometimes violent repression of queer identities are generalized phenomena and are hardly limited to the Arab Islamic world in the way that the crude binary articulated by people like Kirchick would suggest (not to mention actually existing queer communities in Arab cities such as Cairo and Beirut). And as Joseph Massad notes ironically, "We never read stories by AP and other Western news organizations between 1951 and 1977 about how retrograde and repressive Israel was toward homosexuals compared to its Arab neighbors, including the West Bank before and after Israel occupied it. This could very well be because the US and Western Europe also repressed their homosexuals during this period."[55] Israel did not decriminalize sodomy until the late 1980s, and not until the 1990s did it started more systematically to liberalize LGBTQ rights, a point to which I return shortly.[56]

But the real issue here isn't a legal one in any case: it is that according to the narrative circulated by the likes of Kirchick and Halevi, there is no queer life in Palestine. "If we are to believe Kirchick, there are no queer Palestinians: they've all been murdered by Palestinian 'Islamofascists,' and the 'lucky few' who survived have fled to gay-friendly Israel," write Haneen Maikey and Jason Ritchie. "In fact, there is a vibrant, organized community of queer Palestinians who are working hard to create a just, democratic Palestinian society that respects the dignity of every person."[57] One of the most important elements of Palestinian queer activism, indeed, is that it refuses to separate LGBTQ rights from a wider range of other human and political rights. It's precisely in this sense that queer Palestinian activism is inseparable from resistance to Zionism, ethnic cleansing, apartheid, and colonialism.[58]

Zionist pinkwashing, on the other hand, does not serve merely to cover up and justify Israeli violence against Palestinians, though it certainly does that; it also occludes the very presence of a queer Palestinian culture, which exists on its own terms independent of—and specifically aligned against— the Zionist presence in Palestine. "The disavowal and erasure of (queer) Palestinian bodies and subjectivities constitute pinkwashing," Heike Schotten and Haneen Maikey argue. "This invisibility of Palestinian bodies and images is matched only by a hypervisibility when they do appear.

Palestinians are seen only as 'backward' or 'threatening,' while queer Palestinians only become legible as either 'gay' or 'victims of culture.' Invisibility and hypervisibility are results of the ongoing erasure of Palestinian belonging."⁵⁹ This dis-appearance of queer Palestinians operates on several levels. First, it sustains the pinkwashing narrative that Israel is the only regional space where one can find an LGBTQ presence, let alone LGBTQ activism. Second, it sustains the Orientalist claim that aligns Israel and Zionism with white, Western, liberal culture. Third, it builds on and contributes to what is always the primary Zionist discourse and material practice: the removal of Palestinians—in this case queer Palestinians—from Palestine. Pinkwashing must actively dis-appear Palestinians in the process of proclaiming the diversity and openness of Israeli society and the Israeli state. Or, to put this the other way around: the loud proclamation of gay rights in Israel draws attention to itself as a positive value—diversity—while actively occluding and denying the Palestinian presence, in this case the queer Palestinian presence. That is to say, the affirmation of gay Israel is coextensive with the denial of queer Palestine and queer Palestinians—and hence inseparable from a larger Zionist discourse that aims at the transfer or elimination of Palestinians in general.

In fact, the affirmation of gay Israel has by now become fully integrated in the broader Zionist project of settler-colonial apartheid. Little wonder, then, that pinkwashing and what Puar has identified as homonationalism have been seized upon by the Israeli government and its wide network of affiliates and organs in other countries around the world.⁶⁰ It bears repeating, however, that we are addressing here quite recent developments. LGBTQ rights were severely repressed—both legally and socially—in Israel from the state's earliest decades all the way through the late 1980s. It was not until the 1990s that more extensive liberalization of LGBTQ matters took place in domains including above all family rights and rights within the Israeli army (though severe religiously motivated homophobia remains a strong presence in the state away from the relatively liberal bubble of Tel Aviv).⁶¹

All of the reforms that took place were, of course, not simply handed down by a beneficent state but were rather the result of extensive campaigning by gay Jewish activists (so that the state now "smugly lauds itself for rights and achievements that it actually resisted"⁶²). It should also be clear, however, that from the beginning the struggle for Jewish LGBTQ rights in Israel was never posed as a challenge to the state's normative discourses of racism and settler colonialism; on the contrary, the demand, if anything, was for Jewish gays and lesbians to be able to participate in these forms of discourse and their material institutions as well. LGBTQ activism in Israel was and is—with *very* few exceptions, such as the queer Israeli group Black Laundry—aimed at gay and lesbian inclusion in the state project and everything that project stands for; in other words, allowing for gay and lesbian inclusion in an oppressive racial order that otherwise remains perfectly intact, or even becomes stronger as a result.[63]

Thus it is hardly a coincidence that the two chief domains of early LGBTQ activism within Israel were for abolishing the army's discrimination against gay soldiers and for demanding same-sex parenthood and particularly motherhood for lesbians.[64] With the liberalization in these two particular areas in the 1990s, Anat Lieber observes, Jewish gays and lesbians "achieved unprecedented success in the legal, political, and cultural arena, and lesbians and gay men attained at least partial inclusion in the institutions equated with realizing one's citizenship, i.e. the army and motherhood, and in the national collective." However, she continues, "though lesbians and gay men contested the 'naturalness' of the subjects that can embody civic virtue and broadened their definition, they challenged neither the venues to inclusion in the Israeli regime of citizenship, nor the boundaries of the national collective."[65] Gay and lesbian rights in Israel thus served to *strengthen* rather than weaken the broader Jewish-Zionist program of the state. Indeed, "the fact that these struggles focused on institutions that lie at the center of the Zionist-nationalist ethos, such as the army and family, can explain the role that rights in this context began to play later on, along the axis of homonormativity, homonationalism, and pinkwashing."[66] If anything, the state's claims to including gays and lesbians within its racial and colonial framework reinforces this framework precisely by mobilizing that act of inclusion and its associated value, diversity, in opposition to the Other of the national cause, namely the supposedly noninclusive, nondiverse, homophobic Palestinian.

There is no contradiction, then, between queer rights and Zionist racism. Quite the contrary: a discourse of queer rights reinforces Zionist racism like a shot in the arm. Homonationalism is easily assimilable into other forms of nationalism, which in Israel are necessarily premised on racial and colonial discourses. "Homonationalism is the discursive process through which both state and non-state actors bring sexual diversity into the very definition of the nation-state so as to legitimize the exclusion and/ or repression of others who are portrayed as lacking in this crucial criterion of 'tolerance of sexual diversity,'" Milani and Levon explain. "Pinkwashing is the public face of this homonationalist discourse, the way through which Israel can present itself to the rest of the world as a beacon of sexual liberalism in the Middle East, and concomitantly 'wash away' neo-colonial policies toward Palestinians."[67] The mobilization of queer rights within the Zionist project is intended to reinforce and extend it.

Indeed, this affiliation of queer rights with the Israeli state and its policies helps explain the insistence on the part of most gay and lesbian activists and organizations in Israel on the separation of "social" (i.e., gender rights) from "political" issues (i.e., the racial-colonial constitution of the state). Thus, for the most part, the Israeli LGBTQ community is perfectly happy to operate within a racist paradigm.[68] Or, as Jason Ritchie argues, for liberal Zionists, including LGBTQ Zionists, "representations of Israel as a gay-friendly refuge for victimized queer Palestinians function as a way to evade the fundamental contradiction between racism and liberalism that defines Israeli nationalism." Thus, he adds, "'properly domesticated' Israeli queers validate the discourses of Israeli national security, rationalizing the marginalization of Palestinians as a result of the backwardness of Palestinian culture rather than 'racist practices of the Israeli state.'"[69] As Aeyal Gross puts the same point, "Homosexuals are 'enlisted' alongside 'good citizens' against what is perceived as a threat to 'Western' citizenship. This process, which uses the struggle for LGBT rights to distinguish 'us' as liberal and democratic as opposed to the 'enemy,' makes LGBT rights not necessarily identifiable, any longer, with progressive politics."[70] In fact, LGBTQ rights in Israel are specifically identifiable with the harsh politics of institutionalized apartheid and colonial racism. There's even an official gay faction within the far-right ruling Likud party.[71]

Moreover, the relationship between the state's posture toward LGBTQ Jews and its posture toward Palestinians is not merely a matter of attitude or ideology. At exactly the same time that the state started to liberalize its policies regarding Jewish gays and lesbians—allowing openly gay soldiers to serve in the army unhindered by official forms of discrimination, for instance—Israel also began a massive intensification of its occupation of Palestinian territory captured in 1967, as well as its repression of Palestinian citizens of the state in the territories occupied in 1948. "During the 1990s," Rebecca Stein notes, "Israel's gay communities were being recognized in unprecedented ways in Israeli legal spheres, while changing Israeli policies vis-à-vis the occupied territories were creating new forms of unrecognition for its Palestinian population. Gay communities were enjoying new forms of social mobility within the nation-state while the literal mobility of Palestinians from the occupied territories was being increasingly curtailed."[72] For instance, with the advent of the Oslo period of the 1990s, Palestinians were no longer allowed to circulate between and among the territories occupied in 1967 and those occupied in 1948. Palestinians from Gaza were cut off from Jerusalem (as they remain to this day); Palestinians from the West Bank could no longer visit relatives who had survived the ethnic cleansing of 1948 and had remained in Nazareth, Haifa, or Jaffa; and in turn Palestinians from Nazareth, Haifa, or Jaffa were no longer able to visit the major cities of the West Bank, which the Oslo Accords had classified as Area A and hence off-limits to Israeli citizens, including second-class Palestinian citizens. Meanwhile, of course, Jews could come and go between the West Bank, Jerusalem, and pre-1967 Israel with total freedom. But at least openly gay soldiers could now man the Israeli roadblocks and checkpoints prohibiting the movement of Palestinians!

Israeli homonationalism and pinkwashing have thus been at the service of the colonial state from the advent of LGBTQ liberalization in Israel, and the organs of the state have not wasted a moment to broadcast this fact—a process that continues up to the version of pinkwashing evident today. "It goes without saying," claims one of the endlessly self-congratulatory justices of the Israeli High Court, "that the treatment of the gay community is one of the measures of Israel as a liberal-democratic state, in contrast to the situation in the overwhelming majority of Middle-Eastern states, near and far, where members of the gay community are persecuted both by the state authorities and by society."[73] Such claims reflect the ways in which Israel mobilizes the politics of LGBT rights and sexual freedom as it attempts to brand itself as progressive and liberal by virtue of its status as gay-friendly.[74] And, from the late 1990s onward, a loose collection of epithets and slogans has morphed into a minutely orchestrated campaign of imaginative engineering as Israel presents itself to Western audiences as a liberal democracy like their own. As a result, "victories for civil rights, which are gained with hard labor, and often with the government's representatives explicitly objecting to them in the courts, are quickly co-opted by the government in its efforts to present Israel's liberal credentials. Gay rights have essentially become a public-relations tool."[75] And this message has been broadly and loudly disseminated via Israeli embassies and consulates around the world since the early 2000s.

Mobilizing queer rights in the service of Israel is not undertaken by the state alone, however. One of the most striking recent episodes of pinkwashing involves the work of the gay pornographer Michael Lucas, beginning with his 2009 porn film *Men of Israel*, which claims to be the first full-length porn enterprise—gay or straight—shot using Israeli actors and on locations throughout the country. "If you think about it," Lucas explains to a reporter from Israel's most widely circulated daily newspaper, "porn is the only way to get attention to Israel. Because media is doing very good job of turning people off from Israel, because, again, all they see is constant disaster. I want to show them what I see, Israel through my eyes, which is what Israel is."[76] The film, in other words, "is free PR for Israel, and it's much better than the PR they're getting on the news."[77] He adds: "Nobody goes to Israel for Golda Meir, I'm so sorry. . . . Gay people, and straight people, want beautiful beaches, beautiful nature, beautiful men and women, good food, good hotels. Israel shouldn't be mistaken about why people go there. They need me."[78] Lucas's project thus sits squarely in the terrain occupied by more mainstream efforts at pinkwashing, recapitulating its main themes—and indeed the broader themes articulated by Brand Israel in general—one by one.

These themes include, as previously noted, the Orientalist contrast between Israel as a shining beacon of Western modernity and the surrounding wasteland of Islamic despotism, though Lucas expresses this point somewhat more bluntly than his more intellectually sophisticated peers. "Israel is surrounded by the jungle of Muslim countries, which are incredibly brutal, uncivilized and have no freedom for their people and lots of oppression," he says. "And this [Israel] is only a little, tiny island of democracy and Western values."[79] Gay rights in particular here serve as a measure of access to rights more generally. "It is common knowledge that Palestinians are violent murderers of gay people," Lucas says, so that "support for Palestine [is] in correlation support for the deaths of gay people."[80] Israel, on the other hand, "a state of liberty surrounded by countries of intolerance, stands strong in supporting the sexual rights of gay men."[81]

There are five main settings in *Men of Israel*, which alternate between indoors and outdoors.[82] Taken together, the combination of settings covers a range from the metrosexual modernity of Tel Aviv to the pastoral landscape of a quasi-biblical Palestine. The sex scenes are shot so as to make their backgrounds and contexts integral to the scenes themselves: sex itself is here inseparable from the broader geographical and local context in which it takes place. It's not just that the background is visible: it is that the background is in effect the *protagonist* of the sex scenes; the actors are mere props to enable the framing of the territory to which the film wants to establish a claim.[83] Thus the scenes shot in and around Tel Aviv emphasize its modernity, its pulsing economic success, and its urban sophistication; those shot in other locations emphasize the country's claim to a primitive pastoral chic.[84] In both cases, however, the political effects are clear.

One of the scenes of *Men in Israel* was shot in the ruins of a Palestinian town forcibly depopulated during the ethnic cleansing of 1948. (Max Blumenthal suggests that this scene of "desecration porn" takes place in the ruins of Lifta, just outside Jerusalem.[85]) In Lucas's account of the scene, of course, there are no Palestinians, let alone any ethnic cleansing: the scene is "a beautiful ancient township that had been deserted centuries ago." Its ancientness did not, however, "stop our guys from mounting each other and trying to repopulate it. Biology may not be the lesson of the day but these men shot their seeds all over the village."[86] Lucas's attempt at humor may be crude, but it unintentionally reveals something interesting: traditional forms of Zionism—let's say heteronormative Zionism— going back to the ethnic cleansing of Palestine in 1948, and even to the planning for the Zionist settler-colonial project all the way back in the 1920s and 1930s, were predicated on the transfer of the Palestinians from their land and their replacement by Jewish-Zionist settlers.[87]

The logic of this classic heteronormative Zionism was fundamentally biopolitical, based not just on the conquest of the land but on the heterosexual reproduction of a Zionist settler population in Palestine.[88] The heavily biblical overtones of "seed" and the land evoked by Lucas offer what is in effect a postmodern pastiche of that earlier heteronormative Zionism: a project that worked up to a point but then seemingly lost its way. The drive now is no longer to biologically repopulate and seed the land—as it had been for the early Zionists—but to shift to another mode in which "seed" can be spilled because it's no longer what is at stake. Actually, more than merely a pastiche, what Lucas offers is an inversion of both the biblical injunction not to spill seed and the classically modernist ethos of earlier settler Zionism, with its all of its tedious collectivist, nationalist, pioneering, forward-looking myths about itself. In that earlier mode of Zionism, the whole point of conquest and clearing the land of its indigenous inhabitants was to repopulate the land, to redeem the stereotype of the sickly, sallow, weak European Jew with the vision of the "new Jew," bronzed and sweating, working the land, pickaxe in hand, rifle on his back: the "FIGHTING JEW" announced by Menachem Begin (one of the architects of the 1948 ethnic cleansing) in his memoir.[89] In that moment, biology—both the act of seeding the land to render it fertile and the basis for a rejuvenated Jewish population—really *was* the lesson of the day. In Lucas's version of all this, however, spilling seed—waste—has become a gesture of triumph. In gay porn as in straight, after all, the climactic money shot involves an ejaculation over the body of the partner. But here Lucas has symbolically shifted it: the ejaculation is really over the *land*, and the partner is, again, little more than a prop for that exercise. His actors' spilling of their seed is deliberately, wantonly, strategically unproductive in a biological sense: and in that unproductiveness lies its productivity in a figurative or symbolic sense. Spilling seed here marks territory that has already been captured: territory that is secure, that is held not in order to then reproduce but as an end in itself. Or at least so Lucas would like to believe.

Lucas's version of Zionism seeks to supersede that earlier heteronormative form with all its symbols, drives, and motivations as expressed in the political personalities who seemed to sum it up. After all, as he himself puts it, people no longer want Golda Meir and that generation of Israeli politicians (Ben-Gurion, Rabin, Peres, and the rest) who actively participated in the ethnic cleansing and settlement of Palestine; they now "need"

Lucas himself instead. And the idealized model of Israeli masculinity held forth in his film is no longer the settler with his pickaxe struggling with the gnarly oaks and prickly pears of the indigenous Palestinian landscape to "make the desert bloom," but the gay porn actor laying claim to the same land but without the pretense, let alone the tedium, of biological reproduction. Lucas may think he is smarter than the older heteronormative Zionism he wants to supersede, but, as with pinkwashing and indeed Brand Israel in general, the only people who would buy this claim at face value are those who are already sold.

In any case, Michael Lucas's crude redux of pinkwashing did not stop with *Men of Israel*. He followed up that hard-core porn film with a documentary offering a softer version of the same thing: *Undressing Israel: Gay Men in the Promised Land*. And since then his company has been offering gay tours of Israel that feature, aside from all the usual gay attractions (Tel Aviv beaches, clubs, etc.), a bonus "that many a gay tourist would not want to miss—a visit to an IDF [i.e., Israeli army] base and a memento picture with a sexy soldier taken by a professional photographer."[90] Israel here is made available as a space of militaro-techno-sexual modernity, a "gaycation" in which one can presumably fantasize about reenacting the scenes shot in *Men of Israel* as well as all the politics that attend those scenes.[91] But more is at stake here as well. If Israeli soldiers can be offered as models of gay male Israeli masculinity,[92] the state itself is and has to be involved in this production. "I don't see any problem with a group of gay tourists visiting an IDF [i.e., Israeli army] base," Michael Lucas boasts of his gay tours of Israel; "I am doing what the State has not been smart enough to do—marketing the beautiful side of Israel to the world."[93] For all his insufferable self-congratulation, however, Lucas is not as smart as he would like to think: the state has been doing exactly the same things—including making its "hot" soldiers available for snapshots with gay tourists.

Starting as early as 2005, for instance, the state backed a campaign to have World Pride—an international event that had itself launched for the first time only in 2000—held in Israel. That event was called, with no apparent trace of irony, "Love Without Borders." The 2005 event was postponed due to the rise in tensions over Israel's redeployment of its forces from within Gaza to surround and besiege it instead; and in 2006 the parade part of the postponed festival was canceled because of tensions attending Israel's indiscriminate bombardment and invasion of Lebanon that summer. Although Israel's decision to host World Pride was, as Jasbir Puar captures it perfectly, "irritatingly strategic,"[94] it was also something of a failure given the visible and tangible overlap between the Pride events and Israel's colonial and occupation policies. It was also immediately clouded by global calls for a boycott, so that the state's loud proclamations of its devotion to diversity and inclusion were simultaneously wrapped up with international calls by queer organizations—such as QUIT (Queers Undermining Israeli Terrorism)—highlighting the strategic purpose of Israeli pinkwashing.[95] "We support the rights of all lesbian, gay, bisexual, transgender, intersex and other queer-identified (LGBTIQ) people to love and live in freedom, and to demonstrate publicly to demand their/our rights," the boycott call noted. But, it added, "these rights should not be placed in competition with the long struggle of the Palestinian people, including Palestinian LGBTIQ people, for self-determination, for the right to return to their homes, and the struggle against apartheid and the occupation of their lands."[96] From the beginning, then, Israeli attempts to use pinkwashing to occlude apartheid and occupation have backfired in that the resistance to pinkwashing has drawn even more attention to the crimes that are supposed to have been occluded.

This failure has not kept the Israeli state or its overseas affiliates and organs from persisting in that uniquely dogged, single-minded way of theirs. Israeli embassies and consulates were involved in promoting the 2005–6 Pride events and have been working assiduously on other, similar events ever since. With Israeli government and Brand Israel support, the "Israel Pride Month" was launched in San Francisco in 2010: in the guise of a grassroots effort, it was "an event instigated, funded and administered by the Israeli government."[97] Stands promoting gay Israel were established at other Pride festivals around the world (e.g., Berlin, Stockholm, Toronto).[98] In 2010, Pride Toronto was infiltrated by Israeli agitators who attempted (and failed) to have the local group Queers Against Israeli Apartheid (QAIA) banished from the event; indeed, as QAIA points out, Zionist lobbyists attempted to have all of Pride Toronto's funding revoked "in order to silence Palestine solidarity voices at the 2010 festival."[99] Over and again, Israel's voluble commitment to gay rights is consistently exceeded by its determination to suppress and negate Palestinian rights, and gay rights, too, if that's what it takes.

The mission to make queer rights central to the promotion of Israel has been embraced not just by the state but by its overseas arms and affiliates. Stand With Us—undoubtedly the crudest of all the countless Zionist *hasbara* outfits active in the United States (which is saying something)— quickly jumped on the bandwagon with its inimitable clumsiness. It organized an iPride event in Israel in 2009 (an event far more interested in promoting Israel than in actual queer rights)—doing so without the assistance or input of gay people. "'The idea is to improve Israel's image across the globe,' according to Noah Meir, coordinator of iPride," a reporter for the *Jerusalem Post* noted. "'We decided to improve Israel's image through the gay community in Israel; we found that the issue is not familiar around the world,' said Meir, whose team members are all heterosexual."[100]

Indeed, although it was not previously known for its zealous defense of gay rights, even Stand With Us had cottoned on to the fact that pinkwashing was the new trend in *hasbara*, and it threw itself into the campaign for queer Israel without reservation. It pitched a proposal for a workshop on "gay liberation in the Middle East" to the US Social Forum meeting in Detroit in 2010. The proposal was naively accepted by the forum organizers, who took its innocent-sounding pitch at face value, but when its content—the crudest form of hasbara—and the organization behind it were revealed, a campaign was mounted by Arab and other queer organizations to have the workshop rescinded. Stand With Us is trying "to convince the world that [Israel] is not a brutal settler-colony state, but rather a free democracy where human rights in general, and LGBT rights in particular, are respected and enshrined," Arab queer groups pointed out; it "deceptively uses the language of LGBT and women's rights to obscure the fact that institutionalized discrimination is enshrined within the state of Israel."[101] The workshop was ultimately canceled, but that hasn't stopped Stand With Us from extending its campaign. "In the Middle East[,] sexual orientation is a matter of life and death," one of its pamphlets screams. "Members of the LGBTQ community living in the Middle East are vulnerable to violent attacks." Israel, in contrast, it hastens to reassure us, "is a sanctuary for the LGBTQ community," boasting pride parades, gay members of parliament, openly gay soldiers, and above all the city of Tel Aviv, "consistently rated among the most LGBTQ-friendly travel destinations in the world."[102] Although Stand With Us represents the lowest common denominator of crude Zionist *hasbara*, it here regurgitates the main themes of Israel's claim to queer-friendly superiority to the tyrannical, violent, extremist, fundamentalist, and just generally bad lands surrounding it, giving pride of place to Tel Aviv.

The effort to package and sell Tel Aviv as one of the world's great gay cities became central to Israeli pinkwashing discourse from the late 2000s onward. In 2010, the Israeli Tourism Ministry and the Tel Aviv municipality worked together to brand Tel Aviv as an international gay vacation destination, spending almost $100 million.[103] "Israel is without a doubt the best country in the Middle East for gay and lesbian individuals to live," boasts the "Gay Tel Aviv for Beginners" page of the Tourist Israel website. "In addition to the fact that gay people can serve openly in the Israeli military, Israeli governments have been promoting social equality for LGBT people for more than a decade. It should come as no surprise then that Israel's capital of cool, Tel Aviv, has gained a reputation as one of the world's top destinations for gay men."[104] Tel Aviv is in this way held up as embodying forms of sexual and libidinal freedom that repressed Palestinians (and Arabs in general) cannot possibly imagine, and hence (especially with an eye on that global network of Western cities to which it aims to aspire) as the binary Western opposite of the degraded Oriental Other. At the same time, Tel Aviv is also supposed to be open and welcoming, ready to embrace all forms of difference.

Indeed, the idea that Tel Aviv is a kind of welcoming refuge from the harsh fundamentalist climate of the rest of the Middle East is a persistent theme in the city's branding of itself. "Tel Aviv–Yafo is a city of tolerance and pluralism, science and progressive thought," the municipality website announces. "The city has an open atmosphere and warmly embraces everyone—Muslims, Christians and Jews, secular and religious, young and old, legal and illegal immigrants."[105] One might get carried away here and actually start to fantasize that the city eagerly welcomes back the tens of thousands of Palestinian refugees from the city of Jaffa—95 percent ethnically cleansed in 1948—or Sheikh Muwannis or the other villages on whose expropriated lands, and on the basis of whose forced disappearance, Tel Aviv was developed. But I return to this point later in the chapter.

The Tel Aviv pride parade plays a pivotal role in the attempt to boost the city's bona fides as an international gay destination and indeed as the "Gay capital of the Middle East," as the city officially proclaims itself.[106] The first Tel Aviv Pride was held in 1998, and it has grown steadily ever since, having assumed a central position in the branding of Israel as a diverse and tolerant country. By 2017, the Israeli Foreign Ministry could boast that "Tel Aviv hosts [the] largest gay parade ever held in the Middle East." The Tel Aviv Pride Parade "is not just a celebration, but also an important declaration of support," the Foreign Ministry quotes the city's mayor as boasting. "Tel Aviv, which has already been acknowledged as the world's 'most gay-friendly city[,]' will continue to be a light-house city—spreading the values of freedom, tolerance and democracy to the world."[107] Notice again that the proclamation of Tel Aviv's diversity is consistently aligned with its claim to project this message—and the broader values of tolerance and democracy with which it is inevitably bound up—regionally and globally.

These claims have proved central to the city's international branding project. In 2009, the International Gay and Lesbian Travel Association announced that it was holding a conference in Tel Aviv with the goal of promoting the city as "a world gay destination."[108] A series of contests and competitions followed, strategically placed in various travel and airline websites and with the usual Israeli *hasbara* troll farms all too predictably engineering the results. In 2012, Tel Aviv won the "Best Gay City" competition organized by American Airlines (which did not even fly there at the time).[109] The same year, Tel Aviv was named the "world's best gay city" following a readers' poll on Gaycities.com. The extent to which the poll was rigged cannot be doubted: cities with historical gay legacies were absurdly overshadowed by Tel Aviv's 43 percent vote: New York struggled to achieve 14 percent; Madrid and London were split at 5 percent each, and San Francisco, of all cities, didn't even feature at all.[110] These results are simply not credible as a genuine assessment of global queer attitudes.

Western press coverage was the last piece to fall into place following all this engineered buzz and the faux "readers'" polls. "Welcome to Tel Aviv, the gayest city on earth," writes Christopher Muther in the *Boston Globe* in an article that would turn out to be a pivotal and often cited piece in 2016—one that both invokes the engineered polls and has in turn been invoked by Israeli *hasbara* outlets. "I've had the good fortune to visit plenty of LGBT-friendly utopias, and I couldn't imagine Tel Aviv snatching the title, tiara, and sash away from locales such as San Francisco,

Berlin, or Amsterdam as the place to go for gay," he added. "Well, folks, it's
time to set out a plate and a fork, because I'm about to eat my words."[111]
There have been plenty of other media puff pieces about the gay vibrancy
of Tel Aviv. "Passionately secular and avowedly carefree, Tel Aviv–Jaffa is a
24/7 city where the search for the perfect cup of coffee and a commitment
to L.G.B.T. pride seems to take precedence over Israel's complicated politics," we read in a *New York Times* article. The piece refers to "ancient,
cobblestoned Jaffa" as "home to Arab community life for centuries," but
carefully steps around the calamitous history of Jaffa in 1948 and goes
out of its way to avoid using the word "Palestinian" to identity Jaffa's (surviving) generically "Arab" inhabitants, whose city was "united with Tel
Aviv in 1950" (an interesting turn of phrase to describe ethnic cleansing,
mass expulsion, and violent social engineering). But Jaffa clearly shines as
a sidekick to Tel Aviv's vibrant queer party scene. "If you want to find a
taste of peace in the Middle East, the dance floor at Anna Lou Lou, a cultural center and underground bar in Old Jaffa, is a good place to look," we
read. "Utopia reigns at this smoky, hipster-happy party spot, where locals
of every stripe—Muslim and Jewish, gay, straight and undefined—shake
their sweaty selves to electro-Arab and African beats well into the wee
hours."[112] Again and again, the value of Tel Aviv is inclusion, diversity,
combination, tolerance, mutuality, and freedom.

It's impossible, in reading this kind of stuff, to tell at any given moment
whether one is looking at a government proclamation, a *hasbara* pamphlet, bad advertising, or the journalism of the *Boston Globe* or *New York
Times*. There is a consistency to the coverage of the gay scene in Tel Aviv
and a strange recapitulation of Israeli and municipal government talking
points about the city and its relation to the broader cultural and political
context: a simultaneous assertion and denial of place.[113]

"Tel Aviv invites you to have fun, be free and feel fabulous!" the Tel Aviv
Gay Vibe proclaims. "Like her sisters all over the world—New York, Berlin,
Paris and Madrid[—]Tel Aviv draws the free-spirited people from all over
the country, allowing them to live their lives as they choose," the site con-
tinues. "Gay, Lesbian, transgender or bisexual—At all ages, people are free
to live, love, work, create and enjoy the cultural and social oasis that is Tel
Aviv."[114] This kind of assessment—as with the journalistic pieces—casts
Tel Aviv simultaneously as a metonym for Israel (standing in for the state

in international branding efforts) and as displaced from its far more repressive hinterland and connected to a network of Western "sister" cities.[115] And a reading of the photographs, promotional websites, marketing brochures, and other materials branding Tel Aviv as a gay utopia reveals the role that muscular virility plays in generating a global image of Israeli masculinity and hence of the state itself. The particular connection between the supposedly gay-friendly Israeli army and the haven of Tel Aviv, whose liberties that army is taken to protect, plays an important role here, so that the link between the muscular gay Israeli beach lover and his warrior-like double (a link also articulated by the Michael Lucas projects) is constantly being evoked. "On one hand, the virile muscular body is strategically deployed as affective bait that exploits global middle-class gay men's obsession with masculinity . . . in order to seduce visitors to Tel Aviv and Israel with the promise of sexual freedom and a carefree experience," Milani and Levon argue. "On the other hand, his inner warrior-like nature is ready to embark on a war to defend sexual rights, which are taken as proxies of the outer boundaries of the civilized world."[116]

This is an important observation, but something is left out of the analysis. Actually, there are several important points at stake in this play on the overhyped virility of the Israeli gay male body that is integral to so much Israeli pinkwashing. Most obviously, the body in which Israeli LGBTQ freedom *in general* is visually packaged and sold to the world is largely specifically *male*. Looking back over all the materials I read and watched to research this chapter, I can't recall a single image of lesbian women, for instance—and I can't think of a single example of marketing Tel Aviv or Israel in general as a specifically *lesbian* paradise. The marketing materials, the awards, the contests invariably feature images of muscular and toned *men*—and they seem to be aimed specifically at gay men, not, for example, lesbians or transgender people. Tel Aviv is, after all, pushed specifically as the *gay* capital of the universe: it's really the *G* in LGBTQ that matters in pinkwashing, almost if not entirely to the exclusion of other forms of identity. Partly this is indicative of the bad faith of pinkwashing in general, which should come as no surprise given that it is not primarily interested in gay and lesbian (or anyone else's) rights: it's interested in mobilizing those rights in order to safeguard and protect the interests of a state project, and mobilizing them only to the extent necessary to transact the forms of denial that enable that state project to sustain itself through both local and international support and affiliation.

But something more interesting is at stake here as well. Consider the investment, in all the pinkwashing visual materials, in a badly clichéd version of the gay muscle fetish. Part of that work involves establishing a link between the gay men cavorting on the beaches of Tel Aviv and the gay soldiers manning the ranks of the Israeli army: gay masculinity at the beach and gay masculinity in the Israeli army are shown to be two sides of the same coin. After all, in most of the material marketing Tel Aviv as a gay city, a tie is repeatedly established between gays in the Israeli army and Israel's supposed "capital of cool." The one is tied inexorably to the other: Israel's army protects the gay vibrancy of Tel Aviv. From whom does it protect it? From "the more religious and restrictive" neighbors to the east, and indeed not only does Tel Aviv welcome "gay tourists with open arms," but it also offers "safe refuge for those from the LGBTQ community of surrounding countries in the region"[117] (although it's unclear how these last are to negotiate their way there through the walls, trenches, fortifications, and snipers' nests of the gay-friendly Israeli army).

At work here is a strange double move: on the one hand, there is an attempt to boost the claim to a certain kind of masculinity of gay Israel by militarizing it—a tendency best exemplified by Lucas's marketing of the "sexy" soldiers at Israeli army outposts to gay tourists. Gay, pinkwashed Israel, in other words, is strong, taut, virile, able to spill its seed at will. On the other hand, by militarizing pinkwashing, this kind of material inevitably also draws attention to the Israeli army: that is, to military occupation, racial violence, bombing civilians, bulldozing family homes, sniping at children, and all the other things that the Israeli army stands for. This form of pinkwashing thus ends up inadvertently highlighting Israel's occupation and the colonial violence of the Zionist project in general. It is almost as though this form of violence *needs* to be summoned forth in this strand of pinkwashing in order to be denied all the more forcefully: as though the foreclosure, in order to work, fundamentally needs to tangentially acknowledge that which is to be repressed. Let me put this another way: the relationship between Israeli pinkwashing and colonial violence is not coincidental; it is dialectical. Pinkwashing enables colonial violence; and, in turn, colonial violence (now) requires pinkwashing.

This is a variant of the broader logic of denial at play in pinkwashing in general. As with the other forms of denial explored in this book, pinkwashing has a double characteristic: its work toward erasing the Palestinian presence in and claim to Palestine is transacted through its loud affirmation of all the positive values (diversity, freedom, openness, etc.) that gay Israel is said to represent. The more loudly Israel's claim to inclusivity and diversity is proclaimed, the more the Palestinian presence is occluded and denied. And nowhere is this logic on view more clearly than in the marketing of Tel Aviv as a gay destination. What's submerged out of sight to make this vision of utopia possible in the first place is the Palestinian presence in and claim to the land on which Tel Aviv was settled. Through its insistent affirmation of rights, diversities, freedoms, and openness, this image of gay Tel Aviv enacts its violent denial of Palestine and the Palestinians.

That is exactly why Tel Aviv and Eurovision are a perfect match. One might wonder, first of all, why Israel competes in Eurovision at all, given that it is a non-European country. The Eurovision Song Contest was launched in 1956 by the European Broadcasting Union, an alliance of European television and radio stations into which Israel insinuated itself just as it also insinuated itself into European branches of world football and other sports, and just as many European airlines consider Tel Aviv a European rather than Middle Eastern destination. For most of its history, the Eurovision Song Contest was a relatively minor event celebrating minor pop music bands; few of its winners have gone on to any kind of prominence (ABBA, winner of the 1974 competition, is the exception that proves the rule). It was only in the 2000s that the contest became a large-scale event, drawing crowds of tens of thousands.[118]

And it was around the same time—the late 1990s and early 2000s—that the contest gradually evolved into a celebration of queer camp.[119] As Catherine Baker points out, Eurovision gradually developed into a locus of gay and lesbian fan culture, and a site of LGBTQ visibility, at the very moment when Europe was also redefining itself as more open and inclusive. Eurovision became a queer event, Baker argues, in connection with a surrounding narrative of political progress and sexual liberation in Europe in general. "Eurovision thus entered a context where certain state governments and European institutions were constructing LGBT equality as a matter of

European identity and national pride," Baker writes. "Eurovision, during the 2000s, became a key site for producing and contesting narratives of the relationship between 'gay'/'LGBT' equality (a tellingly ill-defined distinction in this context) and national/European identities."[120] Guaranteeing gay and lesbian freedom was a condition of possibility for defining a state's claim to European identity. (We must leave to one side here the question of how liberal and democratic the EU actually is as an institution and how genuine is the discourse of freedom and diversity claimed for European identity. The nakedly racist treatment of minorities in France, Italy, and other EU countries, and the EU's draconian handling of the economic crisis in Greece suggest otherwise.) European states are allegedly LGBTQ friendly; so, presumably, a state that can claim to be LGBTQ friendly can also claim to participate in the glow of inter-European cultural identity.

This explains Israel's insistent—almost pathological—participation in Eurovision, a competition in which it has been one of the most consistent winners in recent years, having won four times, as though its prominence in that domain could redeem it somehow, absolve it of other sins. In this sense, the Tel Aviv Eurovision contest ought to have been a crowning success: Israel's response to a global call for boycotts and sanctions, a way for Israel to prove its openness, diversity, even its supposed Westernness in the face of mounting international criticism for its system of apartheid. Instead, the contest was—precisely because of the attention it drew to Israel—a failure.

The failure was a financial one first of all. Since they became mass events, Eurovision contests have normally generated a massive surge in tourism for the host cities: fully booked flights and hotels at premium prices, tens of thousands of foreign tourists spending money at restaurants, clubs, hotels, and so on. Yet, just a couple of weeks before the Tel Aviv event, thousands of tickets for the performances were still unsold, despite the fact that the venue was far smaller than the one in Lisbon the previous year (about a third the capacity), which had been packed, and hotels and short-term vacation rentals had plenty of availability as the expected surge of visitors failed to materialize; prices were cut by up to 70 percent in a desperate bid to try to generate last-minute interest.[121] By some counts, barely 6,000 visitors actually arrived—far fewer than the 20,000 that had been expected. Heavily inflated prices were one cause—but the international boycott call was also a major reason.[122] The Icelandic Eurovision fan club, for instance, normally travels in a group of up to 150 members to support their country's entry (Eurovision being something of an obsession in Iceland); fewer than a dozen showed up in Tel Aviv. Similarly, the Irish constituency was down from the 190 who had been to Lisbon in 2018 to 25, of whom only 12 actually bought tickets.[123] The organizers ended up giving tickets away for free in a propaganda exercise.[124]

More significant, calls for boycotting the Tel Aviv Eurovision generated at least as much attention as the event itself, negating whatever *hasbara* win it was supposed to have delivered. Indeed, given the active participation of international queer organizations in global protests against the event, Eurovision Tel Aviv backfired spectacularly in reaching the very constituency it wanted to appeal to. Across Europe and around the world, dozens of LGBTQ organizations rallied in support of the boycott call issued by alQaws and other Palestinian and Arab queer organizations, refusing not only to go to Tel Aviv but to attend Eurovision watch parties in Europe itself. "Israel's regime of military occupation, settler colonialism and apartheid is shamelessly using the Eurovision competition as part of its official Brand Israel strategy, which tries to show 'Israel's prettier face' to distract attention from its war crimes against Palestinians," notes a boycott call signed by sixty queer organizations in Europe and around the world. "Eurovision has attracted the interest, passion and support from the LGBTQIA community for decades and Israel sees in this a great opportunity to forward its pinkwashing agenda, the cynical use of gay rights [to] distract from and normalize Israel's occupation, settler colonialism and apartheid."[125] Netta Barzilai, the winner of the 2018 competition, who brought the event to Tel Aviv the following year, launched a promotional European tour to try to generate support for European attendance at the 2019 competition; her shows were dismal failures, drawing crowds of protestors far outnumbering her meager audiences at those concerts that weren't canceled altogether for lack of interest.[126]

If the Tel Aviv Eurovision was supposed to have been the crowning event of Israeli pinkwashing, its failure stands in for the failure of pinkwashing in general. Pinkwashing is similar to the other forms of denial explored in this book in that it transacts denial of Palestinians through the affirmation of a positive value (in this case, diversity). It's different, however, for some very specific historical and political reasons. First, unlike the other projects to which it might loosely be compared, it is a late arrival: like Brand Israel in general, it is an attempt to transact denial in a kind of retrospect, after the fact. Israel planted over the ruins of ethnically cleansed Palestinian towns with evergreen forests at a moment when its claims to innocence still had a certain kind of global purchase, especially on the European and American left. Brand Israel and pinkwashing, by contrast, come far, far too late.

"The transformation of a country's image can only come after the country is transformed," notes Jeremy Kahn. "Throwing millions at public relations firms, hiring marketing consultants, creating snappy slogans or cool logos is basically a monumental waste of time, money and energy. Israel . . . recently spent three years and millions of dollars developing and test marketing an advertising campaign. And yes, Israel does indeed 'start with I,' as the country's new tag line helpfully points out. But so does Intifada—and it will take more than a new marketing campaign to get potential investors and tourists to forget Israel's ongoing conflict with the Palestinians."[127] Indeed, trying to reverse engineer Israeli apartheid so it can be made to look better than it is is not only fraught with difficulties: it runs the risk of generating even more negative coverage than what it is trying to obscure, deny, or elide in the first place. Pinkwashing—and the Brand Israel project of which it is the major focal act—is what denial looks like when it's too late, too crude, too obvious, too forced. Only those who are already persuaded, or those who simply don't care one way or the other (and hence are impervious to marketing initiatives), will take it seriously.

This is an important point: pinkwashing (like most of Israel's current and ongoing attempts at denial) works on those who practice it, not on those at whom it is ostensibly directed. We are witnessing a colonial pathology here akin to those examined by Frantz Fanon in *Wretched of the Earth*. The relentless persistence in engaging in these forms of denial despite their manifestly abject failure as public relations or *hasbara* exercises intended to capture or persuade others serves as a reminder of the overall thesis of this book: that the subjects of denial are those who engage in the denial themselves. (I return to this point in the book's postscript.)

Pinkwashing has, however, unintentionally helped draw new attention to Israeli apartheid and, in so doing, helped generate a new form of activism

in Palestine and around the world. It has also allowed writers and activists
to develop a fuller account of the racial and sexual dynamics informing
Zionist settler colonialism in general. "With its racist and dehumanizing
intentions, pinkwashing is built upon a historically specific colonial logic of
Zionist Israeli Jewish supremacy," argue Lynn Darwich and Haneen Maikey.
"Exposing this logic and emphasizing other (ab)uses of gender and sexuality
in the service of Zionism are essential to the broader project of decolonizing
ourselves."[128] Tracing the Orientalist binaries and other forms of racism
integral to Israeli pinkwashing, for instance, also allows for a fuller understanding of how Zionism works in general, and hence for more effective
forms of resistance to it. "It would be an error to promote antipinkwashing
activism as a new salvation for the somehow boring mainstream LGBT
organizing," Darwich and Maikey add. "Rather, the question is how queer
analysis is also responsible for resisting Israel's Zionist project and its manifestations, from ethnic cleansing and occupation to apartheid and colonialism."[129] What pinkwashing has helped develop, in other words, is a whole
new form of resistance to the Zionist project in Palestine. Decolonial queering, as Walaa al Qaisiya has put it, has now become an essential component
of Palestinian resistance to Zionism.[130] One cause is the added networks of
organization and activism that have been added to the international struggle for Palestinian rights, and another is that Palestinian anti-pinkwashing
activism has helped make visible the forms of denial woven into Zionism
more generally.

4 Tolerance

All the Muslim graves have been removed; they've gone.
The site has been clean for more than a year.

— Rabbi Marvin Hier, Simon Wiesenthal Center

It was a glorious afternoon in May 2004, and the advocates, fund raisers, and backers of the newly launched Museum of Tolerance in Jerusalem could not have asked for a more auspicious groundbreaking ceremony. Dozens of important guests were in attendance to mark the realization of the project by the Los Angeles–based Simon Wiesenthal Center (which had for some years already been running the original Museum of Tolerance in LA), including the building's world-renowned architect, Frank Gehry; the self-styled "dean" of the Wiesenthal Center, Rabbi Marvin Hier; the Israeli president, Moshe Katsav; and the governor of California, Arnold Schwarzenegger. "In the darkness that pervades the Middle East," proclaimed the governor in the ceremony's keynote address, "this building will be a candle to guide us."[1] Schwarzenegger's words spoke to the museum's lofty proclamations about itself. The complex aims to offer, according to Rabbi Hier, "a great landmark promoting the principles of mutual respect and social responsibility."[2] The museum's marketing literature says that, in the face of a "rising crescendo of ethnic tensions, civilizational clashes and the use of religious justification for acts of terror," it intends to provide "a unique institution that will focus on issues of human dignity and responsibility."[3]

Following the groundbreaking ceremony, everything seemed to be going well for the development of the Jerusalem branch of the Museum of Tolerance, including fund raising toward the $200 million cost from mostly Jewish philanthropists in the United States—until a legal challenge was presented to Israel's High Court in February 2006 that led to the suspension of construction. Workers excavating the site had come across human remains and were quietly removing them when news leaked to the local media, which broke the story, precipitating a major crisis.

The site for the Museum of Tolerance, it turns out, includes a cemetery—in fact, the largest and most important Muslim cemetery in all of Palestine—that had been in continual use for hundreds of years from the time of the Crusades until the uprooting of Palestine in 1948; it contained the graves of family members of living Palestinians (including relatives of people I know). Palestinian and Muslim individuals and organizations had been pointing out this fact and warning of the consequences from the time the museum project was announced. They had even managed to suspend excavation (for two days) in 2004, but otherwise their protests had been dismissed—at least until the news broke that excavators had been digging up human remains and then hurriedly (and improperly) trying to dispose of them.[4]

What followed is one of the most remarkable—and surely one of the most profoundly indicative—episodes in the entire conflict between Zionism and the Palestinians. The project leaders refused to consider any alteration in the museum plan following its encounter with a cemetery that had been in active use until 1948 (and was still being visited by the family members of those buried there). Rabbi Hier, the directors of the Wiesenthal Center in Los Angeles, and the museum's backers in Israel were adamant that the project would go ahead as planned, on the original site, cemetery or no cemetery; they could not see what all the fuss was about. "All the Muslim graves have been removed; they've gone," Rabbi Hier told the *Jerusalem Post*. "The site has been clean for more than a year."[5] (Notice his shameless gloating over an act of ethnic cleansing.) Palestinians and Muslims, on the other hand, were asking how, in all seriousness, a "Museum of Tolerance" claiming to represent "mutual respect" and "human dignity" could be built on top of a dispossessed people's graveyard.

. . . . .

The Ma'man Allah (Mamilla) Cemetery lies just to the west of the old city of Jerusalem, close to Jaffa Gate. Covering some fifty acres by the early twentieth century, it is estimated to have been established in the seventh century and to contain the remains of companions of the Prophet Muhammad as well as warriors of Salah al-Din's (Saladin's) army. The cemetery's boundaries were not clearly delineated until the mid-nineteenth century. Jerusalem, like most ancient cities, buried its dead outside the city walls, and there was no need to lay out cemetery boundaries until urban development started spilling over the walls of the old city, which started to take place in this case in the 1840s.

By the 1860s, the cemetery's borders were clearly delineated from the emerging residential district to the west of the old city by a wall and a surrounding road. According to Hebrew University archaeological historian Yehoshua Ben-Arieh, these delineations are clearly visible in maps dating from this period, as well as in the first aerial photographs of Jerusalem. During the last sixty years of Ottoman rule, through the three decades of the British Mandate in Palestine and the first twenty years following the creation of Israel and the concomitant uprooting of Palestine in 1948, the cemetery's boundaries, notes Ben-Arieh, "remained intact and were not violated."[6] Highly detailed maps—indicating buildings, contours, roads, and trees—from the time of the British Mandate show that the dozens of buildings constructed in the vicinity of the cemetery during the late Ottoman period never intruded across its boundaries. This remained true of nearby construction during the Mandate period as well.[7] In the 1920s, for example, the Palace Hotel was built on land adjacent to the cemetery, on the other side of Mamilla Road, but its (Jewish) architect was careful not to encroach on the grounds of Mamilla cemetery.[8]

It was during the Mandate period that the cemetery was entered in the official Jerusalem land registry as one single tract of land: Bloc No. 30036, Plot No.1.[9] It was registered in the name of the Trustees of the Waqf, the Muslim religious endowment funded by the charitable donations that are an integral part of the Islamic faith and that once held up to 10 percent of the land in Palestine, including schools, cemeteries, religious monuments, and mosques, many of which were converted to meeting halls, bars, cafés, discotheques, and barns by their new Jewish occupants after 1948.

Mamilla cemetery fell to the Zionist militias that would coalesce into the Israeli army during the uprooting of Palestine in 1948; so did most of the rest of Jerusalem (though not the old city).[10] Multicultural, multiconfessional Palestine was deliberately uprooted in order to clear the space for the creation of a state with an exclusively Jewish identity, to be populated— that is, once most of the Muslim and Christian Palestinians had been driven away—largely by newly arrived European Jewish colonists and settlers.[11] As chapter 1 details, the lands, homes, livestock, furniture, personal effects, clothes, dishes, family heirlooms, papers, books, photographs, and all the other personal possessions of the Palestinians driven from their homes and expelled beyond the borders of what would become the state of Israel and blocked from returning after the fighting ended—and ever since—were confiscated by the agencies of the Jewish state and eventually transferred to the newly created "custodian of absentee property," to be distributed to Jewish immigrants.[12] What befell the rest of Palestine was also the fate of Mamilla cemetery, along with the other properties of the Waqf, which were transferred to the custodian of absentee property and placed under Israeli control; they remain under state control, or under the control of "national agencies" such as the Jewish National Fund, to this day.[13]

At first, Israeli authorities and state planners respected the boundaries of the cemetery that had been established under Ottoman rule.[14] Mamilla's protected status started to erode in the late 1950s and early 1960s, however—a time when the Palestinian citizens of Israel were subject to martial law and were, hence, ill-equipped to protest. First, a road was paved through the cemetery to connect two neighboring streets. Then, in 1960, a parking lot was built on a small part of the cemetery: a project approved by an Israeli-appointed Muslim official (who was subsequently arrested and removed from office because of corruption).[15] In 1985, the Ministry of Transport established a parking lot on another, larger section of the cemetery; further excavation was involved, and it was again during the installation of sewage lines. Dozens of graves were destroyed during these excavations, and human remains removed and scattered.[16]

All over municipal Jerusalem, and indeed throughout Palestine, the same fate was befalling Muslim and Christian cemeteries: they were, as former deputy mayor of Jerusalem Meron Benvenisti points out, "turned into garbage dumps, parking lots, roads and construction sites."[17] It was only a matter of time before the same thing happened to Mamilla, its historical significance notwithstanding. In 1967 the Waqf proposed the restoration and rehabilitation of Mamilla; Israeli authorities rejected that idea, just as they have blocked the preservation or restoration of Muslim and Christian sites elsewhere in the country. "Throughout Israel there are hundreds of sites that were once Muslim graveyards, whose remains are still evident at a few dozen of them," notes Benvenisti. "The rest have vanished, whether because the tombstones crumbled or because the sites were used for roads, farming or building institutions and residential buildings. The Muslim cemeteries' condition is so outrageous that if it existed in another civilized state it would raise a public storm."[18] From time to time, he adds, conflict erupts "between the al-Aqsa Association for the Construction of Islamic Holy Places based in [the Palestinian Israeli town of] Umm al-Fahm (and other Israeli-Muslim groups) and Israeli bodies . . . over the damage to these graveyards and the efforts to preserve them. Open burial sites are scattered throughout the country, human bones are strewed about, and tombstones are shattered, covered with garbage."[19] While Israel takes great pains to preserve Jewish cemeteries, it is much less invested in the preservation, or even the acknowledgement, of Muslim and Christian sites. (Curiously, the state's contempt for Christian churches, cemeteries and other sites seems not to bother the legion of so-called Christian Zionists in the United States).

In 1992 the custodian of absentee property transferred the cemetery to the municipality of Jerusalem. The Palestinian Muslim community and religious institutions protested that transfer, but to no avail. In the same year, city officials established Israel's Independence Park on a large section of the cemetery. Construction involved the excavation of graves and human remains and the planting of trees and shrubs. Crumbling tombstones can still be seen between the trees of Independence Park.[20]

Today, Independence Park embodies and expresses Israel's uneasy attitude toward the Palestinians: an unstable mixture of acknowledgement, repression, denial, erasure, and resentment of the fact that, despite all the denial and repression, Palestinians still exist and refuse simply to disappear. The sense of incompletion captured in the park also conveys the difference between Israel and other, more successful settler-colonial

Muslim graves near site of Museum of Tolerance, Jerusalem. Photo by author.

projects.[21] In this case, the removal or eradication of the indigenous population to make room for the incoming settler population was not completed successfully. Palestinians constitute a fifth of the population of pre-1967 Israel—and about half of the total population of the territories over which Israel rules (and Palestinians, including those forced into exile in 1948, outnumber Israeli Jews by two to one, as mentioned in chapter 2). If Israel's Independence Park expresses the current unsettled state of Israeli attitudes toward Palestinians, the museum project, among other things, aims to resolve these tensions and contradictions by removing the last remaining traces of dissonance and symbolically cleansing (to use Rabbi Hier's terminology) the settled site once and for all; to secure a sense of Jewish belonging by erasing the traces of the Palestinian Other.

.   .   .   .   .

In February 2004, the local media reported that the Israeli government and the Jerusalem municipality had approved the construction of the Museum of Tolerance on part of the site of Mamilla cemetery. Protests from Palestinians and Muslims went unheeded, and the groundbreaking ceremony was held in May of that year. Protests were stepped up when the actual excavations began in September. Especially vocal were Palestinians in Jerusalem whose relatives were buried in the cemetery, including, for example, Mohammed Hamdi Bader, who used to visit his grandfather's grave in the cemetery regularly in order to pray by it. Bader says that he supports the idea of a museum of tolerance. "But you can't build this museum on any graveyard, regardless of religion," he says. "How can a museum carrying the name of tolerance be built on a graveyard?"[22] That month, Palestinian-Israeli human rights organizations representing the Baders and other families whose relatives are buried in the cemetery secured an order from a Muslim religious court halting of the work. However, excavation was resumed two days later on the grounds that—according to the municipality, the Israeli government, and the backers of the Museum project—the Muslim court had no authority to issue such orders.

After news broke in February 2006 that human remains were being disinterred, the case was taken to Israel's High Court, which ordered a temporary halt to construction in the spring of 2006 and appointed an arbitration panel. In May of the same year, the authorities sealed off the cemetery and threatened to prosecute anyone entering the area, including those, like Mohammed Bader, attempting to visit their relatives' graves, or anyone attempting to maintain the cemetery. That order prevented legitimate visits by Muslims, but it did not prevent the nocturnal vandalization of graves by Jewish groups, including the spray-painting of racist graffiti and the destruction of several graves and tombstones.

On 29 October 2008, the Israeli High Court gave its final go-ahead to the construction project, thereby bringing to an end all legal attempts to stop the project. "Moderation and tolerance have prevailed," declared Rabbi Hier of the Wiesenthal Center. "From this half-century parking lot in the center of west Jerusalem will rise an institution that offers hope and reason to all the people of Israel and the world," he added.[23] There would be "protests for two or three days," Hier conceded, but then things would go back to normal.[24] Palestinians and Muslims in Jerusalem did indeed organize demonstrations against the court's decision. The mufti of Jerusalem, Sheikh Mohammad Hussein, said it was hard to believe that the project's backers would want to build a museum of tolerance "whose construction constitutes an act of aggression."[25] "We came to announce to the entire world in the name of all Palestinians in Gaza, the West Bank, those within the Green Line [i.e., inside Israel] and in the Diaspora," Sheikh Kamal Hatib declared at one of the protests, that "we will not reconcile with you and will not forgive you for violating the graves of our mothers, fathers, and grandparents."[26] The protests notwithstanding, work on the Museum of Tolerance immediately resumed.

The High Court suggested, however, that the project engineers construct an underground—horizontal—separation barrier between the foundation of the museum building and the remaining bodies below, thereby separating the living Jews in the structure above from the dead Arabs in the ground beneath their feet.[27]

.   .   .   .   .

Such a separation barrier—a wall on the horizontal plane—would, of course, perfectly mirror *the* separation barrier—a wall constructed on the vertical plane—that Israel has built in and around Jerusalem and along the length of the West Bank. I have described the wall in great detail elsewhere.[28] Here I need only point out that it constitutes merely one component of a complex of physical and bureaucratic mechanisms and procedures designed to impose nearly absolute Israeli control over the movement and lives of Palestinians in the occupied territories, in total disregard for Israel's responsibilities as an occupying power under the Fourth Geneva Convention and the other constitutive documents of international humanitarian law, which require it to facilitate rather than to disable the inhabitants' conduct of everyday life. The illegality of the wall was confirmed by the advisory opinion that the International Court of Justice in the Hague issued in 2004, though the ruling had little impact on Israel, which has been violating other requirements of international law for decades, so far with total impunity.[29]

We can think of the wall as expressing a kind of apartheid because of the principle of ethnic separation it involves (see chapter 2). Apart from the wall, the other major components of Israel's "matrix of control" in the West Bank and East Jerusalem are the hundreds of roadblocks and checkpoints

Separation wall, Jerusalem. Photo by author.

maintained by the Israeli army (totaling 593 by 2020, in addition to a further 101 barriers to Palestinian movement in the city of Hebron alone and countless midnight raids and "flying" checkpoints randomly set up in the West Bank),[30] and the pass and permit system the army imposes on the Palestinian population. These mechanisms severely restrict—and often suspend altogether—the movement of Palestinians within the West Bank and cut them off from East Jerusalem and Israel (not to mention Gaza).

On the other hand, there is a network of bypass roads *connecting* the sprawling network of Jewish colonies in the West Bank and East Jerusalem to one another and to Israel while at the same time *disconnecting* Palestinian towns and villages from one another and the outside world, because Palestinians are not allowed on (or even near) the bypass roads, which are for Jewish settlers (who are, moreover, not subject to the grid of roadblocks and checkpoints or the pass system, all of which stymie the circulation of Palestinians).[31] Thus the combination of Israel's wall, the apartheid permit system, and the bypass roads *enable* the free movement of Jews while—and by—*disabling* the movement of Palestinians.

Indeed, the enabling of the one population is inseparable from the disabling of the other, for, as the Israeli architect Eyal Weizman observes, the whole point of the matrix of control is to superimpose two separate political geographies—one Jewish, one Palestinian—on the same physical landscape. The Jewish parts of the West Bank, Weizman explains, are seamlessly tied to one another and incorporated into Israel; the Palestinian parts of the West Bank, on the other hand, are fractured and broken and fragmented, shards of territory cut off from one another and the outside world. "The geographic space, which is contiguous for Jews, is a fragmented mosaic for Palestinians," notes the recent B'tselem paper on Israeli apartheid.[32] The result is an Escher-like representation of geography, best understood in terms of what Weizman calls the "politics of verticality."[33] Weizman's notion is not merely figurative but literal as well. For example, where the West Bank's unlit, broken, potholed, or altogether unpaved Palestinian roads cross the well-lit, well-paved, and vigilantly patrolled Jewish bypass roads, they plunge beneath them into tunnels. Jews traverse the landscape *above*; Palestinians, *below*.

Israeli apartheid, in other words, functions in the horizontal plane as well as in the vertical. One effect of this is, whenever possible, to render Palestinians invisible to Jewish colonists and to Israelis driving within eyesight of the West Bank (and, if not invisible, then at least part of the background over and against which the modern infrastructure is built). Thus, Jewish colonists traversing the West Bank, or Israelis driving on Highway 6, roughly parallel to the West Bank, often do not see Palestinians: they are in tunnels below, or on the other side of the twenty-four-foot-high separation wall.

Seen from the Palestinian side, the wall is, unmistakably, a wall. Its brutalist design communicates unequivocally to the Palestinians what Israel thinks of them. Seen from the Israeli side, however, the wall is often not really a wall: in many sections, it is smoothed into the landscape, and its scale is disguised by shrubs, trees, and landscaping that gradually rises and falls, offsetting the severity that is so brutally—and expressively— naked on the Palestinian side. From the Israeli point of view, the effect is not only to render the Palestinians on the other side invisible but, even if only in fits and starts, to render the process of rendering them invisible *itself* invisible. When possible, then, the wall as the signifier of erasure is

Separation wall around Qalqilya, viewed from the east. Photo by author.

Separation wall around Qalqilya, viewed from the west. Photo by author.

itself erased in turn—as though there were some magic trick that could erase the Palestinians from the landscape without the trace of that erasure being evident.

In other places, the wall is written into the landscape in the sense that it is painted over (from the Israeli side) in such a way as to render it as pure background. In some cases, a pristine landscape is painted on the wall, replacing not only the actuality of the wall but also the undesirable real landscape of living Palestinians; in others, the wall is painted over with decorative arches to disguise it as something other than what it actually is, even as something that connects (like a Roman aqueduct) rather than separates. None of these attempts to disguise the wall really succeed, however; as Tom Mitchell points out, they are easily subverted.[34]

Nevertheless, what these adjustments to the wall on the Israeli side express is the same unstable combination of acknowledgement and denial, knowledge and repression (both self-repression and repression of the Other) that can also be seen at work in Israel's Independence Park. On one hand, there is a desire to do away with or deny the Palestinian Other—to retroactively fulfill the Zionist dream that Palestine might be "a land without a people for a people without a land"—while also denying that such a denial is taking place (by disguising its traces). On the other hand, once the willing suspension of disbelief wears off, or once the Palestinians intrude themselves yet once more on the scene from which they were supposed to have been evacuated, there is the returning knowledge that the Other is, despite everything, actually really still there—and that even more denial (or perhaps some other, more effective method of dealing with this stubborn and unrepentant Otherness) is therefore necessary.

.   .   .   .   .

The vertically oriented apartheid expressed by the wall applies to housing units as well as to roads and walls in the West Bank, though here visibility and invisibility play a different role in the project to secure a Jewish sense of homeliness in Palestine. Many of the Jewish colonies in the West Bank are built along the central mountain ridge that bisects the territory along a north-south axis, or on other hilltops. Not only do they command a prospect of the Palestinian Arab landscape below, but their very location is an integral element in Israel's strategy of control over the occupied territory. "A belt of settlements in strategic locations increases both internal and external security," noted Mattiyahu Drobles, the author of Israel's 1978 revised West Bank colonization plan; "therefore, the proposed settlement blocs are spread out as a belt surrounding the mountains, starting along the western slopes from north to south, and along the eastern slopes from south to north, within the minority [*sic*] population as well as surrounding it."

Drobles refers to the Palestinians as a "minority," even though they compose the majority of the population of the West Bank. This suggests their new status—their minoritization in geographic and spatial as well as political terms—as a disenfranchised group trapped—pinned down—in a smooth Jewish-Israeli space surrounding them on all sides, from which they are excluded by virtue of not being Jewish. "Being bisected by Jewish settlements," Drobles explained on a different occasion, "the minority population will find it hard to create unification and territorial contiguity."[35] Jewish colonies, according to Drobles, should thus be implanted in order to maximize damage to the preexisting Palestinian communities of the West Bank, by squeezing them ever *inward* and *downward*, cutting them off from the hilltops. As with the road network and the wall that would come only later, Israeli colonies from the beginning separated Palestinians vertically as well as horizontally.

Because of their role in the politics of verticality, the Jewish colonies in the West Bank were conceived not only in strategic terms but also as integral elements in Israel's tactical military control and surveillance of the Palestinian landscape. Here, however, the point is precisely to render the Palestinians visible (rather than invisible), but only when they intrude into the Jewish geography. The Jewish colonies above keep the terrain below "under perpetual surveillance," as Tom Mitchell puts it, and the "fractured, agonized appearance" of the landscape itself can be thought of as the product of the struggle to control it in visual terms.[36] Indeed, as Weizman and his colleague Rafi Segal point out, the integration of the colonies into Israeli tactical and strategic planning permeating the visual field is literally built into their design from the inside out. The Israeli Ministry of Construction and Housing's 1984 guideline for settlement construction, for example, recommends building homes along the West Bank's mountain ridge in order to maximize the outward view of the surrounding landscape, while orienting inward views toward the colony's inner core, with concentric rings surrounding each mountain peak. "With respect to the interior of each building, the guideline recommends the orientation of the bedrooms towards the inner public spaces, and that of the living rooms towards the distant view," Weizman and Segal explain. "Vision," they continue,

> dictated the discipline of design and its methodologies on all scales. Regionally, a strategic function was integrated into the distribution of settlements around the entire territory, creating a "network of observation" that overlooks the main traffic arteries of the West Bank [most of which are now off-limits to Palestinians and constitute the core of the Jews-only bypass road network]; topographically, it was integrated into the siting of the settlements on [mountain] summits; urbanistically, it was integrated into their very layout, as rings around the summit, and in the positioning of homes perpendicular to the slope; architecturally, it was integrated into the arrangements and orientation of rooms, and finally into the precise positioning of windows."[37]

Given this elaborate design, it is hardly any wonder that Jewish colonies in the West Bank and East Jerusalem—Har Homa, built on Jabal Abu Ghneim, is a typical case—often have a fortress-like appearance in terms of visual function, and sometimes aesthetically as well.

Thus the components of Israeli colonial architecture (the bypass roads, the wall, and the colonies themselves) alternate between making the native Palestinians visible and making them invisible—sometimes marking them as to-be-seen and other times as to-remain-unseen: erased, replaced, quite literally deterritorialized, written out of the space of the would-be Jewish state.

·   ·   ·   ·   ·

The original choice of Frank Gehry as the architect for the Museum of Tolerance project needs to be seen and evaluated in two seemingly (but not really) contradictory ways at once. On one hand, precisely in the sense in which Daniel Libeskind would have been the obvious candidate—because of his work on the Jewish Museum in San Francisco, the Danish Jewish Museum, the Jewish Museum in Berlin, and several buildings in

Israel—the selection of Gehry made no sense at all. On the other hand, he would have been the perfect person for the job. I explain both positions and show how they can be reconciled.

Let's begin with why the selection of Gehry seemed not to make sense. Far from being associated with specifically Jewish-themed projects, his work has come to be seen as both consummately self-referential and homogeneously global. Rather than addressing the specificities of this particular location and historical context, the resulting edifice would have looked like so many of Gehry's later projects (from Bilbao to Los Angeles)— almost as though it had been beamed down from outer space without regard to local context. Indeed, the presence of a new Gehry structure in any city, in effect, lifts a site out of its immediate context and ties it to the global network of other high-profile Gehry sites—the Guggenheim in Bilbao, Walt Disney Concert Hall in Los Angeles, the EMP building in Seattle, the new Guggenheim in New York, and so on—as the locus of a certain kind of cultural (and financial) capital that functions on a global scale. According to the art critic Kriston Capps, these latest projects express one of the recent trends in architecture in which, "in lieu of con-text-driven work, the field's high stylists (Gehry foremost among them) have focused instead on developing drag-and-drop designs that any project can be made to fit."[38] There is, Capps points out, a "Gehry look," with which cities and global corporate clients want to be associated; but it has little or nothing to do with the specificities of a particular site.

Thus, any one of Gehry's recent titanium-clad buildings, featuring what Hal Foster identifies as "the non-Euclidean curves, swirls and blobs that became his signature gestures in the 1990s,"[39] is instantly recognizable as his, no matter where it is located. A Gehry building actually draws atten-tion to itself and away from the site it occupies; it can even draw people to the site in spite of the site itself—which was exactly why Gehry's plan for Disney Hall was seen as the anchor for the rejuvenation of a downtown Los Angeles that had been "abandoned" by the city's cultural and financial elite ("Build It and They Will Come," reads one of the funding appeals for Disney Hall published in the *LA Times*[40]). There is, as Foster puts it, a kind of "anti-contextual" energy in Gehry's recent work, quite at odds with his early work, still best exemplified by his own house in Santa Monica. "The gestures of his early houses," Foster explains, were often idiosyncratic, but they were also grounded in two ways—in an LA vernacular of common materials and against an International Style of purist forms. As these gestures began to lose the specificity of the former and the foil of the latter, they became not only more extravagant (almost neo-Expressionist or neo-Surrealist) but also more detached: they became signs of "artistic expression" that could be dropped, indifferently, almost anywhere—in LA, Bilbao, Seattle, Berlin, New York. Why this curve, swirl or blob here, and not that one? If there is not much in the way of apparent constraint—of formal articulation derived from a resistant material, structure or context—architecture quickly becomes arbitrary or self-indulgent.[41]

And that is exactly why—on the other hand—it made *perfect* sense for Gehry to have been chosen as the architect for the Jerusalem museum: his design would have drawn the site out of and away from the specificities of the local context. The Museum of Tolerance is based in Los Angeles; Gehry is an LA-based architect. In a way, this entire project is really a projection not just of a certain kind of American Zionism but specifically of a Hollywood-infused LA strand of Zionism. With Gehry in charge, the former site of Ma'man Allah Cemetery would become much closer (in a sense) to Los Angeles than to, say, the Mount of Olives, on the other side of Jerusalem. The logic of separation in play in the museum plan would be made complete by this last stage of removal from local context and the ground occupied. Occupation would in fact be turned into removal and symbolic transfer of bodies and indeed of the entire site. The doubts and hesitations expressed in other Israeli projects (Independence Park, the wall) would be transcended in an effort to enable the construction of a form of belonging or claim to the land that, at once, finally erases the last traces of the Palestinian Other and lifts the very land, as it were, away from itself and plugs it immediately into global space. This is emphasized in the artists' impressions of the design, which occlude the project's urban context: this museum could be anywhere in the world—and that is part of the point.

But on this point another set of contradictions now has to be taken into account. Although Hal Foster and others argue that there is a kind of self-referential arbitrariness in Gehry's late style, Gehry himself insists that his work is always site sensitive, and so do many of his admirers (Foster's point, indeed, is that that very insistence itself suggests its opposite). "The important urban idea is to fit a building into the fabric of the city," Gehry says; "it takes time to get the body language of a building, to fit it into an environment."[42] J. Fiona Ragheb writes that "Gehry's building looks to its physical site for its definition, twisting and bending in order to root itself more firmly into its surroundings."[43] Jean-Louis Cohen says that Gehry's buildings are designed with "what he calls the specific 'body language' of each city" in mind. "Only when it is grasped, sometimes intuitively, does the city's architecture find its place in Gehry's work."[44]

In looking at Gehry's design for the Museum of Tolerance, both principles seem to be in play: on one hand, the design had nothing to do with the specificities of this site and its environment or with its proximity to the old city; on the other hand, there are elements of the design that do engage with Israeli colonial architecture. The design also differed markedly from the playful, deceptively "sculptural" look of billowing sheets of titanium cladding that—however misleadingly—seem to express Gehry's freedom of artistic expression and even "freedom" as such.[45] The Museum of Tolerance was much more angular than any of Gehry's other contemporaneous projects. Rather than conjuring up movement, freedom, waves, or billowing sails (as with Bilbao or Disney Hall), it suggested castles, fortresses, and watchtowers—and, above all, walls. This design was about location, surveillance, power, and control—not freedom. (The artist's impressions of Gehry's designs have been expunged from the Museum of Tolerance website, but they are widely available on other sites.[46])

It is in this sense, then, that Gehry's design for the museum actually did seem to consciously integrate all of the major elements of Israeli colonial architecture. And it involved the same kind of play of the visible and the invisible that are at work elsewhere in occupied East Jerusalem and in the West Bank. The centerpiece of Gehry's design was the Grand Hall (the naming of which was on offer for a donation of $10 million), which was to have been surrounded by sixteen titanium "Pillars of Tolerance" (also once on offer to donors for $1 million each). "Frank O. Gehry saw the Grand Hall as the starting point of his design because of its openness on all sides," the museum's website said. "To him, it symbolized the 'living room' of Jerusalem. The exterior of the 118-foot building was supported by 16 sculptured titanium pillars, which could be seen from miles away. Before visitors entered the Grand Hall, they would see the name of a different donor inscribed on the outside of each of the pillars."[47] The circular Grand Hall had windows and entry doors all along its 360-degree circumference; every other structure in the complex faced toward it, so it commanded the entire visual field. In this sense, its design recapitulated the panoptic and surveillance features that, as Eyal Weizman points out, have become essential to Israeli colonial architecture in the occupied and colonized Palestinian territories.

"Protected" by its titanium walls, the symbolic glass and steel "fortress" at the heart of the museum complex would have functioned as an observation site from which to track the movement of bodies in and through the complex. "Families and children are constantly in view, in your face, so that you never escape from the issue of what this place is all about," Gehry said of his plan for the Grand Hall. As for what the place is "all about," he has a clear sense of that: it is about the transfer and circulation of bodies. "I was trying to make a building that had body language," says Gehry. "People can come from all directions, and all kinds of people can come."[48]

In this sense, too, Gehry's design perfectly recapitulated the politics of exclusion that are evident throughout Palestine: *some* people can come from all directions, *some* people can be surveyed coming and going, *some* people can enter the visual field dominated by the Grand Hall, *some* people could feel at home in the "living room" of Jerusalem—but by no means would "all kinds of people" have access to the museum or to the particularized sense of belonging that it wants to convey. Palestinians from the West Bank and much of East Jerusalem, let alone Gaza, *cannot* come to the museum, because they are blocked from access to Jerusalem by the wall and the other mechanisms that Israel uses to control the movement of Palestinians. But that act of exclusion was invisible—indeed, irrelevant— to the design.

In this sense, what Gehry says perfectly aligns the living Palestinian bodies who are excluded from access to the museum (because they are separated from the museum by a barrier built on the vertical plane) with the dead Palestinian bodies in the soil beneath the museum complex (who, as the court's suggestion is taken up, will be separated from it by a barrier built on the horizontal plane). Not only are Palestinian bodies rendered invisible, but (again, perfecting the logic only partially enacted by the wall in the West Bank as seen from the Israeli side) the process by which they are erased, removed, or transferred is itself rendered invisible. Thus the foundational act of erasure and re-placement is placed beyond scrutiny and legibility; or rather it is placed *before* what is seen in the visual and textual field, as a condition of possibility for what will be seen, said, and read.

Thus the logic of occupation and colonization cuts seamlessly across from the surrounding colonial context to the museum itself. If the museum was to have been like a home with a "living room," as its marketing literature put it, the residents of this home would be—just like the residents of the homes in Jewish colonies in and around Palestine—all of one kind, to the exclusion of *other* kinds of people (see, for instance, the discussion of Eshchar in chapter 2). A sense of belonging is enabled for the privileged national self at the expense of the Other, who has been "managed" out of sight. For, in the context of occupation and colonization, "all kinds of people" actually means (without admitting it) "only Jewish people" because of the invisible process of exclusion and erasure by which the universal is restricted to the particular. In exactly the same sense, when the Israeli government expropriates land from Palestinian families in order to build a Jewish colony, it always does so officially "for public use." It never says that the universal formulation "the public" actually refers in the particular sense to the specifically Jewish public (Palestinians are excluded both from Jewish colonies in the West Bank and from so-called Jewish community settlements inside pre-1967 Palestine). Thus, in a situation where only the particular is visible (because its Other has conveniently been covered over, buried underground, or transferred elsewhere), the particular seems to *become* the universal—a point to which I return in a later section of this chapter.

What Gehry's design enabled, then, was an act of self-contemplation (perfectly expressed in the self-referential circle of titanium-clad pillars with their donors' names engraved on them) founded on a violent act of exclusion symbolized by the walls so essential to the plan. In this sense, too, the choice of Gehry as architect made perfect sense: the architect best known for his self-referential structures was chosen to design a building that is thematically all about a form of self-referentiality constructed on the premise of the physical and symbolic exclusion of the Other; a sense of the homely predicated on the evaporation of the Other.

Walls were among the design's most prominent features: the so-called "pillars of tolerance," which would have been *visible* from miles away (or so the marketing literature said), and which, as I mentioned, resembled nothing so much as the slabs of *the* wall; the wall surrounding the entire complex; and the wall that seems to hang, suspended, in the artist's impression of the visitor center.[49] It made perfect sense not only that walls should feature so prominently in Gehry's design but that in the museum design *the* wall is repeatedly summoned forth and echoed back across Jerusalem. In artists' impressions of Gehry's design, what looks much like a scale replica of a section of Israel's West Bank wall seems to hover in midair outside the entrance to the visitor information center. What is so politically laden out there (i.e., a few hundred meters away) is here so relieved of its burden that it actually floats, the shabby concrete transformed by the alchemy of Gehry's design into the pure essence of separation, so that the hovering wall is freed of the mud, dirt, and graffiti contaminating its real-world counterpart. The "Pillars of Tolerance" themselves would have rendered Israel's wall in shiny curved titanium cladding rather than drab, rectilinear concrete. Just as the Jewish geography of the West Bank is smooth and unrestricted while the Palestinian geography is striated and closed, the wall here would have seemed open and lit, rather than forbidding and closed; enabling panoptic vision, rather than shutting down the visual field as the wall does in the West Bank. In Gehry's design, that which is separated is so utterly separated that it has disappeared into thin air—the separated Other is so far gone that the self constructed through the process of its removal is left all alone in blissful self-contemplation.

Here, then, is the resolution to the apparent contradiction implied by Gehry's design: look at it one way, and you see Bilbao, Disney, late capital, freedom of expression; look at it another way, and you see the wall. The design takes the building blocks of Israeli colonial architecture and translates them into the realm of freedom by which this site would be—wants so desperately to be—tied to Bilbao and LA. One kind of viewer, one kind of subject, is tied down and hopelessly fixed; the other is free. One moves, the other is bound.

·   ·   ·   ·   ·

In this sense, the project represented by the Museum of Tolerance fits in neatly—even perfectly symmetrically—with another project taking place today in Jerusalem, on the opposite side of the Old City from Mamilla cemetery. The Bustan neighborhood of the Palestinian district of Silwan, in East Jerusalem, consists of about ninety buildings and is home to about one thousand Palestinian residents. Most of the homes were built without permits in the 1980s and 1990s, though a few were built prior to Israel's 1967 occupation of East Jerusalem. They were built without permits because the Jerusalem municipality, while doing everything possible to facilitate the illegal colonization of East Jerusalem by Jewish immigrants—for example, by expropriating land from Palestinian families and granting immediate permission for Jews to build homes there—only under exceptional circumstances grants building permits to Palestinian residents of the city, even on land that has belonged to their families for generations.[50]

This is but one component of the long-standing Israeli project to Judaize and de-Arabize the city, which John Dugard, former UN special rapporteur on human rights in the occupied territories, referred to as "a cynical exercise in social engineering."[51] It is a project structured in terms of a recurring difference between Jews and non-Jews, and specifically in terms of the replacement of the latter by the former: a form of ethnic cleansing on a small scale and moving at a slow pace. Israel carries out this social engineering partly by, whenever possible, stripping Jerusalem Palestinians of their residency papers, thereby preventing them from living in (or even subsequently visiting) the city in which they were born; partly by making it illegal for a Palestinian from the West Bank to marry and live with a spouse from Jerusalem; and partly by making it as difficult as possible for Palestinians to register the birth of children born in Jerusalem (none of these kinds of measures are ever directed against Jews, whether residents of Israel, Jerusalem, or the West Bank).[52] But it is also carried out by making it very difficult for Palestinians to find and secure property in Jerusalem—adding to the pressure on them to move out of the city and live on the other side of the wall in the West Bank, thereby running the risk of being stripped of their Jerusalem residency (Israel's layers of exclusion are all self-reinforcing).

According to current or former Israeli officials of the municipality of Jerusalem, the distinction between establishing homes for Jews and denying them to non-Jews has been essential to city planning since 1967. "A cornerstone in the planning of Jerusalem is the demographic question," noted Israel Kimchi, director of planning policy for the Jerusalem municipality, in 1977. "The city's growth and the preservation of the demographic balance among its ethnic groups was a matter decided by the Government of Israel. That decision, concerning the city's rate of growth, today serves as one of the criteria for the success of the process of Jerusalem's consolidation as the capital of Israel."[53] Amir Cheshin, former Israeli advisor on Arab (i.e., Palestinian) affairs to the mayor of Jerusalem, explains: "The planning and building laws in East Jerusalem rest on a policy that calls for placing obstacles in the way of planning in the Arab sector—this is done more to preserve the demographic balance between Jews and Arabs in the city, which is presently in a ratio of 72 percent Jews against 28 percent non-Jews."[54] As the percentage of Jews to non-Jews (that is, Palestinians) began inevitably sliding away from the desired ratio, Israeli policymakers struggled to devise ways to reverse the trend, with the 72 to 28 ratio firmly in mind as a desirable outcome.[55]

The inevitable result of all the official bureaucratic limitations and controls on Palestinian growth and development in Jerusalem is a turn to what Israel considers "illegal" construction.[56] Palestinians have built thousands of housing units since 1967 without official permits. But they have done so at considerable risk. Between 2004 and 2008 alone, Israeli authorities punitively demolished 402 Palestinian homes in Jerusalem.[57] There are today around 9,000 Palestinian homes that have been built "illegally" in Jerusalem. All of them are subject to demolition.

Clearly, Silwan is only one case among many. What makes it unusual is that, rather than targeting a single family for punitive home demolition as the Israelis usually do, they are going after an entire neighborhood, threatening a thousand Palestinians at once with instant homelessness and displacement—a scene more typical of Gaza than of Jerusalem. And they are doing so not on the pretense that they are merely enforcing city building codes, but in order to help clear space for an exclusively Jewish archaeological park that is taking shape literally beneath the foundations of the Palestinian homes of Silwan.

Jewish colony in Silwan, East Jerusalem. Photo by author.

The archaeological park, the so-called City of David—only one of a network of such parks intended to consolidate Israel's hold on Jerusalem[58]—is being run by Elad, a secretive Zionist organization with ties to overseas funders such as Irving Moskowitz as well as to the fundamentalist colonists' group Ateret Cohanim. The latter organization has been working alongside Elad to establish a Jewish colony in the middle of the Palestinian neighborhood, by buying Palestinian property (usually by means of extortion), or by fabricating documents claiming ownership and forcing Palestinian families out, or by taking advantage of Israel's Absentee Property Law (the same one under the pretext of which Mamilla cemetery was taken over) to obtain properties in Silwan from the Jewish National Fund, to which they were transferred by the custodian of absentee property in the 1990s.[59] There are by now around 250 Jewish colonists in Silwan, surrounded by thousands of Palestinians in the broader adjacent area.

In 1998, the municipality of Jerusalem transferred control of the City of David archaeological park to Elad, which now runs the archaeological digs there, while simultaneously bringing massive pressure to bear on the Palestinian residents to move out—a move that the municipality itself embraced in late 2004 and early 2005 when Uri Shetrit, the city engineer, directed the municipality's building supervision department to demolish all the Palestinian houses (but not those of Jewish colonists) in Silwan. Demolition orders were secured in early 2009, and made global news headlines partly because then secretary of state Hillary Clinton was visiting Israel at the time; she called the plan to demolish the Palestinian neighborhood "unhelpful."[60] If the demolitions were to go forward, they would be the largest carried out in Jerusalem since 1967 (when another Palestinian neighborhood, the Maghrabi district, was summarily bulldozed to create space for Jews to worship). A renewed push for large-scale demolition of Palestinian family homes in Silwan began in 2021, and at this writing their fate still hangs in the balance.

The City of David site offers a textbook example of what Norman Klein identifies as a scripted space. "Scripted spaces are a walk-through or click-through environment (a mall, a church, a casino, a theme park, a computer game)," Klein explains. "They are designed to *emphasize* the viewer's journey—the space between—rather than the gimmicks on the wall. They audience walks *into* the story. What's more, this walk should respond to each viewer's whims, even though each step along the way is prescripted (or should I say preordained?). It is gentle repression posing as free will," he adds; "from front to back, the choices are defined; yet somehow the walk is supposed to feel open."[61] In this case, the space offers a "mysterious, magical journey between ancient shafts, walls and fortresses at the City of David, the place where Jerusalem began."[62] The story of the City of David originated, the organization proclaims, "over 3,000 years ago, when King David left the city of Hebron for a small hilltop city known as Jerusalem, establishing it as the unified capital of the tribes of Israel. Years later, David's son, King Solomon, built the First Temple next to the City of David on top of Mount Moriah, the site of the binding of Isaac, and with it, this hilltop became one of the most important sites in the world." Today, "the story of the City of David continues. Deep underground, the City of David is revealing some of the most exciting archeological finds of the ancient world. While above ground, the city is a vibrant center of activity with a visitor's center that welcomes visitors for an exciting tour to the site where much of the Bible was written."[63] What is distinctive about this scripted space, like the ones at work in the JNF tree-planting sites discussed in chapter 1, is that it is designed to deny the Palestinian presence in and claim to Palestine not merely by occluding that presence through home demolition, bulldozing, removal of human and material traces, and the like, but also by affirming the value of the Jewish claim to the land—in this case a Jewish claim that, we are told, has an unbroken three thousand–year legacy, as though no other people (the Moabites, the Canaanites, the Jebusites, the Philistines) had been here before the Jews, and no other people afterward, least of all the Palestinian Arabs. The project is designed to frame and structure attention, to draw visitors' gazes *this* way and not *that* way, to have them focus on *this* rather than *that* detail, to channel them in one direction while occluding all other possibilities. And it is designed to do so with extreme violence, blasting away anything—and anyone—that stands in the way of construction of its carefully curated narrative space.

Israel's deliberate destruction of Palestinian family homes is nothing new. The point is that in Silwan the demolitions would be carried out in order to make room for the development of an archeological park by a secretive private organization that uses heavy earth-moving equipment to blast through layers of cultural artefacts—scattering, destroying, or simply trashing material and human remains in the process[64]—in order to get to a supposedly "Jewish" layer allegedly containing King David's palaces and ancient Jewish graves.

As Nadia Abu El-Haj has scrupulously shown, much of the self-fashioning essential to Israeli archaeology hinges on matching a priori textual evidence with material dug out of the earth to come to the most tenuous (and tendentious) conclusions. "In such arguments and interpretations," she points out, "the key (historical) texts and the key (archaeological) evidence remain in a circular relationship of discovery, explanation, and proof. The history produced through this work of archaeology relies on an already-existing story, which is used, in turn, to interpret the evidence found. Once so interpreted, the empirical evidence comes full circle to stand as *independent* proof of the story itself."[65]

This is certainly true of the dig sponsored by Elad in the City of David. And even mainstream Israeli archaeologists, including several from Tel Aviv University, themselves have been casting doubt on the company's claims, which are clearly politically rather than academically motivated. But a dispute carried on in academic journals has little impact on the fortunes of Elad, which now draws some 350,000 tourists a year to the City of David, whose very presence adds to the pressure building on the Palestinians of Silwan, even if what the tourists are here to see is a Disney-like sham. According to the Israeli archaeologist Yonathan Mizrachi, there is no evidence tying the site to King David; all that is known is that the archaeological remains can be dated to the Canaanite period; what their actual function was—or whose they were—is anyone's guess.[66] "Even if we did find a Hebrew inscription saying 'Welcome to King David's palace,' that would not justify Elad's political aims," Mizrachi points out. "The residents of Silwan and their ancestors have been living here for hundreds of years and their rights cannot be ignored."[67] None of this affects what has been happening on the ground, however. The neighborhood's once open spaces are now all closed off to Palestinian residents, and even as Elad continues to make spurious claims about what it is discovering underground, aboveground the municipality of Jerusalem has been busy changing street signs in Silwan, eliminating long-standing Arabic names and replacing them with new Hebrew ones.

It must be noted that although Elad is leading the charge, it is not acting alone. It is working closely with the Israel Antiquities Authority. And, in disposing of the Palestinian neighborhood in Silwan, it has the full support of the Jerusalem municipality, the Israeli court system, and ultimately the full power of the state of Israel.

Thus, on one side of the Old City—in Silwan—living Palestinians are being removed to make room for dead Jews; and on the other side of the Old City—in Mamilla cemetery—dead Palestinians are being removed to make room for living Jews. It is little wonder that the white tents into which the disinterred skeletons removed from Mamilla were taken bear such a resemblance to the white tents that have been the hallmark of the Palestinian refugee for over six decades—or the white tents no doubt being prepared to house the residents of Silwan once Israel's bulldozers move in on their homes.

.   .   .   .   .

The museum will not be built according to Frank Gehry's plan, however. After I published a previous version of this chapter as an essay in the academic journal *Critical Inquiry*, Gehry suddenly announced his with-drawal from the museum project.[68] This was after he had very unpleasantly responded to the manuscript of my *Critical Inquiry* article, having been invited to reply by the journal's editors, and, moreover, after he had asked the Museum of Tolerance itself to respond to my essay (which it did, with crude stupidity). "The program *seemed* legitimate, and I was assured by everyone that there was to be full representation of all sides in developing the museum exhibits, and that complete freedom of expression would be accepted within the walls of the new building," Gehry wrote in response to my article.[69] Furthermore, he added, "the fact that there was an existing parking garage, already built, seemed to validate the idea that this site did not have a sacred character. We designed the building for that site and respected all the bound-aries of the adjacent [*sic*] Muslim cemetery and in fact designed the building as an overlook to the cemetery so that the relationship between the new building and the cemetery expressed respect for it. Construction began and bones were found on the site, which some argued were part of a former bur-ial site." The summer after our lopsided debate in print, and after his with-drawal from the project, Gehry reached out to arrange a meeting. Although I was initially reluctant to meet him because of the unpleasant tone of our print encounter, I responded to his invitation and visited him for a couple of hours at his studio in Los Angeles. In his published response to the essay and in public, Gehry said that he withdrew from the museum project "for sched-uling reasons." In private, he told me otherwise. Given my knowledge of the forms of deception, duplicity, mendacity, prevarication, equivocation, and denial engaged in by the Museum of Tolerance and its parent institution in LA, I have no doubt that he was misled.

In any case, following Gehry's withdrawal, although one might have imagined that the museum project would have been abandoned, it was unfortunately contracted again to another architect, albeit at least with-out the global status and brand recognition of Frank Gehry. The new firm was Tel Aviv–based Chyutin Architects. The firm's exterior design changed significantly from Gehry's, but all of the accounts of the museum concept, the display and exhibition spaces, the rationale behind the museum, and so on remained largely intact.

Absolutely none of the controversy preceding and attending Gehry's withdrawal from the project is reflected in the material published by

Chyutin Architects or any of the other firms awarded the construction, interior design, or gallery contracts. It was as though the page had been wiped clean, the surface restored, the site itself purged of any of its historical associations—the denial emphatically denied. Chyutin's materials refer to "Independence Park" and to surrounding streets. Muslim graves and Palestinian protests are entirely occluded. "We wanted the MOTJ building to stand," the new architects claim, "in the warm embrace of the urban fabric and the park around it, shining as a jewel set to the skyline of Jerusalem. We wanted the MOTJ building to be integrated into the landscape without overshadowing the preexisting urban setting on the one hand, while asserting its own unique character on the other, an iconic structure that reflects transparency and openness and generates visual interest at close and distant views."[70]

Following these textual cues, the artists' impressions of the project emphasize the building's relationship to its landscaped environment, and, like the textual description, the accompanying images comprehensively erase not only the graveyard that the museum is being built on but the remains of Mamilla Cemetery that still envelop the project site, especially to the southeast, and in which one can still see plenty of graves, however derelict their present state. The visual images attempt to naturalize the site; instead of the ruins of graves, we see a pristine natural landscape; instead of tombs, trees—and, significantly, not local trees, but trees from a temperate climate. These trees would fit right into a canvas by Constable or Turner.

Although the graves are clearly visible from the museum site, in the artists' impression they've been removed from the picture.[71] The image of a young man, arms folded, and, separately, a young woman, also with her arms folded, looking at the trees covering the graves that aren't there anymore could have come straight out of one of the scripted spaces of the Galilee villages bulldozed and planted over with trees that chapter 1 describes. These characters could have walked right out of the typescript of the short story "Facing the Forests," which I also discuss there. Cleansed from the space, the graveyard is gone, replaced by a forest that is there to enable a form of self-contemplation that Wordsworth himself might have approved of. Or so, at least, we are asked to believe. The textual description skates very close to an admission of the forms of occlusion the design draws on. It aims, we are told, to include "a sunken archeological garden, enclosing the remains of the roman aqueduct discovered at the site's center," thus simultaneously foregrounding the status of the archaeological site that the museum does indeed occupy while pushing the date of the site back off to ancient times—which is to say also ancient Jewish times, the time of the Jewish presence in Jerusalem, and comfortably before the medieval inauguration of Mamilla as a Muslim cemetery.

The mere disappearance of the graves is not actually the most interesting aspect of the Chyutin plan drawings and artists' impressions, however. Even more striking is the logic of the design itself. It places public spaces, a theater, a restaurant, and a gift shop all on the ground floor or the upper floors. Beneath, two belowground floors host "the children and the adult museums [*sic*] exhibition spaces—the so-called 'dark box.'" At no point does this textual description seem to notice its own presumably unintentional ironies, so, just to spell this out: the museum's display spaces will be contained in a "dark box" emplaced in a deep hole excavated into a cemetery from which bodies, bones, shrouds, and coffins have been removed in order to build the museum. That is to say, the "dark box" affirming the wonderful values of "tolerance" recoded as the history of the Jewish people will take the place of the actual dark boxes containing the bodies of Palestinian and other Muslims formerly buried in the graveyard.

These people, in other words, want to remove coffins and bodies to bury a self-congratulatory "dark box" monument to their own alleged "tolerance" literally in the space formerly occupied by corpses in someone else's graveyard, which they have just desecrated—and they are doing so without betraying the least awareness of the macabre ironies involved in their endeavor. If one had set out consciously to fabricate the most exaggerated possible version of the denial of denial and the affirmation of denial, one could scarcely have imagined such a project. Honestly there's very little more that I can or need to add: it speaks for itself.

The story does not end here, unfortunately. A few years after the Chyutin firm started work on the project, it too had a falling-out with the Wiesenthal Center, apparently over finances. An Israeli journalist writing about the current state of the project reached out to Michael Chyutin for comment but was rebuffed and told that "he is in an arbitration proceeding, and the matter is sensitive and difficult."[72] In any event, the Wiesenthal Center has apparently handed the Chyutin plans to yet another firm—Aedas, a multinational design and construction outfit, in connection with the local architect Yigal Levy—to actually complete the work as planned. Aedas has built corporate and transportation structures primarily in China; its website does not mention the Jerusalem project. Guy Nardi, a journalist who has written about the museum project, reports that he was unsuccessful in his April 2018 attempts to reach not only Chyutin but also Levy, who referred him to the Wiesenthal Center in Los Angeles, where after a long delay a staff member told him that "the financers were suffering from 'press trauma,' and would not talk."[73] When Nardi approached a member of the Jerusalem city council for information, he discovered only further mystery and a touch of outrage. "It's outrageous that space zoned for public buildings in the heart of Jerusalem was given away without knowing what is planned for it and whom it will serve," he was told by the council member. "According to the museum's website, the place will be managed by rabbis. Even though the building involved is supposed to serve the entire public, an orthodox religious building will be built there, with separation between men and women. Despite my inquiries, we received no explanation of the content that will be there."[74] When Nardi approached the deputy mayor of Jerusalem about the museum project, he was told that the deputy mayor had tried to contact the developers several times "but they refused to cooperate." The Wiesenthal Center, said the official, "is a foundation that is ostensibly very serious. They raise a lot of money, and this is an enormous building. I asked for the plan and the content, and proposed building a museum of Israel music there. They didn't answer me, and that's worrying. It arouses questions and doubts."[75] Hier told the *Jerusalem Press* in 2010 that the project would be completed by 2013;[76] in 2016 he told the *Hollywood Reporter* it would be done by 2017. I am writing this in 2021 and they are now saying 2022, but who knows?

The website of the Simon Wiesenthal Center in Los Angeles once had an elaborate section on the Museum of Tolerance in Jerusalem project. That is where the images and textual descriptions of the Gehry design, discussed above, originated, though the website itself has been taken down and redesigned several times since the collapse of the Gehry design. For some time after the collapse of the Gehry project, the website had a page headed "MOTJ-OLD" that read "Museum of Tolerance Jerusalem— OLD," but little else. As of spring 2021, the "About the Project" page on the current Museum of Tolerance website has an artist's impression of the Chyutin design and a bizarrely misplaced 2019 financial statement for the SWC Museum Corporation showing $26,000,000 in fund raising for that year and total assets of $151 million. Other pages show, in no particular order, a few photos of the construction site, one artist's impression of the Chyutin design, and an oddly inset quotation from Benjamin Netanyahu ("Very elegant—a beautiful fit for the city of Jerusalem").[77]

The ever-changing website includes the 2019 fund-raising pamphlet outlining the museum's vision. "For 2,000 years, the Jewish people have returned to their Promised Land," the pamphlet begins. The museum, we are told, will offer "a journey through the values that inspired and nurtured the Jewish people throughout the millennia."[78] The main exhibition, A People's Journey (which was part of the original, Gehry design), "begins as visitors board the legendary ship, Exodus 1947, where visitors 'meet' Holocaust survivors, many of them orphans and Jewish volunteers from the US, the UK and North Africa. At key points throughout the 7 pavilions in A People's Journey, visitors return to the story of the Exodus to see how the values which kept the Jewish people alive for thousands of years also sustained the desperate passengers during their difficult voyage." The pavilions include "Standing Up to Evil," "Respect for Humanity," and the culminating "Return to Zion." If the whole thing sounds like the cheesiest possible Hollywood production, that's no accident. "Since its inception, the Museum of Tolerance in Los Angeles has maintained a unique relationship with the entertainment community," the pamphlet boasts. "Some of the best-known names from the world of film and television will narrate the films and interactives in each of the 7 pavilions." But the point of the pamphlet is not simply to provide a narrative of the museum project; it is to raise more funds on top of the tens of millions of dollars already invested in this project. "To accomplish our goal, we are looking to partner with philanthropists and visionaries from the United States and around the world who will support this once-in-a-lifetime project. Donors to the Museum of Tolerance Jerusalem will have the additional privilege of linking their name in perpetuity in the center of Jerusalem, the eternal capital of the Jewish people." Presumably they mean linking their name to perpetuity? Or in perpetuity to the center of Jerusalem? The whole thing is badly thought through, clumsily written, and sloppily proofread; it exudes that misplaced sense of smarmy self-satisfaction that seems to hang over everything connected to the Simon Wiesenthal Center.

Here it must be pointed out that not everyone committed to Zionism endorses the museum project. Indeed, there have been denunciations of the project—or, rather, its intransigent choice of site[79]—from individuals who are otherwise committed to Zionism (as well as American Jews who have long been critical of Israeli policy, including Richard Silverstein[80]). Several prominent Jewish Israelis and Jewish Americans—including Bradley Burston, Reuvin Rivlin, Gershon Baskin, Yehoshua Ben Arieh, Meron Benvenisti, and Eric Joffe—have published their opposition to the idea of building a Jewish museum on a Muslim cemetery. But their voices are the exceptions to the overwhelming public complicity and state and official support for the project.[81]

And, in any case, most of the Jewish-Israeli opposition to the choice of building site—and for the most part it's only the choice of site to which they object, not the idea of having a museum of Zionism packaged as a museum of tolerance—actually aims to reinforce Israel's claims to Jerusalem, rather than seeing the whole museum episode as a way to open up and think through anew the inherently problematic nature of Zionism's exclusive claim to the city (and to Palestine itself). This kind of opposition to the museum site ends up reinforcing the very same chauvinist blindness of which the museum project is only one manifestation among a whole range of others.[82]

The assumption underlying many of these protests against the choice of the museum site is that, if it were not for the museum project, the legitimacy of Israel's claim to Jerusalem would not be at issue, and Israel's "moral claims" on the city would remain intact. It is as though it took the museum to raise doubts and questions—or as though the museum suddenly outweighed four decades of the minutely thought-through bureaucratized violence directed against the Palestinian population of Jerusalem by the Israeli state. Such critics are more worried about the appearance of impropriety than the substance; building on the cemetery is problematic because it manifests what is (to them) an otherwise invisible injustice. It's not the *fact* of injustice itself that matters, in other words, it's the *appearance* of injustice. We could here reiterate almost word for word Thomas Paine's fierce rebuttal of Edmund Burke in *Rights of Man*: he "is not affected by the reality of distress touching his heart but by the showy resemblance of it striking his imagination"; he "pities the plumage, but forgets the dying bird."[83]

The point is that the museum is not something that came from out of the blue: it embodies a tendency that is manifested across the spectrum of Zionist politics as one way of dealing with the Palestinian "problem." Which is precisely why so much of the (little) criticism that the museum siting has generated in Israel or among Zionists unwittingly reiterates the museum's own claims. The specificity of the choice of site is seen to be an issue; but the problematic nature of Israel's unique and exclusive claim to Jerusalem as what it calls "the eternal and undivided capital of the Jewish people," the forcible removal of the indigenous Palestinians in 1948, the denial of their right of return, the "social engineering" that has made Jerusalem what it is today—those issues, which are at the heart of what the museum is ultimately all about, are pointedly *not* addressed in most of the Jewish criticisms of the choice of site. They are repressed all over again. It is in this sense that the museum represents a certain psychic formation in its purest form: not everyone can be so pure!

·   ·   ·   ·   ·

"The most sublime act is to set another before you," William Blake once wrote.[84]

What's happening in Jerusalem is the exact opposite of what Blake called for: what is being facilitated is a form of self-contemplation premised on and made possible by the removal of the Other and the denial of the Other's very existence. Indeed, what will be on offer within the Museum of Tolerance is a form of self-contemplation so cleansed of the traces of Otherness that the Jewish self—at whom this project is primarily directed—comes to think of itself as universal, as though there were literally no one else in the world because every last trace of Otherness has been obliterated and cleansed. The themes that Gehry's design elaborated in visual terms are also to be addressed in textual terms in the museum's content, at least according to the early brochures made available by the museum as well as the most recent iterations of its ever shifting website.

Like the City of David project, the entire museum amounts to one of Klein's scripted spaces. In this case, the presumably Jewish visitor will be conducted through a series of exhibitions not about what one might imagine "tolerance" to mean but rather about the history of the Jewish people. The extreme violence involved in the excavation of a graveyard, the hurried removal of corpses, body parts, bones, and human skulls—all that material denial will be denied and then finally covered over (in every sense of that term) with an affirmation of the value of the visitor for whom all this monumental violence was inflicted. After all, as Rabbi Hier triumphantly put it, "the site has been clean for over a year."

Let me give some examples of how this is to be played out in the museum, which, according to the original marketing literature available on its website from 2003 to 2011, will take the tendencies already built into the Los Angeles Museum of Tolerance (MOT) to their ultimate extreme. "In the [Los Angeles] MOT's bare whispers and loud silences about the Middle East, Israel's current woes are also tacitly figured as continuous with the situation of the Jews throughout history—that is, as besieged by enemies for no reason other than being Jewish," Wendy Brown argues. "No other context is offered for hostility toward Israel, its policies or its actions. Jews are depicted as persistently in need of tolerance and, at the same time, as advocates of a tolerant world."[85] According to Brown, the LA museum thus positions Jews and Israel as the ultimate embodiments of tolerance and, indeed, as defenders of civilization and humanism against an intolerant and barbaric Other.[86] How, she asks, in her trenchant critique of the LA museum, "are Palestinians made to appear as enemies of tolerance while Jews are only ever victims of intolerance? How is Israel depicted such that it is not a problem for tolerance? How is tolerance constructed such that Israel is not a problem for it? That, is, how is Israel identified with tolerance?" The Jerusalem Museum of Tolerance will have its answers to those questions—and it will frame them in terms much more extreme, even absolute, than what the LA museum has been able to. For if Otherness haunts the fringes of the LA museum, it will be altogether purged from the Jerusalem one, and the conclusions derived as a result will be much purer, once they are on display in the setting upon the ruins of Mamilla cemetery, than what is on offer today on Pico Boulevard in Los Angeles.

The aim of the Jerusalem institution is, we are told in the original marketing literature for the project, which has been updated over the years but retains the same vision, to offer "a social laboratory that speaks to the world and confronts today's important issues—issues like global anti-Semitism, terrorism and hate. A place that will remind *us* that greater than any external threat is the internal divide that separates *us*. A place that will reinforce the idea that Jewish unity is not a slogan, but an essential recipe for survival in the 21st century."[87] The remarkable thing here is the seamlessness of the move from universal statements about what might have seemed—at first glance—like matters of global concern affecting all people everywhere, to statements that make it clear that this is not an institution interested in the global and the universal after all, but rather an institution that, by excluding the Other, reframes the particular as the universal (there's no one else left, after all). Not "hate" in general is at stake, for example, but hatred of Jews specifically. The slippage from universal to particular is so subtle that one almost doesn't even notice it, but it's clear that the "us" and "we" being addressed here does not include everyone in the world, but only Jews. However, the passage that begins by addressing "the world" ends by invoking "Jewish unity," as though there were no difference between Jews and "the world," or, rather, as though there were no other kinds of people in the world. Consider the original description of one of the main installations in the museum:

> The Social Laboratory is the dynamic hub of the Museum's outreach to the world. Its exciting interactive environment challenges visitors to confront the contemporary complex issues facing humanity. Here visitors are placed on the fault lines of regional and global conflict, becoming active players in real-time scenarios, confronting such threats as radical ideologies and global terrorism, and the resurgence of antisemitism. Compelling high-tech exhibits engage visitors in finding common ground and understanding between different communities, including religious and secular, immigrants and veteran residents, and the poor and affluent. The vital experience in The Social Laboratory puts into practice the essential values of Judaism—mutual respect, social and personal responsibility—that have sustained the Jewish people and impacted the world.

Here again there is a remarkable slippage between "the world" and "the Jewish people." The "threats" facing "humanity" are actually the threats facing "the Jewish people," or rather Israel itself (for the museum does not recognize a distinction between the Jewish people and Israel; or, as Rabbi Hier puts it, "Israel didn't start in 1948. Israel is part of the Jewish people"[88]).

Thus "radical ideologies" and "terrorism" refer not to ideologies and violence directed against just anyone (ideologies and violence directed by Israel against the Palestinians, for example)—that is, as universal phenomena—but, on the contrary, ideologies and violence that are taken to be directed against Jews and Israel in particular—hence "the resurgence of antisemitism." The language that follows also clearly refers to Jewish communities inside Israel—differences between religious and secular Jews, for example, or new immigrants and "veteran residents," the latter an especially telling and probably unconscious formulation—for only in a place like Israel and the occupied and colonized territories are "residents" to be thought of in militarized terms as "veterans," hence "veteran residents" (Jewish colonists are heavily armed; almost all are army veterans as well).

If it is not already abundantly clear that the Museum of Tolerance in Jerusalem aims to recode the particular as the universal, the original description of the institution's central and most important exhibit (the current version of the project is somewhat different in style but not substance, as the 2019 pamphlet quoted above reminds us) will surely drive that point home:

"A People's Journey." This experiential historical walkthrough, using the ship *Exodus* as a metaphor, dramatizes the seminal events and the pivotal moments in Jewish history. A People's Journey takes the Museum visitor on a voyage through the ages—an evocative environmental multi-media 1.5 hour presentation of the *Golden Age of Spain*, the *Spanish Inquisition*, the *Protestant Reformation*, the *Dreyfus Trial*, and *Theodor Herzl's Zionist Conference in Basel*, immersing the visitor among heroes and amid layers of memory. The exhibit serves as a gateway, connecting the past and serving as an introduction to the challenges confronting the modern State of Israel in the Museum's second section, the Social Laboratory.

By this stage in the museum's account of itself, the conflation of the universal and the particular has been taken to its logical conclusion. The point is that this is not simply a museum dedicated to Jewish history (there would be nothing wrong with that, apart from its being built on top of a Muslim cemetery). It is not even simply a museum dedicated to an attempt to rewrite all of Jewish history in teleological and specifically Zionist terms, with Israel cast as the alpha and omega of Jewish life. It is, rather, a museum that, having purged itself of the last traces of the Other, seeks to represent a Zionist teleology in terms of universal values—to rewrite Zionism *as* a universal value. What is on display, then, is not Zionism as such but rather Zionism as translated into the realm of value and recoded as "tolerance." Otherwise, why not simply call it the Museum of Jewish History, or the Museum of Zionism? Why call it the Museum of Tolerance?

What is interesting about the deployment of the term "tolerance" here is not simply that Zionism is presented as the expression of "tolerance," whereas resistance to Zionism (that is, resistance to the ethnic cleansing and racism through which Zionism has expressed itself to the Palestinians since 1948) is presented, ipso facto, as "intolerance." It is also that the term "tolerance" itself is used as though it could be redefined as exclusive rather than inclusive. For the notion of Otherness and the existence of an Other are both built into the very concept of tolerance—which is, by definition, tolerance of some *other*. UNESCO's 1995 Declaration of Principles on Tolerance—the closest we get to an international convention, even if it is aspirational rather than binding—defines the term as "the appreciation of diversity, the ability to live and let *others* live, the ability to adhere to one's convictions while accepting that *others* adhere to theirs, the ability to enjoy one's rights and freedoms without infringing on those of *others*."[89] Otherness saturates the term. Moreover, as David Theo Goldberg has argued, the discourse of tolerance is generally expressed from a position of power and is articulated by those in power toward the less powerful or the altogether powerless.[90] The language of tolerance is used to admit the particular into the universal; here, however, it is being used the other way round.

For this is clearly a museum founded by a Jewish institution that seeks to represent Jewish history (framed in a particular way) for a Jewish audience ("us"). It is not about the Other at all: it is about the self. More than that, it is a museum about a Self that has been constructed in a formerly Other space from which the Other has been systematically eradicated. Morally speaking, the museum makes a mockery of the usual understanding of tolerance as we use that term in English. It is best, however, to understand this gesture not simply in moral terms—as an act of hypocrisy or grotesque self-satisfaction, for example. That may be in part what it is, but there is much more at stake in the project as well, both symbolically and politically speaking. What is at stake is the play of the universal and the particular that are essential to the discourse of tolerance in the first place—but that, again, are here altered and reframed, though in profoundly and, I think, unconsciously telling ways.

Just consider one last time that this edifice is to be called the Museum of Tolerance, and that the from the beginning the whole project has been wrapped up in a relentlessly self-congratulatory discourse of "mutual respect," "social responsibility," "human dignity," and so on. It is not mere bullshit to package the merciless desecration of another people's cemetery as an affirmation of "respect" and "dignity." For one thing, as with everything connected to this project, the act of denial and erasure of the Palestinian Other is so clean, pure, and total that it is no longer recognizable as such; in fact, it is an act of denial that—far more successfully than Israel's Independence Park or its West Bank wall or those greenwashed villages explored in chapter 1—denies itself in turn. And, moreover, just as in the other episodes explored in earlier chapters of this book, this double denial is sustained through the tireless affirmation of the values of "respect," "dignity," and, above all, "tolerance" itself. The primary act of erasure, destruction, obliteration, and denial is rendered invisible to its proponents by being presented as an expression, an affirmation, of "tolerance" and "human dignity." The relentless affirmation of the value of tolerance completely occludes the monstrous racial violence involved in the project; the violence and racism will be inscrutable to the liberal Hollywood (and other) backers of the project and eventually the visitors to the site if and when it ever opens. For this is a project aimed at people who can bathe in the glow of wonderful values they attribute to themselves without for a moment having to come to grips with grisly material circumstances that they make possible precisely by being entirely oblivious to them.

Indeed, the point here is that the museum project is a breathtaking endeavor not because of the audacity that it represents—not simply because of the way this self-congratulatory act of self-contemplation is founded on, premised on, quite literally and materially *built* on a violent act of exclusion and denial—but because the deep, appalling irony of this foundational gesture is completely invisible and inscrutable to the presumed audience and backers of the museum project, who are, it bears repeating, American Zionists, not Israeli ones. When they say that they don't see a problem with building a "museum of tolerance" on a dispossessed people's graveyard, or that "moderation and reason have prevailed" when people are prevented from visiting their relatives' graves—or that Zionism is a force of "tolerance"—they must be seen to be *absolutely sincere*. This is not just an act of hypocrisy—which is exactly why we need to go beyond a moralistic approach in trying to understand it.

This whole project expresses that form of denial to which American supporters of Israel are particularly prone: a form of Zionist consciousness that has been built not merely on the denial of denial but on the affirmation of a self-congratulatory set of values (tolerance etc.) that enables the denial by sweeping it out of view and occluding it. This form of affirmative denial is what renders liberal American supporters of Israel so particularly intransigent. This is why even the most principled criticisms of Israeli policy are so often received with the eruptions of blind rage that cloud discussion of the Zionist conflict with the Palestinians in the United States: when that which has been for so long denied is forced back into the view of the consciousness that has denied it, the reaction is sheer fury, rather than intelligent and articulate counterargument (of which there is such a paucity in contemporary American Zionism).

It is in this sense that the museum project is a perfect example of a scripted space, as Norman Klein defines it. In this case, the lone Jewish self is to be ushered into a space from which the Other has been purged in order to contemplate his or her own ethical goodness, his embodiment of the very spirit of "tolerance." This is a form of "tolerance" ideally suited to the self-righteousness of the paranoid self.[91] And it is especially true in this sense that we can see not merely the denial of denial but affirmation as denial in play here: the Museum of Tolerance does not just deny the denial of the Palestinian presence; it does so through its paranoid emphasis of its own ethical value, its commitment to "tolerance" as self-validation in a world from which every last trace of the Other has been forcibly removed. After all, the site is "clean."

The museum is to be built for people wrapped up in the most debilitating form of denial. They would have no idea of the profundity of the historical, material, and psychical layers of denial on which they stand. It's worth reiterating one last time the fact that the Museum of Tolerance and

Muslim graves with Museum of Tolerance in background. Photo by author.

the Simon Wiesenthal Center of which it is an arm are American, not
Israeli, Jewish institutions. They are focused on American "implicated
subjects," to use Michael Rothberg's term (see the introduction), not
Israeli Jews. And it's no coincidence that this institution, so obsessed with
the fabrication of this particular scripted space, should have such strong
connections to Hollywood, the motherlode of soundstages, backdrops,
scene fabrication, and the like, without which, as Hier once admitted, "I
don't know how we would've made it."[92]

One corner of the Mamilla cemetery in Jerusalem is today taken up by
a giant construction site—a huge excavation and the hulking frame of an
enormous incomplete building. Whether or not this grotesque institution
ever opens its doors, the damage to what remains of the cemetery has
clearly been done. For now, this huge project, frozen in time as it seems, is
a perfect monument to what this book seeks to articulate—but in an
incomplete state. We see in it the process of denial of denial in formation,
as yet unfinished, with all the resulting gaps, holes, blank spots. And, more
important, this project in its present state of incompletion allows us to see

the work that goes into the manufacturing of the denial of denial, the affirmation of denial: the manipulations, the excisions, the occlusions, caught
in the very act, as it were, and frozen there—a scripted space as yet still in
formation, the embarrassing props, levers, pulleys, screens, overlays still
in place, the scene still raw and far, far too revealing; tolerance shorn of
whatever redeeming character it might be said to possess and revealed as
little more than an emptied-out and barren wasteland.

Conclusion

The previous chapters trace what is in effect an archaeology of an emotional-political—a psycho-geographical—formation that is rapidly disappearing before our eyes. What I set out to explore in this book is the contradiction between Israel as a racial, colonial, and apartheid state and Israel as the object of affection of the European and particularly American left from at least the 1960s on. For several reasons, that contradiction is beginning to resolve itself.

Two major reasons for this unraveling are steadfast Palestinian resistance to Israel's system of occupation and apartheid, and the emergence of a new movement from the terrain once dominated by older Palestinian formations, notably Hamas and Fateh. I am referring here to the emergence of the BDS (boycott, divestment, and sanctions) movement, building on the call for international support issued by hundreds of Palestinian civil society organizations in 2005.[1] The boycott call is simple and easy to understand; it is closely modeled on the successful boycott and sanctions campaign directed against the former Apartheid regime in South Africa. The demands of BDS are an end to the military occupation of Palestinian territory; the elimination of racial discrimination within Israel; and the right of return of those Palestinians ethnically cleansed from their homeland in 1948, along with their descendants. Although the BDS movement is agnostic on the question of whether these aims can be accomplished in one state or two, it is clear that Israel as the presently constituted racially violent enterprise that it is would, at a bare minimum, need to be reconstituted as a state of equal citizens: something categorically at odds with the Zionist project. Partly as a result of this, the BDS movement has indirectly strengthened the growing calls for a one-state solution of the question of Palestine—that is, the establishment of a single democratic and secular state encompassing the territory of historical Palestine, a position that I personally support.[2] The movement for Palestinian rights has thus shifted to a set of demands for justice, equality, and rights, with clarity and a broad international appeal that the Zionist establishment—in defending the indefensible inequality and violent injustice on the basis of which Israel was founded—has rightly designated as a mortal threat to its very existence as a project of racial exclusion and violence.

This development has led directly to the second major reason for the unraveling of the historical contradiction this book sets out to explore. The shift in the conflict between Zionism and the Palestinians from a confrontation between an occupying power and an armed national liberation movement to a confrontation between a people demanding equality and rights and a state representing grotesque inequality has greatly enhanced the visibility and appeal of the Palestinian movement and its intersections and overlaps with other, similar movements. This tectonic shift was predicted years ago not only by Palestinians but by certain canny Israeli politicians as well. "We don't have unlimited time," the former Israeli prime minister Ehud Olmert was warning his compatriots as early as 2003. "More and more Palestinians are uninterested in a negotiated, two-state solution, because they want to change the essence of the conflict from an Algerian paradigm [of armed resistance to occupation] to a South African one. From a struggle against 'occupation,' in their parlance, to a struggle for one-man-one-vote. That is, of course, a much cleaner struggle, a much more popular struggle—and ultimately a much more powerful one."[3] Developments since Olmert issued his warning have proven him right: on an international level, the Palestinian struggle is now more closely affiliated with movements for rights and equality by other marginalized or dispossessed movements, which are gaining in popular support and the sympathy of the left, such as Black Lives Matter in the United States and indigenous peoples' struggles in the United States and elsewhere. In fact, the Palestinian flag is unique as a national symbol that has become affiliated with the cause of justice more generally: hence its prominence in protests—such as Occupy Wall Street and environmental justice movements—that might seem to have nothing directly to do with Palestine itself. Israel has, concomitantly, seen the base of its own global support shift from the left to the right, nowhere more clearly than in the United States.

This is not the place for a broad discussion of US support for Israel, but suffice it to say that, without US support, Israel would be unable to sustain the traumatic violence it imposes on the Palestinians, and quite possibly it would be unable to sustain itself as an enterprise at all.[4] The United States has, after all, provided Israel with financial aid to the tune of hundreds of billions of dollars, diplomatic and political support, and essentially blanket coverage in the UN Security Council provided by the timely use of its veto. (The United States has used its veto around seventy times in the Security Council. Around fifty of those vetoes were to protect Israel; most of the rest were used to protect Apartheid South Africa and Rhodesia in the 1970s and 1980s. Very few were to protect actual American interests.[5])

US support for Israel is based, however, not simply on national interests (in fact, I would argue—though again this is not the place to develop such an argument at length—that US support for Israel actually contradicts and undermines genuine US national interests) but on the mobilization and maintenance of broad-based popular support for Israel as a state. For most of the years since at least the late 1960s, American support for Israel has been premised on a narrative of "shared values," liberal principles, a common status as (supposedly) Western liberal states: a narrative that has resonated most strongly in liberal sectors of US society (leading people such as Jane Fonda to pledge their support for Israel when, at face value, they have nothing to do with it at all—except insofar as they are, like Fonda, champions of liberal values). Only in the recent past (since September 11, 2001) has the justification of that support been articulated in terms of war, surveillance, drone attacks, antagonism to "Islam," and fighting "terrorism," an argument that in general appeals more to the right wing and adherents of the Republican party in US politics than it does to

liberals and the Democratic party, where support for Israel has tradition-
ally been strongest for decades.

Indeed, before our very eyes, even as Republicans have been throwing
themselves fully behind the Zionist project—including unveiling policies
that had been unthinkable for even the most ardently sympathetic
Democratic administrations—support for Israel on the left or liberal end
of the political spectrum in the United States and Europe is waning as
quickly as it is growing on the right. The 2020 election wins of Democratic
politicians who have been critical of Israeli policy, including Rashida Tlaib,
Ilhan Omar, and Jamaal Bowman (who decisively defeated Representative
Elliot Engel, for decades one of Israel's most devoted servants in Congress),
is evidence of this shift in attitudes among Democratic voters, at least at
the grassroots level (elites at the highest levels of the party continue to
resist change on this as on so many other issues). More and more once
committed liberal Zionists could no longer just go along with the charade.
"Israel has all but made its decision: one country that includes millions of
Palestinians who lack basic rights," wrote Peter Beinart in a landmark *New
York Times* piece in the summer of 2020 announcing his abandonment of
an effort to reconcile his Zionism with his deeply felt liberal values. "Now
liberal Zionists must make our decision, too. It's time to abandon the traditional two-state solution and embrace the goal of equal rights for Jews
and Palestinians."[6] When the Israeli human rights organization B'tselem
published its 2021 paper saying that Israel has become an apartheid state,
the news wasn't the assessment of apartheid: Palestinians and others
(myself included) had been saying so for years. The news was that recognition of apartheid had finally filtered into liberal Jewish consciousness.
Even the *New Yorker*—long a bastion of uncritical support for the Zionist
project—carried a piece, by Masha Gessen, acknowledging this new
reality.[7]

This shift has not yet reached the highest level of US politics, however.
Over four years, Donald Trump—or more precisely not Trump, who had
no particular interest in Israel or Zionism himself, but his son-in-law and
"advisor" Jared Kushner and a range of other hangers-on (including the
Republican megadonor Sheldon Adelson, also a committed Zionist)—
rewrote the playbook of US policy in the Middle East by moving the US
embassy to Jerusalem, legitimating the annexation of that territory and of

the Golan Heights, cutting off even nominal relations with and aid to Palestinians, and publishing, under Kushner's guidance, a "peace plan" that would relegate the Palestinians to the abject role of a subject people. In 2021, Trump's replacement, Joe Biden, signaled a return to the same old, same old of the pre-Trump mainstream of US politics, only now the words—and the renewed verbal commitment to a two-state solution that has been dead and buried for over a decade—sound even more hollow. No one believes the old platitudes any longer; no one listens to them. Biden's State Department people just mouth the words because that is what they are supposed to do.

Meanwhile, Israel itself has been unpeeling one layer after another of the forms of denial and equivocation that formerly gave it cover among its left-leaning supporters overseas, thereby enabling that support in the first place and sustaining it over the years. These are the forms of denial explored in this book. In 2018, for instance, the Israeli parliament passed the Jewish Nation-State Law, which made explicit certain formerly implicit forms of discrimination against non-Jewish citizens of the state. In material terms, the law changed nothing: it simply affirmed what was there all along, shifting from de facto to de jure discrimination. The Israeli prime minister and other major politicians have repeatedly and explicitly said that Palestinian ("Arab") citizens can look elsewhere for the fulfilment of their national aspirations rather than continuing with the fiction that Israel is an inclusive, properly democratic state. And, rather than perpetuating previous governments' nominal or verbal commitments to a two-state solution, the present regime in Israel has committed itself to the annexation of some or all of the territory occupied in 1967 without admitting the Palestinians resident in that territory to citizenship: in other words, to formal, rather than implicit and sotto voce, apartheid.

This shift from denial, equivocation, and agonizing hairsplitting to the outright embrace of explicit racism is hugely significant. Israel's calculation seems to be that in the age of Trump, Bolsonaro, Duterte, Modi, and company, the era of denial is over: that we have shifted permanently to a world of violent, racist, right-wing populism, that it is better to go with the shifting tide than to hang on to something else. This shift, in other words, amounts to the admission that the forms of denial explored in this book are no longer effective, that they correspond to a different era, that we have moved on from affirmations of sharing, equality, cooperation, and solidarity—Birkenstocks and granola and Amos Oz on a kibbutz in the Galilee—to a much harsher world of racism, inequality, and brutal violence.

This shift involves something much broader than the question of Palestine: what is at stake, rather, is the very form of imperial and racial discourse in our moment. The form of denial explored in this book expressed a certain logic of empire itself: not the older, nineteenth-century imperial logic of racial hierarchies and superior or inferior civilizations, but rather a new, postmodern discourse of empire in which crude power is dressed up in the language of progressive values such as sustainability, democracy, inclusion, and tolerance (words that I chose for the chapter titles of this book). Israel has bet that it can do away with these trappings of liberalism and progressivism and just come out as the violent racial enterprise that it was all along, securing new support for itself among those committed—in the United States and Europe—to building walls, deporting immigrants, exterminating Muslims, breaking up families, violently policing minority communities, and crushing dissent.

In the short term, this calculation seems to be working, and Israel has extracted forms of support—such as the official endorsement of conquest and annexation—from its explicitly racist Republican supporters (most recently Trump and Sheldon Adelson, eventually the likes of Nikki Haley and Michael Pompeo, who are eagerly waiting in the wings), forms that liberal Democratic politicians had once kept firmly off the table. In committing itself to this new, nakedly racist agenda of violence, religious and cultural antagonism, suppression of rights, and so on, these hard-core Zionists have abandoned all those forms of denial and occlusion that sustained the Zionist project for decades.

I would like to think that they are making a critical mistake, and that the world we live in is not nearly so bleak as they seem to imagine. Either way, there is no mistaking the fact that a massive generational shift in perceptions of Israel is taking place around the world, especially in the places that nourished the Zionist project from the beginning, namely Europe and the United States.

This shift in perceptions could be detected, for instance, during and after the crisis that swept all of historical Palestine in the late spring of 2021.[8] In May of that year, over all the territory across which the Israeli state seeks to project its power—from Acre in the north to Gaza in the south, and from the coastal cities of Jaffa and Haifa up to the hills east of Jerusalem—a new set of political circumstances came into sharp focus for a global audience.

The large-scale violence that erupted in spring 2021 (as opposed to the ongoing, daily small-scale violence of life under occupation and apartheid) did not simply take place—as it so often has in recent years—in absurdly lopsided "exchanges" of fire in and out of Gaza, pitting homemade Palestinian rockets against the large-scale devastation that only a modern army and air force can inflict. It also took place across what Benjamin Netanyahu referred to as the "second front," in cities long under Israeli control. Mobs of Jewish supremacists, sometimes protected and sometimes actively assisted by state armed forces that had been promised blanket immunity by Netanyahu, unleashed a campaign of terrorization against Palestinian citizens of the state, smashing their shops, marking the doors of their houses, breaking into their homes, dragging them from their cars, and beating them savagely in the street. Such events are routine across the West Bank, where settler violence against Palestinian residents—carefully documented and tabulated each week by the United Nations Office for the Coordination of Humanitarian Affairs—is protected by the Israeli army and invariably goes unpunished by the state. But, especially on this scale, such unbridled violence is more unusual on the other side of the 1949–67 armistice line, in cities like Haifa or al-Lydd.

Clearly, for an ever increasing number of Jewish Israelis, the "enemy" is no longer simply Hamas or Islamic Jihad, or even the Palestinians living the misery of military occupation in Jenin or Nablus, or the burial alive in the open-air prison that is Gaza to which the implacable logic of a profoundly racial state has condemned them, but also the second-class citizens of the state itself, who have long been seen as a "demographic threat." With his carefully calculated talk of a second front, Netanyahu did his best to capitalize on this attitude. But it would be naive to blame him for originating it, as so many do when they bemoan the state's rightward turn in recent years—as though the putatively left-leaning politicians of the past were innocent of such attitudes, or as though official Israeli racism were only a recent phenomenon, rather than one hard-baked into the institutions and apparatuses of the state from the moment of its inception.

That moment of inception (which Palestinians refer to as the Nakba) is what Palestinians relived last spring, coincidentally on the anniversary of its commemoration: an inception that was never really—and will never be—completed, but that has continued in fits and starts ever since 1948. It is no coincidence that survivors of the Nakba said that the sight of anti-Palestinian pogroms in the major cities in 2021 brought back all the trauma they experienced in 1948: the terror of such pogroms is exactly what drove them into the sea in Jaffa or Haifa or on to the bitter march to exile in Lebanon or Jordan. But the spectacle of racial violence that swept across cities from Acre to Jerusalem did not just *look* uncannily like Israel's primal scene; it reminded us that we are still living that same moment of origin—and that we have been all along. The Nakba did not end in 1948, in other words: it continues to this day.

Last spring's crisis began, after all, with the renewal of attention to a long-standing Israeli attempt to expel Palestinian families from Sheikh Jarrah, a Palestinian neighborhood in occupied East Jerusalem that fell to Israeli forces in 1967 and that the state claims as part of its "eternal" capital (that shrill claim to the eternal is the tell-tale sign of Israel's paranoid sense of its permanent unsettledness). As in countless other areas across the land, such as Silwan (discussed in chapter 4), a group of Jewish settlers had been using legal proceedings (or, to be precise, the proceedings enabled by the Israeli legal system, which is totally at odds with the requirements of international law) to take over Palestinian homes and turn their occupants, already refugees, into refugees twice over. That process was on the verge of leading to yet another set of expulsions last spring; indeed, it may have been immediately buried in the headlines about rockets and bombings, but it was in protest against those looming expulsions that Palestinians started marching.

The events in Sheikh Jarrah were so important because they represented a microcosm of the entire conflict between Zionism and the Palestinians, going all the way back to that primal scene of 1948. The removal of Palestinians and their replacement by Jewish settlers has been going on, sometimes on a large scale, sometimes on a small scale—family by family, household by household—for over seventy years. Hundreds of thousands of Palestinians have been forced from their homes over this period, which have subsequently been taken over by Jewish settlers or simply obliterated, their rubble planted over with forests intended to make them disappear, as described in chapter 1. The Sheikh Jarrah expulsions would have represented the addition of just one more drop to a sea of such forced displacements.

The source of the conflict is really not as "complicated" as we are so often told. The reason that it exists at all is that one group of people has for seventy years been seeking to lay claim to territory occupied by another and to remove them by any means necessary. In the past, that tended to be at the point of the bayonet or in the wake of a massacre or pogrom; today it's more likely to come in the bureaucratic form of a court order issued by a legal system—the very embodiment of the banality of evil—that institutionally and systematically privileges the rights of Jews over those of Palestinians. To make this clear: while the Israeli courts and the Israeli state routinely enable the establishment of new Jewish settlements on Palestinian land, there is simply no mechanism in the Israeli legal system for a Palestinian family to reclaim land or property forcibly taken from them by Zionist settlers or the Zionist state or its auxiliaries, such as the Jewish National Fund. On both sides of the 1949–67 armistice line, the state demolishes Palestinian homes and builds Jewish ones. There ought to be no surprises here: the entire program of the state is, and has always been, built around the project of removing Palestinians and replacing them with Jews. Is it any wonder, then, that Palestinians resist—and that they have been resisting since long before anyone heard of something called Hamas?

But if the 2021 lynchings and pogroms that took place in Palestinian communities on one side of the 1949–67 armistice line represented the continuation and extension of the artillery and aerial bombardments pulverizing Palestinian communities on the other side of the line, what that suggests is that the line itself is functionally meaningless. Here it must be stressed that all that the line has ever really denoted is the cease-fire that took place in 1949: it is not an official border, and Israel has famously refused to declare its borders at all. In other words, it no longer makes any sense to use that armistice line as a way of distinguishing the territory often referred to as "Israel" from that referred to as "the occupied territories." The same racial violence, driven by the same logic and in the name of the same cause, encompasses both sides of the line, even if it takes quantitatively different forms (the lynching of a single individual over here, the obliteration of an entire neighborhood or the murder of an entire family over there).

From the perspective of an increasing number of Israeli Jews, then, there is no substantive difference between "here" and "there," this or that side of the 1949–67 armistice line. And while the attitude may be hardening, both enabling and enabled by increasingly right-wing governments, including the one that took over from Netanyahu in June 2021, the infrastructure sustaining it goes back to the 1967 conquest, occupation, and colonization of the remnants of what had been Palestine in 1948. And it has been enabled by so-called left-wing governments as much as right-wing ones. For example, the crippling restriction of Palestinian movement while protecting Jewish circulation among and between the territories captured in 1948 and those captured in 1967, alongside the protection of Jewish circulation within those territories, was a policy instituted in the 1990s—not by the right-wing "hawk" Netanyahu but by the Labor "doves" and "peace makers" Yitzhak Rabin and Shimon Peres.

For Palestinians, too, the 1949–67 armistice line has less and less meaning. The 2021 uprising that started in Sheikh Jarrah spread easily to the great mosques of Jerusalem. When the state and mobs of Jewish supremacists intervened to suppress that uprising, Palestinian citizens from Nazareth and the coastal cities rallied to the cause of Sheikh Jarrah and Jerusalem, abandoning their cars and blocking the highway when Israeli checkpoints tried to bar them. When Israeli forces stormed Al-Aqsa mosque, trampling its prayer rugs with their boots and firing smoke bombs and stun grenades at worshippers, Hamas fired rockets from Gaza; when Israel bombed Gaza, demonstrators poured out of the refugee camps across the West Bank. When lynchings gripped the coastal cities, Palestinian youths came down from Jerusalem to reinforce the embattled communities of Jaffa and al-Lydd. And when they saw their people at home being battered and bombed, Palestinians in the refugee camps of Lebanon and in their far-flung global exile rose up in solidarity.

Israel has tried its hardest to separate Palestinians into discrete groups: West Bankers, Gazans, Jerusalemites, refugees, exiles, and the reviled minority inside the state whose enduring Palestinian identity the mere reference to which is so unbearable to the state that, as we saw in the preceding chapters, it calls them "Israeli Arabs." Indeed, the separations and restrictions that Israel has imposed on the Palestinian people are integral components of its apartheid system. Last spring's events reminded us that Palestinians do not accept these attempts at colonial divide and rule: they are one people with one homeland, even if they experience disenfranchisement and racial violence in somewhat different forms depending on where they live.

Although unspeakable trauma is being inflicted on an entire people, the 2021 crisis also offered a moment of clarity. The combination of the savage Israeli bombardment of trapped and shelterless civilians in Gaza and the widely shared videos of pogroms and lynchings taking place in Haifa, al-Lydd, and Jerusalem stripped the Israeli state project ever more bare of all those layers of denial, equivocation, and mystification with which it has cloaked itself for decades, and that this book examines. The stark reality was there for all to see: you may find and read any one of those recent reports that carefully document Israel's method of apartheid, or you may spend a minute watching that video—widely circulated in May 2021—of Jewish vigilantes trying to break into a Palestinian family home, the father and son desperately trying to barricade the front door while the younger children scream in terror in from the kitchen. The result is the same: the hideous spectacle of a once apparently formidable state project unraveling into the elementary racial violence out of which it was born.

The reaction across the globe was striking. Quite literally millions of people marched for Palestine in cities around the world, from Los Angeles and Santiago to Beirut and Aden, from Paris and Berlin (where authorities attempted to suppress such marches) to Johannesburg and Durban. Celebrities including Mark Ruffalo and even Paris Hilton—not previously known for her political pronouncements—expressed their condemnation of the savage Israeli bombardment of Gaza. Players from the 2021 Football Association Cup winners in Leicester City draped themselves with the Palestinian flag while collecting their medals, and players from other teams, including Manchester City's Riyad Mahrez and Manchester United's Paul Pogba, also carried the Palestinian flag during end-of-season farewells. Comedians and talk show hosts including John Oliver and

Trevor Noah quite bluntly discussed the disparity in power between the Zionist state and the Palestinian people or the clarity of Israel's system of apartheid. Faculty and students—even whole departments—at universities across the United States issued unprecedented statements denouncing Israel's racial violence against the Palestinians. Even in the halls of the US Congress, the word "apartheid" was uttered and links made—by Representative Cory Bush, for example—between Israel's violence against Palestinians and US state violence against black and brown communities. Representative Betty McCollum introduced unprecedented legislation affirming Palestinian rights, with only marginal support among her peers in Congress but solid support from US voters, especially Democratic ones.[9]

In June 2021, more than sixteen thousand artists—not just those whose support for Palestinian rights is long standing, such as Roger Waters and Brian Eno, but other stars whose affiliation with the Palestinian cause is less familiar, including Viggo Mortensen, Alejandro Iñárritu, Jeremy Irons, Holly Hunter, Brian Cox, Julie Christie, Thandiwe Newton, and Viet Tanh Nguyen—signed a letter written by Palestinian artists connecting the dots between the scenes of Israel's violence against Palestinians in the way I do in the preceding pages, linking the expulsions from Sheikh Jarrah, the mob violence and lynchings, the bombing of Gaza, and the overarching system of racial violence and racial privilege tying them all together. *"To frame this as a war between two equal sides is false and misleading,"* the letter states. *"Israel is the colonizing power. Palestine is colonized. This is not a conflict: this is apartheid."*[10]

Last spring's events really were a kind of confirmation that the layers of denial that this book investigates are falling off. Israel's system of apartheid is no longer buried under the shrouds of mystification and equivocation and outright lies that enabled it to secure vital support for most of its history as a state project. Naftali Bennett, the prime minister who took over from Netanyahu in 2021, has committed himself to an explicitly racist agenda with not even the pretense at a two-state solution to which even Netanyahu himself felt compelled occasionally to pay lip service. Israel is now coming out, formally, legally, explicitly, and without any attempt at concealment, as an apartheid state.

The era of denial traced by this book is over, in other words. There will not be a two- or three- or four-state solution. There is only one state in all of historical Palestine. So that one-state solution about which we have heard so much in recent years is not some far-off possibility but an existing reality. The only remaining question is what form that one state should take: apartheid or democracy. Palestinians know their answer to that question—and so do more and more people around the world.

Postscript

"I know what you're thinking about," said Tweedledum: "but it isn't so, nohow." "Contrariwise," continued Tweedledee, "if it was so, it might be; and if it were so, it would be; but as it isn't, it ain't. That's logic."

— Lewis Carroll, *Through the Looking Glass*

On 7 January 2017, the Delegate Assembly of the Modern Language Association (MLA) voted down a resolution endorsing Palestinian civil society's call for a boycott of Israeli academic institutions. The resolution would have been a largely symbolic measure; it would not have directed institutions or individuals to engage in a boycott; it would not have been enforceable.[1] What it would have done is to validate the urgent call for help issued by besieged and embargoed Palestinian scholars, unable to conduct research, attend conferences—or often even simply get to class—because of the array of punitive prohibitions Israel has imposed on their freedom of movement and travel. It would also have affirmed the right of American faculty and students to advocate for the right to boycott Israeli academic institutions without fear of institutional retaliation, given the atmosphere of hostility and the severe administrative repression of expressions of solidarity with Palestinians in the United States. In other words, the resolution would have been a gesture in favor of academic and intellectual freedom: both the freedom of Palestinian scholars (which has been stifled by Israeli institutions working in collaboration with the Israeli state) and the freedom of international scholars to voice their support for the Palestinian boycott call without facing potential repercussions from their own institutions.

At the same session in which it denied this expression of solidarity with beleaguered Palestinian academics, the MLA Delegate Assembly passed two further resolutions connected to the question of academic freedom. One, offering a grotesque misrepresentation of the boycott call (e.g., that it would prohibit "the evaluation of work of individual Israeli scholars," when it would do no such thing), called on the institution to "refrain" from endorsing the boycott of Israeli institutions. Another, upholding the value of "free and unfettered scholarly exchange, including the right of scholars to travel across international borders," called on the MLA to endorse a statement by the American Association of University Professors denouncing the apparent threat to American academic freedom posed by the then incoming Trump administration.[2] These resolutions were later ratified by the full membership of the MLA—in the case of the one calling for the MLA to "refrain" from endorsing the academic boycott of Israeli institutions, by a margin of two to one. A further resolution, promoted by Agnes Mueller of the University of South Carolina, which had sought in the most extraordinary terms to condemn Palestinians themselves—a people living under a brutal military occupation—for threats to academic freedom, was only narrowly postponed.

Taken together, the two resolutions that passed and the one that was voted down committed the MLA to a defense of Israeli and American academic freedom while actively disavowing Palestinian academic freedom, which has materially been under sustained assault since at least the 1980s. As far as the MLA and its members are concerned, in other words, the academic freedom of the privileged is what needs to be protected; the academic freedom of the battered and occupied does not matter. Although I had been a member of the MLA through my academic career to date— and had served on various committees—I, like many others, left the organization after that vote, preferring not to have anything to do with an institution whose membership is so manifestly committed to the oppression of the Palestinian people or to not caring one way or the other (which I feel is even worse, since committing to oppression at least represents a form of actual commitment, however abusive).

Two MLA members had taken the most prominent roles shepherding the pro-Israel resolution through the Delegate Assembly and on to the membership for ratification: Cary Nelson of the University of Illinois and

his sidekick Russell Berman of Stanford University. "This is a good outcome for the MLA and for higher education," Berman said after the membership ratification; "the MLA membership does not want to be pulled into
political controversies that have little or nothing to do with the mission of
the association." Nelson's assessment was much the same. "We believed
from the outset that the majority of members did not want to debate an
MLA foreign policy," he said; "MLA members also do not believe that Israel
is the Darth Vader of nations."[3] Their responses were interesting for a
number of reasons. Most obviously, although both Nelson and Berman
claimed that the MLA should not involve itself in political controversies or
take positions on foreign affairs, the resolution they both supported did
just that by committing the MLA to the defense of Israeli academic freedom while not merely remaining silent on Palestinian academic freedom
but actively "refraining" from supporting it, which is the same in effect as
simply denying it in the first place. In the name of political aloofness, in
other words, Nelson and Berman were engaging in politics; in the name of
neutrality, they were being partisans; and in the name of defending academic freedom for some, they were actually undermining it for others.
Above all, through the very affirmation of the values of academic inquiry,
intellectual freedom, rights, peace, and so on, they were actively denying
the rights of Palestinians. This kind of academic denial is the most slippery
and duplicitous of all the forms of denial this book explores, but Berman
and Nelson give us the perfect opportunity to pin it down and see its logic
at work. The specific occasion for the examination we are now afforded was
an exchange I had with Berman and Nelson, whose response to my critique
of one of them not only proves my point for me but also perfectly embodies
the forms of denial I examine throughout this book.

·   ·   ·   ·   ·

In 2018 I published an essay in *Critical Inquiry* that would form the basis
for chapter 2 of this book. The essay was largely about the Israeli form of
apartheid, but it was also interested in the ways in which Israeli apartheid
is often denied in the United States, including in academic or scholarly
circles. As a case in point, I singled out Russell Berman's public pronouncements during the MLA boycott debate, which frequently indulged in the

forms of denial that this book discusses. Berman sought to reply to my article after it appeared, but, apparently unable to do so by himself, he enlisted the aid of Nelson. Although the journal allowed them the opportunity to reply using its standard protocols, they insisted on more: not merely a response any longer, but a piece equal in word count to my original article. When *Critical Inquiry* declined this request, they took their piece not to another prestigious academic journal (where the same result would likely have obtained), but to an obscure British Zionist venue called *Fathom* (the organ of a lobbying outfit called the Britain Israel Communications and Research Centre). There it was published in full.

In the following pages, I recapitulate my discussion of Berman as it appeared in *Critical Inquiry*, then turn to a reading of the tactics of denial resorted to by Nelson and Berman in their published response. I note from the outset of this discussion that I have no interest in replying to their accusations against me, which primarily take the form of crude and racist ad hominem insinuations. I am, however, interested in their rhetorical strategies and the tactics to which they resort, which capture perfectly the modes of denial this book has been reading, as well as the wider political and institutional context in which this reading must be situated.

Consider, for instance, the position of Russell Berman, whom I single out here because he is by far the most thoughtful, thorough and articulate of the anti-BDS activists within the MLA, so that his argument makes the best possible case for the defense of Israel. The denial that Israel is a settler-colonial and apartheid state is central to his position against boycott, and the way he articulates his argument is a perfect example of the larger syndrome I have been discussing here, and so worth discussing at some length. Berman's contention is that the charge of apartheid is a "slur" and a "falsehood."[4] Unlike an apartheid regime, he argues, "Israel provides for equality before the law." His evidence for this, however, is not actually Israeli law but rather that country's declaration of independence, which, like all such declarations, is aspirational rather than legally binding (the affirmation that "all men are created equal" in the US Declaration of Independence did not, after all, prevent formal and legal inequality for over a century). And yet Berman specifically insists that "Israeli law recognizes the fact that the population includes distinct ethnic groups, but it declares them equal, a bedrock principle of the Jewish state." Why, if he is convinced that Israel guarantees equality before the law, does Berman not actually cite the law and this bedrock declaration of equality? Because *not one single Israeli law—above all none of its Basic Laws, which constitute something like a constitution—* *affirms the formal equality of Jewish and non-Jewish citizens:* there is therefore literally nothing for him to cite.[5]

Berman then goes on to assert that "Israeli law prohibits discrimination in education." Not only does he offer no evidence of this claim, he immediately contradicts it by admitting that "the bilingual character of the society" means that there are "separate Hebrew and Arab [*sic*] schooling options." In other words, there *is* legal discrimination after all. Yes, he adds, but "Arab parents can choose to send their children to Hebrew-language schools." It's hard to know how seriously to take this argument, which is a bit like Betsy DeVos's recent suggestion that historically black colleges in the US "are real pioneers when it comes to school choice,"[6] or like arguing that "the biracial character" of 1960s America meant there were separate white and black schooling systems but black parents could "choose" to send their kids to white schools. Really? Even if it were technically true, are there really no other cultural or political considerations worth mentioning in confronting such a "choice"? Palestinian parents sending their children to a Hebrew-language school—where profound hostility to Palestinian culture and the erasure and denial of Palestinian history are institutionally entrenched[7]—would be condemning them to even more of a sense of social and cultural dislocation and alienation than they already experience surrounded by fellow Palestinian classmates, reduced against their will to the status of a reviled minority in another people's state. Anyway, why should they even have to face such a "choice"? There are plenty of bi- or multi-lingual countries that educate their citizens in several languages at once within a unified system precisely in order to overcome differences and integrate the citizenry. That Israel lacks a unified educational system and so many other mechanisms to help unify the population (such as interracial marriage) is proof that the unity and equality of its citizenry is hardly the bedrock value that Berman claims it is.

But Berman is adamant. "Arab students study in the same university classrooms and reside in the same dormitories as Jewish Israelis," he goes on to say, although even minimal research beyond Israel's reassuring slogans reveals that this faint veneer of equality is belied by the deliberately crafted structural mechanisms—including the segregated and unequal school system—that make it immensely more difficult for Palestinian citizens than Jewish ones to even gain acceptance into Israeli universities, let alone prosper there. "Discrimination at every level of the education system winnows out a progressively larger proportion of Palestinian Arab children as they progress through the school system—or channels those who persevere away from the opportunities of higher education," Human Rights Watch points out in its investigation of the Israeli education system (which is readily available online for anyone who bothers to look). "The hurdles Palestinian Arab students face from kindergarten to university function like a series of sieves with sequentially finer holes. At each stage, the education system filters out a higher proportion of Palestinian Arab students than Jewish students. Children denied access to kindergarten do less well in primary school. Children in dilapidated, distant, under-resourced schools have a far higher drop-out rate. Children who opt for vocational programs are often limited to preparation for work as 'carpenters, machinists, or mechanics in a garage,' as one school director told Human Rights Watch."[8] And the discrimination continues all the way through the university system, with partially segregated housing (universities reserve dorm space, for instance, not for Jews as such but for Israeli army veterans, which excludes almost all Palestinians without technically saying so[9]) and rapidly falling off percentages of Palestinian participation at each successive rung of the Israeli university system: Palestinians constitute 20 percent of the state's population but 10 percent of its recent BAs, 6 percent of its MAs, 3 percent of its PhDs, and fewer than 2 percent of its lecturers, despite the well-known Palestinian commitment to education.[10] None of this highly integrated and structural inequality registers in Berman's assessment that the system treats all students equally, a claim based simply on taking the system at its word.

Similarly, on the question of housing rights, Berman predictably cites the 2000 Ka'adan case (see chapter 2) that, despite all its limitations, is the solitary example of the supposed equality of housing rights in Israel routinely trotted out by Israel's overseas defenders. And, equally predictably, he avoids mentioning the 2011 law [see chapter 2] that essentially invalidated the Ka'adan ruling, such as it is, and yet was upheld by the very same High Court (which is no surprise given that the court has given its approval to almost all of Israel's routine violations of international law).

I could go on and on: Berman affirms the value of "interracial contact" but makes no mention of the laws that prevent Jews from marrying non-Jews in Israel: why can Jews not marry non-Jews if interracial contact and integration is such a "bedrock value" of the Jewish state? He says several times that South Africa didn't allow blacks to vote while Israel lets its "Arabs" vote, but he has little to say about the four million Palestinians who have lived under Israeli rule for fifty years—almost threequarters of Israel's existence as a state—and have no right to vote in Israeli elections, which looks a lot more like South Africa after all. Berman systematically elides the word "Palestinian" in discussing the Palestinians in Israel (he uses the deliberately mystifying Israeli designation "Arab" to refer to them instead). Plenty of Palestinians have written extensively about these questions, and yet Berman, as far as I know, has not cited or quoted a single Palestinian source on the question of Palestine. Trying to understand the question of Palestine without taking into account what Palestinians themselves have to say is a bit like thinking through the question of race relations in the US without consulting a single Black source. It is, however, routine practice in the US academy.

The end result is that Berman is able to look right at a state that officially declares itself to be the state of one people ("there is no Israeli nation separate from the Jewish People") and say, no, really, it's the state of all its people. On the one hand, he admits, the state has "a specifically Jewish character"; on the other hand, he says, it treats everyone equally. That this is a self-evidently illogical proposition surely requires no substantiation: the slogan that Israel is a "Jewish and democratic state" may be deeply and reassuringly satisfying to those who find comfort in such slogans, but anyone thinking about it for even a few minutes will realize the oxymoronic nature of the expression. A state can be either be for one part of its population or for all who live there; it can't be both simultaneously. And in any case, in making a legal distinction between nationality and citizenship, Israel formally identifies itself as the state of the Jewish people—including those in Europe and the US—not the state of its citizens or of those over whom it rules.

The point I am trying to make here is that even as intelligent and technically capable a reader of texts as Russell Berman can look Israeli apartheid in the face and declare that it is not apartheid because of the forms of linguistic evasion built into the system, which readily facilitate the forms of equivocation or simply the uncritical reiteration of official claims and slogans on which his argument depends for its very existence. I believe Berman to be sincere in his protestations; in other words, he's not being disingenuous. Since the Israeli system of apartheid doesn't force him, the way the South African system did its defenders, to acknowledge it for what it is—and, on the contrary, opens up the many rhetorical avenues we see Berman pursuing, and offers endless comforting soundbites affirming the many wonderful values for which the state claims to stand—it is easy to look right through its deeply institutionalized and legalized racism without ever actually seeing it. And so he, like countless others, does; he takes the path of least resistance, which the state opens up for him by its own rhetorical posture, and he chooses not to see it for what it actually is. The key condition of possibility for this position, however, is the ability to cherry-pick what one wants to see and to avoid inconvenient data, laws, Palestinian authors, the instruments of international law and countless international investigations into what is probably the most thoroughly documented and archived conflict in modern history. The question is what would happen if Berman were given an accumulation of evidence to the contrary and asked to present a counter-argument that—even if only as an academic exercise—isn't allowed to ignore or sidestep the presented evidence but actually has to take it on, even if in an attempt to refute it. I'm happy for this essay to serve as such a challenge.

Russell Berman responded to my scholarly challenge indirectly, by ask-ing for Cary Nelson's help and publishing with him a thirty-page farrago of race-baiting and largely ad hominem nonsense in response, to the accu-sations of which, as I noted earlier, I am simply not interested in replying. My intention here, rather, is to focus on a few of the authors' rhetorical moves and gestures in order to show how they unwittingly help prove the overall argument of this book, and to think through the politics of denial in the contemporary United States on the question of Palestine.

DENIAL THROUGH SLIPPAGE; OR, HOW (NOT) TO CONSTRUCT AN ARGUMENT

As scholars, we teach our students how to develop and sustain an argu-ment, and the basic rules of argument in our profession apply equally to a one-page close reading of a poem by William Blake as they do to debates with other scholars. (We also teach them, of course, that ad hominem attack is the surest sign of a lack of evidence to sustain an argument.) Berman and Nelson offer plenty of what looks like evidence; in fact, their piece, at first glance, seems to positively bristle with evidence. However, their "evidence" is usually disconnected from actual argument. It is as though the mere pres-entation of "evidence" is an end in itself, as though the sheer existence of what looks like evidence can stand in for argument, as though the appear-ance of a scholarly apparatus can stand in for actual scholarship. One of their favorite tactics is to offer a stream of impressive-looking quotations—which have the *appearance* of insurmountable evidence—that don't actu-ally engage the argument they claim to be making. Here, the work of denial is performed by this mustering of "evidence."

The way this tactic usually works in their piece is that they take a spe-cific claim I make and, rather than responding to it directly, let alone actu-ally refuting it, they talk about an entirely different matter, backed up with what looks like a mountain of evidence, as though that could somehow magically stand in for a refutation of what I actually say. One of the most egregious examples of this comes when Berman and Nelson try to take on the central claim of my essay: that institutionalized racism is legally woven into the fabric of the Israeli state. Here is my claim as it appeared in print in *Critical Inquiry:* "Nowhere in Israeli law is the right to equality and freedom from discrimination protected; quite the contrary, in fact: dozens of laws explicitly or implicitly discriminate against Palestinian citizens of the state." This argument is backed up with a footnote referring to the database, assembled by the Israeli human rights organization Adalah, of dozens of Israeli laws (sixty-five at last count) that implicitly or explicitly discriminate against Palestinian citizens of the state.[11]

Here is how Berman and Nelson attempt to refute this claim: "Makdisi imagines that 'nowhere in Israeli law is the right to equality protected,' but an objective reading of Israel's Basic Law: Human Dignity and Liberty (1992) proves otherwise, as many rights are thereby guaranteed to all."[12] The authors then enumerate in excruciating detail *all* the protections afforded by this law, which include an affirmation of the sanctity of human life and a prohibition against violations of privacy, private property, or "the life, body or dignity of any person" and against unreasonable search and seizure, arbitrary arrest, and so on.[13] "Israel does not have a formal constitution guaranteeing a right to equality," they admit, but, they reassure us, the aspirations of the state's Declaration of Independence have been incorporated into Basic Laws with constitutional status, including the one on human dignity. "Equality is a fundamental value in Israeli law," they then triumphantly conclude this sequence; "this duty of equality for all citizens of the State of Israel, whether Arab or Jewish, is one of the foundations that make the State of Israel a Jewish and democratic state."[14]

Now let's work our way through this. In response to my specific claim— backed up with specific evidence in the form of a database of discriminatory laws—that Israeli law does not offer protection from racial discrimination and indeed actually enshrines it, they provide a tedious list of quotations and references showing how wonderful Israeli law is on a whole range of issues *that have absolutely nothing to do with equality between Jews and non-Jews,* which was the focus of my claim. Notice that they try to be clever by quoting only part of my sentence, carefully slicing off the part that refers to the particular laws in which racial inequality is manifestly enshrined. Since they have jettisoned that troublesome specificity, they presumably think they no longer have to worry about it, let alone actually deal with it. I refer to particular laws that prove my point; simply by excising that reference, they act as though their elision stands in for refutation.

That's bad enough; worse is their attempt to disprove even the part of my sentence they left intact. "An objective reading of Israel's Basic Law: Human Dignity and Liberty," they say, proves me wrong. But *nowhere in the text of that law, from which they quote abundantly, is there even a passing reference to equality.* And yet even though the law they cite and quote from does not say what they want it to say, and certainly says nothing to contradict my claim—indeed, the glaring absence of any mention of the principle of equality from this Basic Law actually validates my point in the most profound way possible—they feel themselves able to conclude that they have proven me wrong merely by having cited it. But no matter, because a few sentences later they abruptly change course and admit that there is no formal constitutional protection of equality, only to then conclude that, after all, they've thought better of it and decided that equality is a fundamental value in Israeli law, without offering an iota of tangible evidence to show that it is—apart from a few aspirational throwaway lines by an insufferably self-congratulatory Israeli judge that have zero legal bearing.

Berman and Nelson thus seem to think that a claim can be refuted simply by throwing up a cloud of irrelevant citations and quotations and hoping for the best. This, then, is denial by quotation: by quoting snippets of legal texts that offer disconnected bits and pieces of meaningless liberal rhetoric about rights, values, protections, and so on, they are attempting to elide the basic fact of the matter, and the only thing that ultimately matters in an argument between scholars: I have specific evidence to back up my claim, and they have none.

DENIAL THROUGH REJECTION; OR,
"NO" IS NOT AN ARGUMENT

Another major component of Berman and Nelson's response to my argument is simply stony denial. For example, my essay makes the case for treating Israel's system of racial discrimination as a form of apartheid. In making this argument, I refer to the instruments of international law, notably the 1965 International Convention for the Elimination of All Forms of Racial Discrimination (ICERD) and the 1973 Apartheid Convention. Backed with specific evidence and referring to specific laws, my argument shows the extent to which various Israeli legal structures meet the criteria established by those conventions for identifying discriminatory and apartheid regimes. Furthermore, I compare the Israeli system of apartheid with the one formerly established in South Africa; I work carefully through the mendacious distinction established in Israeli law between citizenship and nationality; I quote Israeli laws and judicial rulings that bluntly spell out the privileges specifically reserved for Jewish citizens; I show how organs and affiliates of the state—such as the Jewish National Fund—actively and explicitly discriminate along racial lines (see chapter 2 for details on all of these matters).

Berman and Nelson try to refute this argument primarily by simply denouncing it—and denouncing me personally along with what I argue, evidence be damned. To counter my argument that Israel is a racial state, for instance, they claim that my understanding of race, which I specifically derive from *the* major international convention on racial discrimination (ICERD), to which Israel is a signatory, is misleading and even racist itself. Makdisi, they write, "goes on to say that 'Israel considers all Jews everywhere . . . on the basis of their racial identity, to have 'Jewish nationality.' This," they then draw their breath and intone gravely, "is a dangerous and arguably anti-Semitic argument," adding that just as the Third Reich considered Jews a race, Makdisi "insists that all Jews are of the same stock."[15]

Leaving that nasty race-baiting barb to one side, there is one glaring problem with their line of reasoning: that specific argument—in fact, *exactly the sentence they selectively quote from to claim that I am essentially a closet Nazi*—I derive from a binding *Israeli High Court ruling* that, although I quote and discuss it in my essay, Berman and Nelson strenuously avoid mentioning, let alone refuting. "There is no Israeli nation separate from the Jewish People," the High Court held in its seminal 1972 ruling on Israeli national identity. "The Jewish People is composed not only of those residing in Israel but also of Diaspora Jewry."[16] In other words, as far as the state of Israel is concerned, Israeli *national* identity is inseparable from Jewishness—to the extent of including all Jews everywhere but manifestly and obviously excluding non-Jewish *citizens* of the state—and hence the Jewish population of that state constitutes what ICERD identifies as racial group. That is what I argue in my essay; it is, moreover, a point repeatedly made by major scholars of international law. John Reynolds and John Dugard—two of the world's leading legal authorities on this particular question—deserve quoting again here: the ICERD, they assert, "provides categories that Jewish Israelis and Arab Palestinians may be classified by, even if not clearly discernible under the more ambiguous categories of race or colour" in the "traditional sense." Thus, they conclude, "Jewish and Palestinian identities, while not typically seen as 'races' in the old (discredited) sense of biological or skin colour categories, are constructed as groups distinguished by ancestry or descent as well as ethnicity, nationality, and religion. As such they are distinguished from each other in a number of forms within the parameters of racial discrimination under international human rights law."[17] Like the pronouncement of the Israeli High Court on this question, this quotation from Dugard and Reynolds's analysis is right there in my paper, but Nelson and Berman tiptoe gingerly around it, acting as though it doesn't exist.

What this phase of their denialism represents is decidedly unscholarly: it amounts to little more than an awkward refusal to engage with arguments and evidence that have been placed before them, and instead saying "no, no, no" and resorting to cheap ad hominem insinuations rather than mustering evidence and developing and sustaining a credible counterargument in the way that even a marginal student can be taught to do. No, Israel is not a racist state. No, Israel does not violate the international prohibition against the crime of apartheid. No, Israel cannot be compared to Apartheid-era South Africa. No, there is no difference between the categories of nationality and citizenship in Israel. No, no, no.

DENIAL THROUGH CONFOUNDING; OR, THE
DISTINCTION BETWEEN WOODS AND TREES

But other forms of denial are at play here that are even more insidious. Take Nelson's and Berman's response to my discussion of unrecognized villages, one of the most appalling forms of racist land use deployed by the Israeli state (again, see chapter 2 for details). To refute my argument concerning the unrecognized villages and what they represent in general terms, they seize on one village in particular. A village I refer to as a case in point to understand a larger pattern thus becomes for them something to obsess upon in order *not* to see the larger pattern at work. This is not missing the wood for the trees; it's seeing only a single tree and refusing to recognize that it helps constitute a wood. This particular unrecognized village, Arab al-Naim, they triumphantly announce, was actually recognized in 2000 (as I note myself in my essay). Thus, there is no need to worry about the years of expropriation, abuse, and neglect from 1948 to 2000 in Arab al-Naim. For anyone with even a semblance of a conscience, the point of course is that these forms of abuse have gone on elsewhere in countless other, as yet unrecognized villages, including for instance Umm al-Hiran (a Palestinian town inside pre-1967 Israel, which, as I point out in my essay, was demolished in January 2017 to make room for a new, exclusively Jewish town to be called Hiran) and Araqib, another Palestinian town inside pre-1967 Israel, which, as I write in my essay, was demolished for the 113th time in May 2017. The residents of both towns, like those of all the unrecognized villages, are Palestinian citizens of Israel who, according to Nelson and Berman, are treated as the equals of Jewish citizens of the state. Of course, in these cases and countless others, the homes of non-Jewish citizens are being demolished in order to provide housing and amenities exclusively for Jewish citizens. This corresponds to a generalized condition: as a recent Human Rights Watch report points out, barely 3 percent of land inside Israel falls under the jurisdiction of Palestinian municipalities (though Palestinians account for 20 percent of the state's population)—but 97 percent of home demolitions for code violations take place in those municipalities.[18] This damning evidence constitutes circumstances that are difficult to reconcile with equality as we understand that concept in the English language.

Had Berman and Nelson been the zealous scholars they claim to be, while they were rummaging through my essay desperately looking for errors, they ought to have caught at least *one* factual inaccuracy: Araqib has *not* been demolished 113 times. It has now (as I write in early 2021) been demolished 184 times.[19] But of course they are not interested in that particular fact; they have nothing to say about what it means for a state to repeatedly—obsessively, even pathologically—demolish the homes of citizens who belong to one racial group in order to replace them with homes for members of another racial group. Such forms of racist abuse are, on the contrary, what they intend to cover up and deny. So instead of saying anything about Araqib or Umm al-Hiran or the other unrecognized villages and the vicious racism that their status reflects and embodies, they focus myopically on Arab al-Naim and insist that all is well there—and that, because all is well in that one particular case, all is well everywhere else as well. The tree, in other words, has come to stand in for the forest.

How do they do this? They actually claim to have been in touch, via a chain of settlers living in a nearby Jewish town (built on expropriated Palestinian land of course), with a local Palestinian administrator in Arab al-Naim who, they say, insists that life with the neighboring Jewish town is perfectly fine and, on the contrary, that the Jewish settlers have been very kind and generous in their treatment of the natives whose land they stole. Of course, Berman and Nelson don't refer to the theft and expropriation of land that lies at the very heart of the question of Palestine. But they claim in all seriousness to have found a native who is not only satisfied with his own disenfranchisement, the theft of his land, the expulsion of his people, and the demolition of hundreds of their towns and villages, but is positively grateful to the settlers who undertook all this violence in the quest for a racially pure state free of Arabs, and who, they say, is actually angry at *me*, "someone halfway across the world," who is "involved in misrepresenting the character of two villages engaged in helping each other."[20] Notice how close they come, and yet simultaneously how far they stray, from what is arguably the most important question in play here: how did I, like other Palestinians, come to be "halfway across the world" from Palestine? That is exactly the heart of the matter.

Palestinians are a people dispossessed and forcibly driven into exile. But for Berman and Nelson, there was no ethnic cleansing of Palestine; there were no expulsions; there were no demolished villages; there was no settler-colonial expropriation of native land. All that is there are two villages happily living alongside each other in a balmy dream of peace and innocence. "For Makdisi the story of the villages is one of long-running hatred and discrimination," they write, "while for us it is one of rebirth and reconciliation, of empathy and social responsibility across ethnic lines, a story of hope."[21] The Zionist project in Palestine is, in other words—far from being a form of settler colonialism involving the usurpation of land, the demolition of hundreds of villages, the expulsion of an entire population—a mission of empathy, reconciliation, hope, and joy.

That this quite literally unimaginable (if not altogether nauseating) image of happy natives and benevolent settlers comes straight and unfiltered out of the pages of Theodor Herzl's 1902 Zionist fantasy novel *Old-New Land* is not even the point, however. Rather, Berman and Nelson are deploying this fantasy image in order to occlude the hideous reality of a state that distributes access to land and housing along racial lines, taking from one racial group in order to give to another. In my piece, the unrecognized villages help us understand and think through a larger pattern of dispossession and alienation. For Berman and Nelson, the one village they focus on becomes something to affirm and celebrate *in order to obscure the larger pattern, to deny hideous political realities by affirming the classic liberal values of empathy and hope.* So all the evidence I present in the article and the footnotes about Israeli land policy, systematic home demolition, withholding of municipal services, and so on is ignored; what they want to leave us with instead is an image of the grateful supplicating Palestinian native and his benevolent Jewish masters to whom he is eternally grateful for the kindness they have shown him. Like Herzl's novel, this is denial through sheer fantasy; except that Herzl's fantasy was written before the reality of the Zionist project actually took place, whereas Berman and Nelson's fantasy is written after decades of bitter experience, violence, and cruelty on the ground in Palestine, about which they have absolutely nothing to say because they deny that it exists—because denial is the message.

DENIAL THROUGH WORD CHOICE: OR, THE NOMENCLATURE OF ERASURE

There's something else at stake in this particular passage of Berman and Nelson's text, however, that, hard as it may be to believe, is yet more striking. Here they repeatedly chide me for referring to Palestinians as "Palestinians." They prefer, of course, the nomenclature used by the Zionist settler-colonial state to refer to the native population, so they throw at me

"Arabs" and "Bedouins" and "Druze," but never *Palestinians* (e.g., "these are all, as it happens, Bedouin villages, though Makdisi identifies them as Palestinian"[22]). As I explain in the original article, the by now pathological Israeli insistence on classifying Palestinian citizens as "Arabs," "Druze," or "Bedouins" rather than *Palestinians* plays a significant role in obscuring the continuity of the Palestinian population within the state as well as the seamless fraternity of the Palestinians inside Israel with the Palestinians in the occupied territory and those in exile.[23]

In other words, using the terms "Arab," "Bedouin," and the like is and has been from the beginning an integral component of the Israeli attempt to deny the very existence of the Palestinians as a single people with a single national identity. This is why Palestinians insist on being identified as Palestinians, not as mere members of deracinated and scattered ethnic or religious tribes or groups, which is how the Israelis—and apologists for Israel—prefer to think of them. I make this point quite strenuously in my essay, calling not only on my own status as a Palestinian or my knowledge of fellow Palestinians but on the published declarations of leading Palestinian organizations within the state. Berman and Nelson categorically refuse to engage with this aspect of my argument, or the evidence I provide in support of it: having read my essay, they still seem confused about what a Palestinian is.

Here, for instance, is the opening of the Haifa Declaration, issued by leading Palestinian scholars, intellectuals, and activists inside the state in 2007: "We, sons and daughters of the Palestinian Arab people who remained in our homeland despite the Nakba, who were forcibly made a minority in the State of Israel after its establishment in 1948 on the greater part of the Palestinian homeland, do hereby affirm in this Declaration the foundations of our identity and belonging, and put forth a vision of our collective future, one which gives voice to our concerns and aspirations and lays the foundations for a frank dialogue among ourselves and between ourselves and other peoples." The declaration continues: "Despite the setback to our national project and our relative isolation from the rest of our Palestinian people and our Arab nation since the Nakba; despite all the attempts made to keep us in ignorance of our Palestinian and Arab history; despite attempts to splinter us into sectarian groups and to truncate our identity into a misshapen 'Israeli Arab' one, we have spared no effort to preserve our Palestinian identity and national dignity and to fortify it."[24] I quote this passage in full in my essay, but Berman and Nelson are clearly not interested in how Palestinians identify themselves; they are far more invested in the designations the Israeli state has concocted—and still insists on—for identifying them: a move unthinkable for any contemporary American scholar addressing the members of any other ethnic or national group. This is the equivalent of Nelson and Berman insisting on addressing Black Americans as "Coloreds" or "Negroes" (or worse) today on the basis that they as white men know better than Black people themselves what their identity is or how to identify and address them.

Perhaps this refusal on their part expresses their confidence that they know more about Palestinian identity than the Palestinians themselves. Perhaps? Not *perhaps:* they actually say so bluntly. "A specifically Palestinian identity did not actually begin to cohere until the late 1960s, basically spurred by the 1967 war and Israel's capture of Gaza and the West Bank," they write. "Israel can hardly have stripped them of an identity they did not yet claim." Here they are of course recapitulating Golda Meir's infamous statement that "there was no such thing as Palestinians. . . . It is not as though there was a Palestinian people considering itself as a Palestinian people and we came and threw them out and took their country away from them. They did not exist."[25] Meir, of course, was an active participant in the ethnic cleansing of Palestine; Berman and Nelson are supposed to be scholars. But, in both cases, the commitment to ethnic cleansing is expressed as a denial that there was anyone to be cleansed in the first place, and certainly no one with a specific political and national identity: at most a ragtag assemblage of shiftless and wandering tribes, not a people with a coherent identity and inalienable rights.

Yes, they admit, "in the new millennium many Israeli Arabs have begun to insist on calling themselves Palestinians, but others have not. Neither group, however, shows any interest in living in a Muslim majority country."[26] This passage is actually breathtaking in its arrogance. They literally *are* claiming to know more about Palestinian identity and Palestinian political aspirations than Palestinians themselves; so, no matter how many Palestinian historians have documented the existence of a modern Palestinian political culture dating to at least the 1920s, they don't care: why would they bother reading the work of Palestinian historians when they are empowered to know everything already? And why should they care what Palestinians have to say about their own identity? Even though they admit that there is at least today a Palestinian national culture and that "some" Palestinians insist on calling themselves Palestinians, they prefer to use the official Israeli nomenclature.

Why? Because there is more at stake here than mere arrogance. Every time an Israeli (or an American cheerleader for Israel) refers to the accomplishments of this or that "Israeli Arab" citizen—"look how many Arab lawyers, doctors, judges, and members of parliament there are!"—it is a denial of the Palestinian identity of those people. In fact, the more their supposed prosperity in a colonial and apartheid state for whose existence they ought to be grateful (a Jewish-majority state being clearly preferable to a Muslim-majority state for both Muslim and Christian Palestinians, as Berman and Nelson say, not just because presumably Jews are infinitely more benevolent and tolerant than Muslims but also because they bring with them development, progress, liberalism, and other values Muslim culture lacks), the more their political and national identity is denied and covered up, and the more the colonial and apartheid nature of the state is elided and covered up in turn. This fits the larger pattern of denial through affirmation discussed throughout this book, and *that* is why Berman and Nelson make this move over and over in their piece. For example: "The competitive achievements of Israeli Arabs," they insist, "would require an independent essay, but one might begin by noting that there are currently 18 Arab members of the Knesset."[27]

So Berman and Nelson insist on using an oppressive racial state's official nomenclature for a subject people while refusing to acknowledge that oppressed people's resilient insistence on their own national identity. And in mobilizing this nomenclature in an attempt to prove me wrong, they claim to know more about Palestine and the Palestinians than I do (they even quote Mahmoud Darwish at me chidingly, though it's clear they know nothing about Darwish or Palestinian culture in general). But what I say Palestinians say—both from quoting Palestinian texts in my paper and from having talked to living and breathing Palestinians in their own language, with which Nelson and Berman have not even a passing familiarity—does not matter when confronted with the discourse of their colonial masters as used by Berman and Nelson. The only somewhat surprising thing here is that they seem to positively glow in this racist form of argumentation.

DENIAL AND THE OLD LIE: OR, "ANTI-SEMITISM" AND ARGUMENT

The foregoing is only part of the racial paradigm Nelson and Berman rely upon. The other side of the coin is their desperate, scattershot deployment of a false accusation of anti-semitism in order to invalidate an argument with which they ultimately have no other way to contend. This begins with their tactical deployment of emotionally loaded terms like "demonization" and "delegitimization," staples of the dozens of Israel *hasbara* outlets that have proliferated across the United States and besieged our campuses in recent years. Their pages are interspersed with the odd "Makdisi seeks unreservedly to demonize Israel" or "he cannot resist demonizing Israel" and the like. What is the standard gesture of a *hasbara* outlet, however, ought not be the recourse of the university professor.

What exactly constitutes "demonization," though? The term is routinely deployed by *hasbara* outlets when they seek to rule a critique of Israeli policy out of bounds. Its primary function, in other words, is to evade an argument by preempting it. The *hasbara* manuals distributed to Zionist students on US campuses explain that it's often best for these students to avoid entering into an actual argument with students or speakers advocating Palestinian rights and to "score points" instead. "Point scoring communication ought to give the appearance of rational debate, whilst avoiding genuine discussion," one of these manuals informs its eager readers. "Central to point scoring is the ability to disguise point scoring by giving the impression of genuine debate," it notes, adding that "the aim of the Israel activist point scorer is to make as many comments that are positive about Israel as possible, whilst attacking certain Palestinian positions, and attempting to cultivate a dignified appearance."[28] Right down to the image of scholarly humanism that they desperately try to project in their piece (and certainly including the endless descriptions of how wonderful Israel is and how kindly it treats its "Arabs," who are so grateful to it that they'd rather live in the Jewish state than in an Arab- or Muslim-majority state or the single democratic and secular state that Palestinians are calling for), Nelson and Berman's tactics come straight out of one of these cheap for-hire propaganda manuals. Their references to "demonization" and "delegitimization" are little more than attempts to rule out arguments without actually entering into them.

Lurking behind these phrases, however, is something darker still. Implicit here is that someone who attempts to demonize is clearly motivated not by rational purposes—let alone a commitment to justice and equal rights—but by hatred. The accusation of "demonization" is reserved, in other words, for someone who is actually a kind of demon himself: someone blinded by hatred and prejudice against another people. Notice, then, how Berman and Nelson clumsily shift the emphasis of their purported critique of my essay into a critique of me personally, and how, in so doing, they make the object of *my* critique not the racist settler-colonial state whose policies I am outlining, but rather an entire people.

Thus, they persistently try to shift what I am saying from a critique of specific Israeli policies (on access to land or housing, on education rights, etc.) to a critique of the Jewish people as such. Makdisi, they write, "projects his own racialism onto the Jews with a two-fold insinuation: they see themselves racially and reject others on the same ground." Makdisi "suggests the Jews cannot be trusted." Makdisi's language "invokes the classic anti-Semitic trope, that Jews are duplicitous, deceptive, calculating, conspiratorial, slippery and untrustworthy." And with this we have arrived—as we were inevitably going to do, because that is always the final, desperate maneuver resorted to in all these wretched attempts to negate argument and critique in the American academy—at the accusation of anti-semitism. Makdisi, in short, is an anti-semite who seeks to "demonize" Israel not because he opposes racism, injustice, ethnic cleansing, home demolition, military occupation, apartheid, and inequality—which is what he has a thirty-year public record of saying—but because he secretly hates Jews. This is a move so predictable, so low, so vulgar, so cheap, so pathetic, so utterly unworthy of a response, that I decline to offer one.

Moreover, the personal stakes don't really matter: the accusation of anti-semitism, on which Berman and Nelson were eventually, inevitably, going to fall back, has long been leveled at critics of Israeli policy in the United States. But, having been mostly a tedious annoyance in, say, the

1980s and 1990s, this accusation has recently been weaponized, turned into an administrative and legal mechanism that can be used to suppress academic critique of apartheid: a trend of which Nelson and Berman are but one minor manifestation.

I want this point to be absolutely clear. Hardly a single word of what Nelson and Berman write constitutes an original argument or claim: they merely recycle the same tired old claims, clichés, and fabrications that pour out of a veritable industry of *hasbara* organizations—dozens of which have banded together to form the Israel on Campus Coalition—whose self-appointed mission is to police our campuses and academic institutions and suppress criticism of the Israeli state by any means necessary.[29] In their capacity as writers in defense of Israel, Nelson and Berman are mere channels through which unmediated official state propaganda and the slogans and tactics of professional disinformation outlets flow, which is why it is so easy to point out the places in their arguments that dovetail neatly with the claims of professional *hasbara* outlets, and indeed why their piece was *published* by a professional *hasbara* outlet. They are just deploying the standard, lowest-common-denominator tactics of an array of institutions that stand behind them and whose tedious rhetoric they are essentially transcribing in their own agonizing prose. Their clichéd invocation of the charge of anti-semitism, demonization, and the rest is the surest indicator of this fact.

The latest version of the anti-semitism accusation in response to criticism of Israeli policy centers on a long-standing campaign to formally redefine the term precisely in order to include criticism of the Israeli state. In 2004, the European Monitoring Centre on Racism and Xenophobia (EUMC), an EU agency, developed, in consultation with American Israel lobbying organizations such as B'nai Brith and the American Jewish Committee, a "working definition" of anti-semitism that included "denying the Jewish people their right to self-determination (e.g., by claiming that the existence of a State of Israel is a racist endeavor)" and "applying double standards by requiring of it [Israel] a behavior not expected or demanded of any other democratic nation."[30] According to this definition, showing that Israel is a constitutionally racist apartheid state is "a racist endeavor." In other words, criticizing racism is itself racist. Does this sound familiar? It's one of the claims that Berman and Nelson level against me. Berman and Nelson, however, are only tiny and insignificant elements in a much larger machine of academic, intellectual, and ultimately political repression.

After an extensive lobbying campaign, the United States Department of State agreed to publish this EU "working definition" of anti-semitism on its website. It was initially careful, under President George W. Bush in 2004–5, to note that "the recitation of the EUMC 'working definition' of anti-Semitism should not be construed as an acceptance of that definition, or the statements and examples thereunder, as United States policy."[31] But, under the Barack Obama administration in 2010, the State Department upgraded the definition's status by officially embracing it, even adding to it further examples of "anti-Semitism," including focusing "on Israel only for peace and human rights investigations," "denying Israel the right to exist," "demonizing Israel," and "delegitimizing Israel,"[32] which, as with Berman and Nelson, are now standard-issue forms of attack leveled against those critical of Israeli apartheid.

Meanwhile, the EUMC "working definition" was never adopted as EU policy, and indeed it was eventually dropped by its successor agency within the EU, the Fundamental Rights Agency, which even disavowed it. "We don't foresee adding the working definition to our webpage," an FRA spokesperson said. "The FRA is not a standard-setting body and creating definitions is not part of our mandate. The EUMC working definition of anti-Semitism is not an official EU definition and has not been adopted by the FRA."[33] The damage had already been done, however, especially in the United States, though also in certain European states, such as Germany, where the will to assuage a (rightly) guilty historical conscience for the Holocaust has been conveniently offloaded onto another people.

Heavily promoted by Zionist lobbying organizations, the EUMC "working definition" was pushed on administrators and legislators across the United States in order to develop a legal foundation essentially for outlawing criticism of Israeli policy and banishing it from American university campuses. "What the EUMC referred to originally as a 'working definition' has become a standard for important institutions on both sides of the Atlantic," Seth Berkman points out. "It is cited by the U.S. State Department, the United Kingdom's All-Party Parliamentary Group Against Antisemitism, the Organization for Security and Co-operation in

Europe and a recent report by a University of California commission on campus prejudice. The definition, which was composed with input from B'nai Brith International and the American Jewish Committee, is also endorsed by American Jewish groups and used in reports by the Jewish Council for Public Affairs."[34]

Some of the most damaging instances of the definition's legal implications emerged in legislation adopted by various state governments in the United States that drew on the definition explicitly in order to target academic freedom on college campuses. The California Legislative Assembly, for example, passed House Resolution 35 in August 2012, a bill that cited not only the working definition but the various institutions that had adopted it (including the US State Department). HR 35 directed the California State University system and the University of California "to increase their efforts to swiftly and unequivocally condemn acts of anti-Semitism on their campuses and to utilize existing resources, such as the European Union Agency for Fundamental Rights' working definition of anti-Semitism, to help guide campus discussion about, and promote, as appropriate, educational programs for combating anti-Semitism on their campuses."[35] Similar bills were promoted in other state legislatures. Their effect, if adopted, would be that universities would condemn students and faculty critical of Israeli policy.

Armed with the California House resolution, Zionist lobbying organizations in California immediately began pushing the University of California to adopt the definition—which by then, remember, the EU itself had already disavowed—to criminalize criticism of Israeli policy on UC campuses. In 2015, for instance, a coalition of rabbis and Zionist UC faculty members called on the university system to adopt the definition— by then it was being referred to as the "State Department definition"— explicitly in order to "discipline" those engaging in "anti-Semitic" discourse on campuses, including criticism of Israel.[36] The petition asks UC administrators "to adopt the State Department's definition of anti-Semitism as a means to 'accurately identify' and 'publicly condemn' it in campus debate, protest and discussion," I pointed out at the time in a piece I published in the *Los Angeles Times* (one of many pieces I have written for that newspaper on Zionist attempts to suffocate academic freedom). "That problematic definition conflates principled criticism of Israeli policies with genuine anti-Semitism; if the university accedes to this demand, such criticism—and academic freedom—could be suppressed by administrative fiat."[37] Pushed relentlessly by lobbying organizations, that particular campaign kept gaining momentum, however, until the UC Regents were called upon to adopt a measure that would have directly equated anti-Zionism with anti-Semitism as "hate speech" and thereby administratively banished criticism of Zionism and Israeli policy from UC campuses once and for all.

In early 2016, a UC Regents working group published its "Principles Against Intolerance," which included an extensive discussion of anti-semitism based on the so-called State Department definition and concluded that "Anti-Semitism, anti-Zionism and other forms of discrimination have no place at the University of California."[38] UC regent Richard Blum, one of the proponents of this measure, issued an unveiled threat to his colleagues on the Board of Regents, warning that there would be consequences if the university did not formally adopt the principles equating anti-Zionism with anti-Semitism. "Over the weekend my wife, your senior Senator [Dianne Feinstein] and I talked about this issue at length," Blum warned. "She wants to stay out of the conversation publicly but if we do not do the right thing she will engage publicly and is prepared to be critical of this university if we don't have the kind of not only statement but penalties for those who commit what you can call them hate crimes, call them whatever you want."[39] Blum's statement—a grotesque gesture given that his wife has zero authority over the University of California—made explicit the intention of the weaponized form of the anti-semitism accusation: criticize Israeli policy, and you will be disciplined. "Students that do the things cited here today probably ought to have a dismissal or a suspension from school," Blum added. "I don't know how many of you feel strongly that way but my wife does and so do I."[40] The consequences for faculty critical of Israel were left unstated but presumably equally dire.

As the Board of Regents meeting got under way, supporters of the measure as well as critics made their positions clear. I wrote yet another piece for the *Los Angeles Times* (with Judith Butler in this instance), warning of the consequences of the imposition of this definition on the university system. "In a few paragraphs, the report conflates two distinct phenomena: hatred of Jews on the one hand, and criticism of a political ideology on the other," Butler and I pointed out. "The overall claim is that the latter—objections to the Israeli state, its military occupation, its demolition of homes, its two-tiered system of citizenship—is the new, covert form of anti-Semitism. These are issues regularly debated in public discourse; it is imperative that they be freely discussed in universities as well. But if the report is adopted, scholarship and teaching that include critical perspectives deemed 'anti-Zionist' could be branded illegitimate, and open discussion shut down."[41] In the end, after lengthy debate, the regents ended up softening their position, and the resolution they adopted, condemning specifically "anti-Semitic forms of anti-Zionism," though it was proclaimed as a victory by the forces rallying behind the redefined and weaponized definition of "anti-Semitism," was actually a pretty solid defeat for them.[42] After all, in singling out specifically anti-Semitic forms of anti-Zionism, the new statement of principles makes clear that there are forms of anti-Zionism that are not anti-Semitic, or in other words that anti-Zionism is not by definition anti-Semitism, which is what the organizers of this movement wanted the university to declare.

Unfortunately, the story did not end there. In 2016, an organization called the International Holocaust Remembrance Alliance (IHRA; essentially a club of EU states with guilty consciences for the vicious crimes visited by Europeans on European Jewry, plus Israel and the United States) unearthed the discredited EUMC "working definition" from the dustbin to which it had been consigned and adopted it essentially wholesale, along with its conflation of criticism of Israel with anti-semitism as such.[43] President Obama's US State Department immediately adopted the revitalized zombie definition as well.[44] And it has been adopted by other states, police forces, and organizations across Europe,[45] including the Labour Party in the United Kingdom, despite the resistance of the party's then leader, Jeremy Corbyn. Indeed, when Corbyn attempted to at least add a counterbalance to the worst political tendencies of the definition, he was voted down by the members of the party's National Executive Council. According to the *Guardian* (a newspaper whose own stake in this debate was made clear), "The most controversial passage in the draft statement proposed by Corbyn said: 'It cannot be considered racist to treat Israel like any other state or assess its conduct against the standards of international law. Nor should it be regarded as antisemitic to describe Israel, its policies or the circumstances around its foundation as racist because of their dis-criminatory impact, or to support another settlement of the Israel-Palestine conflict.'"[46] To say that criticism of Israel is not racist, in other words, is "controversial," whereas to say that Israel's manifest and legal-ized racism is not racist is, by this logic, not at all controversial.

Zionist lobbying organizations in the United States are now hard at work pushing state legislatures and, above all, universities to adopt the IHRA definition of anti-semitism. "When an organization denies Israel's right to exist as a Jewish and democratic state; when it demonizes Israel by comparing the Jewish state to Nazi Germany or South African apart-heid; and when in making demands of Israel it applies double-standards that are not applied to any other country in the world, this organization is not seeking justice," writes Natan Sharansky in calling for colleges and universities to adopt the definition. "Rather, it is promoting anti-Semitism, plain and simple."[47] Such mobilizations received a major boost when, in December 2019, Donald Trump, with his partisan son-in-law Jared Kushner beaming behind him, signed a presidential executive order that threatened to withdraw federal funds from universities that fail to combat what the IHRA defines as anti-semitism, including criticism of Israel. "According to this redefined notion of anti-Semitism (which has been pro-moted by Israel's army of advocates in this country for the best part of a decade)," I pointed out in a piece I wrote for the *Nation*, "pointing out the racism of the Israeli state—a state that legally enshrines racial discrimination—would itself be considered a form of racism. Calling for equal rights throughout that state, which institutionally privileges Jews over non-Jews, could similarly be considered hate speech. Students and teachers criticizing Israel's policies, let alone those daring to advocate Palestinian rights, would be silenced."[48] To add to the damage, the man in charge of evaluating whether or not universities are muzzling criticism of Israel, in keeping with Trump's executive order, was none other than Kenneth Marcus, then Trump's assistant secretary of education for civil rights, but also the founder of an organization whose stated purpose is to combat what it calls "anti-Israelism on college campuses." His outfit has tried to use legal means to target the First Amendment rights of those who advocate Palestinian narratives or criticize Israel. He used his former posi-tion to file lawsuits against a series of universities for allowing the advocates of Palestinian rights to speak on campus. The courts have dismissed all of those lawsuits as baseless—but now Marcus was to be the one who would be adjudicating them from his position in the Department of Education, and he would have had the power of a presidential executive order to add to his repressive toolkit.[49] (Thankfully, Marcus resigned shortly before Trump himself left office.)

Within weeks of Joe Biden taking office in 2021, his administration also threw its weight behind the new definition of anti-semitism. "As prior US administrations of both political stripes have done, the Biden administration embraces and champions the working definition," the State Department announced. Just to be sure, the secretary of state added that the Biden administration "enthusiastically supports" the IHRA definition.[50] This, then, is the state of denial in play in the United States today, a state that Berman and Nelson have played their own minor roles in helping to bring about. Ethnic cleansing, home demolition, military occupation, forced expulsion, and grotesque racial inequality are now recoded as "rebirth and reconciliation, empathy and social responsibility across ethnic lines, a story of hope." Quite literally, in other words, denial has become affirmation and affirmation denial; oppression has become freedom, and resistance to oppression itself oppressive; racism is tolerance and anti-racism intolerance. And why not, while we are at it: war is peace, freedom is slavery, ignorance is strength?[51]

DENIAL THROUGH ASSERTION OF A POSITIVE VALUE; OR, HUMANISM AND REPRESSION

The first several pages of Nelson and Berman's piece consist of a paean to what they call "evidence" and "objective scholarship," which they claim to be defending. "Much debate by proponents of the Boycott, Divestment, and Sanctions (BDS) movement in academic and public spheres is not genuine debate but rather the promotion of accusations and slogans directed against the state of Israel," their piece begins. "Efforts at making a detailed, fact-based case are far less common, even full-length books are largely polemical."[52] Their point is not just that they will provide evidence in developing a scholarly argument, but that the very legacy of the humanities, to which they lay claim, is at stake. Operating in the background here is the long legacy of a colonial history throughout which white men like them claimed to be in possession of facts and methods while insisting that unruly natives have difficulties with the truth. They are not only claiming institutional superiority in their defense of "the Humanities" as such (it's in the title of their piece after all) but also, implicitly, asserting racial privilege, since the elevated discourse of factual and scholarly objectivity, used in just this way, has been inextricable from the history of Western colonialism in its encounter with the Orient since at least the time of James Mill, in the early nineteenth century. "For the colonized subject," as Fanon once pointed out, "objectivity is always directed against him." The institutional and racial legacy to which they want to lay claim is an integral component of how they want to position themselves supposedly as genuine scholars.[53]

Of course, they published their defense of the humanities and its rules of scholarship, their impassioned apologia for scholarly standards, peer review, fact-checking, their appeal to "publication venues with area expertise," *not* in a peer-reviewed scholarly humanities journal in anything like the same league as *Critical Inquiry,* but rather in the organ of an obscure British Zionist propaganda outfit that supports "a close relationship between Britain and Israel, based on shared values and interests."[54] As a glance at their tortured prose will show, their piece didn't even receive proper copyediting, let alone peer review.

These men speak the grand language of liberalism and humanism, they use the cover of what looks like rational debate and reasoned response and academic argument to elide and cover over, deny and occlude, the activities of a racial state engaged in a long-standing and merciless project of violent dispossession. The language of liberalism and humanism is intended here as a form of cover: the more it is emphasized, the more the occluded injustice is covered up; the occlusion is transacted through the claim to humanism.

This claim to humanism brings us back to the broader institutional framework in which this entire lopsided "debate" has been taking place— in institutional humanities settings, from the universities in which we teach to the meeting rooms of the MLA. And, as the MLA boycott vote reminds us, the agents of denial—Berman and Nelson are only token examples, and there is, as I've said, an army of professional hasbarists working in well-funded lobbying organizations behind them—are exerting undue influence over our academic and intellectual lives. Denial in its many forms plays a central role in their activities—above all in the affirmation of humanities values (diversity, racial and cultural difference, religious tolerance, and so on) in order to deny and suppress criticism of Israeli policies. Rallying around the claim of "intolerance" has become the new way to protect the truly intolerable.

Notes

1. Omer Bartov drew my attention to the geographical proximity of Yad Vashem and Deir Yassin.
2. Efraim Shalin, "Jerusalem Forest: Nature in Jerusalem," Jewish National Fund, accessed 3 July 2021, https://www.kkl-jnf.org/tourism-and-recreation/forests-and-parks/jerusalem-forest.aspx.
3. "Testimonies," *Ha'aretz,* 16 July 2017.
4. "Testimonies from the Censored Deir Yassin Massacre: 'They Piled Bodies and Burned Them,'" *Ha'aretz,* 16 July 2017.

INTRODUCTION

1. See Article 1 of the ICERD, United Nations Office of the High Commissioner for Human Rights, accessed 26 August 2021, https://www.ohchr.org/en/professionalinterest/pages/cerd.aspx
2. In other contexts, I have referred to this as hard-core Zionism to distinguish it from the more prevalent soft-core variety.
3. Morris is not referring specifically to Lieberman. "My feeling is that this place would be quieter and know less suffering if the matter had been resolved once and for all [in 1948]," says Morris. "If Ben-Gurion had carried out a large

expulsion and cleansed the whole country—the whole Land of Israel, as far as the
Jordan River. It may yet turn out that this was his fatal mistake. If he had carried
out a full expulsion—rather than a partial one—he would have stabilized the
State of Israel for generations." He adds: "If the end of the story turns out to be a
gloomy one for the Jews, it will be because Ben-Gurion did not complete the
transfer in 1948. Because he left a large and volatile demographic reserve in the
West Bank and Gaza and within Israel itself." Benny Morris, interview with Ari
Shavit of *Ha'aretz*, reprinted in *New Left Review* 26 (March–April, 2004).

4. Lieberman, quoted in Ahmad Tibi, "A Harsh Reality for Palestinians," *New
York Times*, 6 April 2009.

5. The 1947 UN Partition Plan, for example, would have left as many Arabs as
Jews in what was proposed as a Jewish state.

6. See Morris, interview with Shavit. See also Benny Morris, "Revisiting the
Palestinian Exodus of 1948," in Eugene Rogan and Avi Shlaim, eds., *The War for
Palestine: Rewriting the History of 1948* (Cambridge: Cambridge University
Press, 2002), 40.

7. "There are circumstances in history that justify ethnic cleansing. A Jewish
state would not have come into being without the uprooting of 700,000 [the
actual figure is closer to 800,000] Palestinians. Therefore it was necessary to
uproot them. There was no choice but to expel that population." Morris, interview with Shavit.

8. Arnon Sofer and Ruthie Blum, "One on One: It's the Demography, Stupid"
(interview), *Jerusalem Post*, 20 May 2004. Sofer is describing the policy of separation between Palestinians and Jews, of which he was one of the architects, specifically with reference to Gaza.

9. In a 1993 essay on the politics of denial, a piece that would evolve into his
book *States of Denial*, the sociologist Stanley Cohen, who was living in Israel at
the time, asks how it could be that there is so little reaction (dissent, criticism,
protest) among Israelis to their army's brutal crackdown on the first intifada—a
crackdown that featured such openly-announced government policies as deliberately breaking the bones of protestors—especially in those sectors of Israeli
society where one would expect such protest to occur. "In the face of clear information about what's going on—escalating levels of violence and repression, beat-
ings, torture, daily humiliations, collective punishment (curfews, house demolition, deportations), death-squad type killings by army undercover units—the
level of shame, outrage and protest [among Jewish Israelis] is not psychologically
or morally appropriate," he writes. Cohen makes it clear that he is not referring
to the solid majority of Jewish Israelis who were (and are increasingly) adamantly supportive of the army's treatment of Palestinian protestors. "My object
of study," he writes, "is the minority: the enlightened, educated middle class,
responsive to messages of peace and co-existence, first to condemn human rights
violations everywhere else in the world." Why, he asks, "when faced by knowledge

of others' suffering and pain—particularly the suffering and pain resulting from what are called 'human rights violations'—does 'reaction' so often take the form of denial, avoidance, passivity, indifference, rationalization or collusion?" The answer that Cohen develops in response to this question involves an investigation of the complex syndrome of denial. This pattern can take several different forms, he suggests. In psychoanalytic terms, he argues, "denial is understood as an unconscious defense mechanism for coping with guilt, anxiety, and other disturbing emotions aroused by reality. The psyche blocks off information that is literally unthinkable or unbearable. The unconscious sets up a barrier which prevents the thought from reaching conscious knowledge. Information and memories slip into an inaccessible region of the mind." In the cognitive or social psychology understanding of denial, "information is selected to fit existing perceptual frames and information which is too threatening to shut out altogether. The mind somehow grasps what is going on—but rushes a protective filter into place. Information slips into a kind of 'black hole of the mind'—a blind zone of blocked attention and self-deception." People in a state of denial, whether that is understood in orthodox psychiatric terms (Freud referred to it as disavowal) or social psychological terms, can look right at a situation and reconcile—really, consolidate—their sense of themselves only by blocking out data, information, and knowledge that would threaten their sense of who they are and what they stand for. And they can sustain this until something (or someone) comes along and forces the disavowed knowledge into view.

Two points are at stake here right away. The first is that in a state of denial, information and knowledge that would threaten the ethical sense of self is at least theoretically available—it's out there—but it is filtered out or sealed off from consciousness. In other words, it's not that the potentially offensive or troubling information is hidden or inaccessible or requires exhaustive research to be revealed: it is plainly available for anyone who can—and wants to—see it. Some of it at least is always registered, even in a state of denial, and there is a simultaneous knowing and not-knowing as the filtering mechanisms do their work. A series of what Freud identified as "perverse arguments" are marshaled as the irreconcilable is temporarily, or at least apparently, reconciled.

The second point is that if the filtering or blocking mechanism fails—for instance, if the offensive information is presented in such a way that there is simply no avoiding it—the very premise of the self constructed on the basis of that denial is threatened, and the result is a crisis. When, in other words, the unthinkable or unbearable knowledge that has been disavowed, filtered out, blocked off, or sealed away is forced into consciousness, a reaction takes place. Whether we classify it as psychotic or neurotic, it involves a loss of self-control and an angry lashing out at whatever—or whoever—initiated the intrusion of the disavowed knowledge.

Cohen argues, however, that there is another mode of denial besides this one of simply closing off and disavowing unbearable knowledge or information.

Drawing on John Steiner's political reading of Oedipus, he suggests that if the first mode of denial involves, as earlier described, almost literally turning a blind eye ("keeping facts conveniently out of sight, allowing something to be both known and not known"), the second, more aggravated mode of denial is far more pathological. Steiner identifies it as the retreat from truth into omnipotence. "This takes a particularly dangerous form," notes Cohen, "of a self-righteousness that exonerates all atrocities and obsessively blames others." According to Steiner's reading of Oedipus at Colonus, "He denies responsibility and guilt and claims that these wrongs were wrongs inflicted *on* him rather than *by* him." Cohen suggests that this second mode of denial can play a role in "the 'new barbarism' of ethnic nationalist conflict, with its delusionary circuits of self-righteous omnipotence and self-vindication by blaming others." In this second mode of denial, the raw facts as such aren't denied or turned away from, as they are in the first mode—they are acknowledged, even embraced, but agency and responsibility are deflected to others: the unspeakable things that first mode of denial simply turns away from and refuses to acknowledge are here in the second mode of denial admitted, not as the fault of the self, however, but as the fault of the other; the greater the violence of the self, the greater his sense of victimhood and persecution—and the greater the need for even more violence.

A certain structure of denial—in both modes—is part of what is at stake in the syndrome that this book explores. But there is more at stake as well. The people Cohen observes who prompted his 1993 essay on denial, which ultimately grew into his book *States of Denial*, are otherwise liberal Israelis who see-but-don't-see the violence of Israeli state policy toward the Palestinians. Just as the essence of white liberal South African consciousness in the era of Apartheid was, as Cohen puts it, "a continuous shutting out of what seemed 'obvious' to any outsider," in Israeli society as a whole, "denial of the injustices and injuries inflicted on the Palestinians is built into the social fabric," Cohen argues. "The Jewish public's assent to official propaganda, myth and self-righteousness results from a willing identification—not fear of arbitrary imprisonment, commissars or secret police. Many topics are known and not-known at the same time. Israel is a country full of 'open secrets.'" The result, he points out, "is a xenophobia that would be called 'racism' anywhere else, an exclusion of Palestinians from a shared moral universe and an obsessional self-absorption: what we do to them is less important than what this does to us." See "Colonel Says Rabin Ordered Breaking of Palestinians' Bones," *Los Angeles Times*, 22 June 1990; Stanley Cohen, "Human Rights and Crimes of the State: The Culture of Denial," *Australia and New Zealand Journal of Criminology* 26 (July 1993): 103; Stanley Cohen, *States of Denial: Knowing about Atrocities and Suffering* (Cambridge: Polity, 2010), 5, 6, 28, 32–34, 157; John Steiner, "Turning a Blind Eye: The Cover Up for Oedipus," *International Review of Psycho-Analysis* 12 (1985); Steiner, "The Retreat from Truth to Omnipotence in Sophocles' 'Oedipus at Colonus,'" *International Review of Psycho-analysis* 17 (1990).

10. "Fact Sheet: Olive Trees—More than Just a Tree in Palestine," ReliefWeb (UN Office for the Coordination of Humanitarian Affairs), 21 November 2012, https://reliefweb.int/report/occupied-palestinian-territory/fact-sheet-olive-trees--more-just-tree-palestine.

11. The distinction that Harry Frankfurt draws between lying and bullshit is pertinent here: the liar, Frankfurt points out, has an awareness of the truth; for the bullshitter the whole distinction between truth and falsehood is irrelevant. See Harry Frankfurt, *On Bullshit* (Princeton, NJ: Princeton University Press, 2005).

12. In his important book *States of Denial*, which emerged partly from his own experience of denial in Israeli society, the sociologist Stanley Cohen explains some of the mechanisms involved. Denial can take several different forms, he suggests. In psychoanalytical terms, he argues, "denial is understood as an unconscious defense mechanism for coping with guilt, anxiety, and other disturbing emotions aroused by reality. The psyche blocks off information that is literally unthinkable or unbearable. The unconscious sets up a barrier which prevents the thought from reaching conscious knowledge. Information and memories slip into an inaccessible region of the mind. In the cognitive or social psychology understanding of denial, "information is selected to fit existing perceptual frames, and information which is too threatening is shut out altogether. The mind somehow grasps what is going on—but rushes a protective filter into place. Information slips into a kind of 'black hole of the mind'—a blind zone of blocked attention and self-deception." People in a state of denial, whether that is understood in orthodox psychiatric terms (Freud referred to it as disavowal) or social psychological terms, can look right at a situation and reconcile—really, consolidate—their sense of themselves only by blocking out data, information, and knowledge that would threaten their sense of who they are and what they stand for. See Cohen, *States of Denial*, 5–28.

13. Liberalism has, of course, long been connected to empire and racial hierarchies, but generally through explicit acts of exclusion. John Stuart Mill, for instance, excluded Asians and Orientals from his passionate elaboration of liberal values because they were, in his estimation, racially inferior. What I am discussing here has a different dynamic because the exclusion is not explicitly spelled out.

14. Edward Said, *The Question of Palestine* (New York: Vintage, 1979), 57.

15. Said, 57.

16. Said, 58–59.

17. Kier Starmer, quoted in "After Corbyn, UK Labour Elects Starmer, Zionist with a Jewish Wife, as Leader," *Times of Israel*, 4 April 2020.

18. Said, *Question of Palestine*, 87.

19. *Oxford English Dictionary*, s.v. "occlude."

20. Ann Laura Stoler, *Duress: Imperial Durabilities in Our Times* (Durham, NC: Duke University Press, 2016), 10.

21. See Michael Rothberg, "Trauma Theory, Implicated Subjects, and the Question of Israel/Palestine," MLA *Profession* (May 2014), https://profession .mla.org/trauma-theory-implicated-subjects-and-the-question-of-israel-palestine /; Rothberg, *The Implicated Subject: Beyond Victims and Perpetrators* (Stanford, CA: Stanford University Press, 2019).

22. See the discussion of Benny Morris and company above.

23. "Structurally, postraciality maintains prevailing conditions of historically produced racial arrangement and power, both domestically and globally, now stripped of their historically inherited terms of recognizability, address, and redress," Goldberg argues. "Ideologically, postracialism (the discursive formation representing the combined conditions of the postracial characterized here) does not solely absolve whites of guilt for past racisms. Rather, it erases the very histories producing the formations of racial power and privilege, burying them alive but out of recognizable reach. They wipe away the very conditions out of which guilt could arise. That denial of denial: there is no guilt because there is nothing recognizable to be guilty about, least of all the guilt itself." David Theo Goldberg, *Are We All Postracial Yet?* (London: Polity, 2015), 100–101.

24. See Wendy Brown, *Regulating Aversion: Tolerance in the Age of Identity and Empire* (Princeton, NJ: Princeton University Press, 2008), esp. 107–48.

25. Donald Macintyre, "Israel Plans to Build 'Museum of Tolerance' on Muslim Graves," *Independent*, 9 February 2006.

CHAPTER 1. SUSTAINABILITY

Epigraphs: Mahmoud Darwish, "A Canaanite Rock in the Dead Sea," in *If I Were Another,* trans. Fady Joudah (New York: Farrar, Strauss and Giroux, 2011), 80. Kamala Harris quoted in, among other sources, "Joe Biden Selects Kamala Harris as Running Mate," *Jerusalem Post,* 12 August 2020. Harris was addressing the Zionist lobby AIPAC in 2017.

1. Emile Habibi, *al-mutasha'il* (1972; repr. Beirut: Ibn Khaldun Press, 1989), 32–33. Translation by author.

2. Walid Khalidi lists 418 villages in *All That Remains: The Palestinian Villages Occupied and Depopulated by Israel in 1948* (Washington, DC: Institute for Palestine Studies, 1992). On the basis of new and more extensive research, Salman Abu Sitta lists 530 towns and villages depopulated in 1948, as well as the homes of Bedouin Palestinians that were more widely scattered in small clusters but collectively constituted the equivalent of a further 125 average-size villages, for a total of 655. See Salman Abu Sitta, *The Atlas of Palestine* (London: Palestine Land Society, 2010), 106.

3. Constantine Zurayq, *The Meaning of the Disaster,* trans. R. Bayly Winder (Beirut: Khayyat, 1956), 3.

4. See Ilan Pappe, *The Ethnic Cleansing of Palestine* (London: Oneworld, 2006); Nur Masalha, *Expulsion of the Palestinians: The Concept of "Transfer" in Zionist Political Thought, 1882–1948* (Washington, DC: Institute for Palestine Studies, 1992); Nur Masalha, *The Palestine Nakba: Decolonising History, Narrating the Subaltern, Reclaiming Memory* (London: Zed Books, 2012); Benny Morris, *The Birth of the Palestinian Refugee Problem Revisited* (Cambridge: Cambridge University Press, 2004).

5. UN General Assembly Resolution 194 of 1948 *"Resolves* that the refugees wishing to return to their homes and live at peace with their neighbours should be permitted to do so at the earliest practicable date, and that compensation should be paid for the property of those choosing not to return and for loss of or damage to property which, under principles of international law or in equity, should be made good by the Governments or authorities responsible." See also Shira Robinson, *Citizen Strangers: Palestinians and the Birth of Israel's Liberal Settler State* (Stanford, CA: Stanford University Press, 2014).

6. Patrick Wolfe, *Traces of History: Elementary Structures of Race* (London: Verso, 2016), 33.

7. See Jala Makhzoumi, "Unfolding Landscape in a Lebanese Village: Rural Heritage in a Globalising World," *International Journal of Heritage Studies* vol. 15, no. 4 (July 2009), 321 (emphases in original).

8. Quoted in Masalha, *The Palestine Nakba*, 6.

9. Quoted in Irus Braverman, *Planted Flags: Trees, Land, and Law in Israel /Palestine* (Cambridge: Cambridge University Press, 2009), 100.

10. See Masalha, *The Palestine Nakba*, 107.

11. Aron Shai, "The Fate of Abandoned Arab Villages in Israel, 1965–1969," *History and Memory* vol. 18, no. 2 (Fall–Winter 2006), 87.

12. Shai, 91.

13. Shai, 93.

14. Meron Benvenisti, *Sacred Landscape: The Buried History of the Holy Land since 1948*, trans. Maxine Kaufman-Lacusta (Berkeley: University of California Press, 2000), 11–54.

15. Rafi Segal and Eyal Weizman, "The Mountain: Principles of Building in Heights," in Segal and Weizman, eds., *A Civilian Occupation: The Politics of Israeli Architecture* (London: Verso, 2003), 92, 93.

16. Uri Eisenzweig, "An Imaginary Territory: The Problematic of Space in Zionist Discourse," *Dialectical Anthropology*, vol. 5, no. 4 (May 1981): 282 (emphasis in original).

17. Braverman, *Planted Flags*, 86.

18. Noga Kadman, *Erased from Space and Consciousness: Israel and the Depopulated Palestinian Villages of 1948*, trans. Dimi Reider (Bloomington: Indiana University Press, 2015), 112; Khalidi, ed., *All That Remains*.

19. Quoted in Kadman, *Erased from Space and Consciousness*, 43.

20. "Biriya Forest: Magic and Mysticism in the Upper Galilee," Jewish National Fund, accessed 10 July 2021, http://www.kkl-jnf.org/tourism-and-recreation/forests-and-parks/biriya-forest.aspx.

21. See Masalha, *The Palestine Nakba*, 122.

22. "Ayalon Canada Park: Biblical and Modern Israel," Jewish National Fund, 10 July 2021, http://www.kkl-jnf.org/tourism-and-recreation/forests-and-parks/ayalon-canada-park.aspx.

23. See Masalha, *The Palestine Nakba*, 128.

24. See Heidi Grunebaum, "Landscape, Complicity, and Partitioned Zones at South Africa Forest and Lubya in Israel-Palestine," *Anthropology Southern Africa* 37, nos. 3–4 (2014): 213–221. Also see her film, *The Village Beneath the Forest*.

25. This is one of Patrick Wolfe's indispensable aphorisms. See Wolfe, *Traces of History*, 23.

26. See Grunebaum, "Landscape, Complicity, and Partitioned Zones," 214.

27. A. B. Yehoshua, "Facing the Forests," trans. Miriam Arad, *Jewish Quarterly* 18, no. 1 (1970), 33, 36.

28. Quoted in Allon Tal, *All the Trees of the Forest: Israel's Woodlands from the Bible to the Present* (New Haven, CT: Yale University Press, 2013), 63.

29. Quoted in Tal, 65.

30. Tal, 86; Braverman, *Planted Flags*, 96.

31. Tal, 81.

32. See Tal, 72.

33. Braverman, *Planted Flags*, 91.

34. See Kadman, *Erased from Space and Consciousness*, 42.

35. Braverman, *Planted Flags*, 89.

36. See Masalha, *The Palestine Nakba*, 120.

37. Tal, *All the Trees of the Forest*, 80.

38. "Forestry and Green Innovations," Jewish National Fund USA, accessed 28 August 2021, http://www.jnf.org/work-we-do/our-projects/forestry-ecology/.

39. Gary Fields, *Enclosures: Palestinian Landscapes in a Historical Mirror* (Berkeley: University of California Press, 2017), 238–57.

40. Mel Salburg, "Jewish National Fund Presents . . . Its First Century," Jewish National Fund, July 10, 2021, http://support.jnf.org/site/News2?page=NewsArticle&id=9938.

41. See Oren Yiftachel, *Ethnocracy: Land and Identity Politics in Israel/Palestine* (Philadelphia: University of Pennsylvania Press, 2006).

42. "Excerpts from the Jewish National Fund's Response to H.C. 9205/04 and H.C. 9010/04," Adalah, December 9, 2004, https://www.adalah.org/uploads/oldfiles/eng/publications/makan/hc9010.pdf.

43. Masalha, *The Palestine Nakba*, 120.

44. Ilan Pappe, *The Ethnic Cleansing of Palestine* (London: Oneworld, 2006), 228.

45. Pappe, 227. Uri Davis makes the same argument even more bluntly. "One cannot understand the priorities of planting trees and forest in the State of Israel if one ignores the central purpose of this policy, which has been to cover-up crimes against humanity by ethnic cleansing and through the destruction of 400 to 500 Palestinian villages," Davis writes. "The first priority of JNF's forestation policy is to hide its war crimes so that Israel can be considered the only democracy in the Middle East. . . . [So] the cover provided through forestation is essential, and the seemingly shared forest is important so that an Apartheid state (i.e., the State of Israel) can present itself as democratic." Quoted in Braverman, *Planted Flags*, 99–100.

46. Grunebaum, "Landscape, Complicity, and Partitioned Zones," 214.

47. See "Harvey Hertz Ceremonial Tree Planting Center," Jewish National Fund USA, accessed July 11, 2021, https://www.jnf.org/visit-israel/day-tours/harvey-hertz-ceremonial-tree-planting-center.

48. On implicated subjects, see Rothberg, "Trauma Theory, Implicated Subjects, and the Question of Israel/Palestine."

49. See Norman Klein, *The Vatican to Vegas: A History of Special Effects* (New York: New Press, 2004).

50. Klein, 12, 11; see also 333 (emphases in original).

51. See Klein, 325–28.

52. See the Jaffa Cakes page on McVitie's website, https://mcvities.co.uk/products/jaffa-cakes.

53. See Benvenisti, *Sacred Landscape*, 164.

54. Quoted in Kadman, *Erased from Space and Consciousness*, 18.

55. For more on Ayn Hawd, see Susan Slyomovics, *The Object of Memory: Arab and Jew Narrate the Palestinian Village* (Philadelphia: University of Pennsylvania Press, 1998).

56. Muhammad Abu Hayja, "Unrecognized Villages," *Journal of Palestine Studies* 31, no. 1 (Autumn 2001): 44–45.

57. "Occupied Palestinian Territory and Israel," Oxfam International, accessed 11 July 2021, https://www.oxfam.org/en/what-we-do/countries/occupied-palestinian-territory-and-israel.

58. See Gary Fields, *Enclosures: Palestinian Landscapes in a Historical Mirror* (Berkeley: University of California Press, 2017), esp. 233–82; Ahmad Amara, Ismael Abu-Saad, and Oren Yiftachel, eds., *Indigenous (In)Justice: Human Rights Law and the Bedouin Arabs in the Naqab/Negev* (Cambridge, MA: International Human Rights Clinic, Harvard Law School, 2012); and Alexandre Kedar, Ahmad Amara, and Oren Yiftachel, *Emptied Lands: A Legal Geography of Bedouin Rights in the Negev* (Stanford, CA: Stanford University Press, 2018).

59. Kedar, Amara, and Yiftachel, *Emptied Lands*, 10.

60. "Renounce Theft of Bedouin Land," *Ha'aretz*, updated 10 April 2018, http://www.haaretz.com/opinion/1.557517 (emphasis mine).

61. For more on Araqib, see Fields, *Enclosures*, 279–82.

62. Abdelraouf Arna'out, "Israel Demolishes al-Araqib Village for 184th Time," Anadolu Agency, 11 March 2021, https://www.aa.com.tr/en/middle-east/israel-demolishes-al-araqib-village-for-184th-time/2172306. Also see Oren Ziv, "Israel Steps Up Campaign against Bedouin Village It Demolished 173 Times," *972 Mag*, 28 January 2020.

63. "'Nakba Law': Amendment No. 40 to the Budgets Foundations Law," Adalah, https://www.adalah.org/en/law/view/496.

64. Wolfe, *Traces of History*, 33.

65. Strakosch and Macoun, "Land, Territory, or Political Difference?" (paper presented at the International Political Science Association Conference, Sydney, 2013), quoted in Wolfe, 36.

66. Wolfe, *Traces of History*, 37.

CHAPTER 2. DEMOCRACY

Epigraphs: Hillary Clinton speech to AIPAC, transcript published in *Time*, 21 March 2016, https://time.com/4265947/hillary-clinton-aipac-speech-transcript. Kamala Harris, interviewed as candidate for California's US Senate seat in 2016, in "Candidates Vying for Barbara Boxer's Seat Speak on Israel, Anti-Semitism, BDS," *Jewish News of Northern California*, 3 June 2016, https://www.jweekly.com/2016/06/03/candidates-for-sen-boxers-open-seat-speak-on-israel-anti-semitism-bds.

1. "Rubio, Colleagues Urge Obama to Cut Ties with Anti-Israel U.N. Organization," Marco Rubio, US Senator for Florida, 26 October 2016, https://www.rubio.senate.gov/public/index.cfm/press-releases?ID=118A8059-B7F1–4BB0-B545-B91475920DCA. See also "Why Marco Rubio and Ted Cruz Think Israel Is a Winning Issue against Donald Trump," *Washington Post*, 26 February 2016.

2. See "AIPAC Policy Conference 2020 Highlights," http://www.policyconference.org/article/transcripts/cruz-2016.asp.

3. John Kasich's speech to AIPAC, published in *Time*, 22 March 2016, http://time.com/4267674/john-kasich-aipac-israel-speech-transcript.

4. See "AIPAC Policy Conference 2020 Highlights," http://www.policyconference.org/article/transcripts/cruz-2016.asp.

5. "Hillary Clinton's Letter to Haim Saban against BDS," 2 July 2015, available on DocumentCloud, accessed 11 July 2021, https://www.documentcloud.org/documents/2158218-hillary-clintons-letter-to-haim-saban-against-bds.html.

6. "Liberals' Darling Elizabeth Warren Defends Israeli Attacks on Gaza Schools and Hospitals," *RT*, 29 August 2014, https://www.rt.com/usa /183744-elizabeth-warren-gaza-israel.

7. Kamala Harris quoted in Philip Weiss, "Israel 'Made a Desert Bloom'—and I Helped—Kamala Harris to AIPAC," *Mondoweiss*, 10 March 2018, http:// mondoweiss.net/2018/03/israel-desert-helped. See also Michael F. Brown, "White House 'Contender' Kamala Harris Stays Silent on Israel's Crimes," *Electronic Intifada*, 28 November 2017, https://electronicintifada.net/blogs/michael-f-brown /white-house-contender-kamala-harris-stays-silent-israels-crimes.

8. Hilary Leila Krieger, "Ileana Ros-Lehtinen: Ready to Play Hardball," *Jerusalem Post*, 23 December 2010, https://www.jpost.com/Features/In-Thespot-light/Ileana-Ros-Lehtinen-Ready-to-play-hardball.

9. "Senator Menendez Remarks at AIPAC Policy Conference," Bob Menendez, 6 March 2018, https://www.menendez.senate.gov/news-and-events/press /senator-menendez-remarks-at-aipac-policy-conference.

10. Kamala Harris quoted in Michael F. Brown, "White House 'Contender' Kamala Harris Stays Silent on Israel's Crimes," *Electronic Intifada*, 28 November 2017, https://electronicintifada.net/blogs/michael-f-brown/white-house-contender-kamala-harris-stays-silent-israels-crimes.

11. Robert Wright, "A U.N. Plan for Israel," *Opinionator* (blog), *New York Times*, 13 December 2010, https://opinionator.blogs.nytimes.com/2010/12/13 /a-u-n-plan-for-israel.

12. See "AIPAC Policy Conference 2020 Highlights," http://www.policy conference.org/article/transcripts/cruz-2016.asp.

13. Barack Obama, "Remarks by the President on the Middle East and North Africa," White House: President Barack Obama, 19 May 2011, https:// obamawhitehouse.archives.gov/the-press-office/2011/05/19/remarks-president-middle-east-and-north-africa.

14. Peter Beaumont, "John Kerry Apologises for Israel 'Apartheid' Remarks," *Guardian*, 29 April 2014, https://www.theguardian.com/world/2014/apr/29 /john-kerry-apologises-israel-apartheid-remarks.

15. "The Presidential Candidates on the Israeli-Palestinian Conflict," Council on Foreign Relations, 20 July 2019, https://www.cfr.org/article/presidential-candidates-israeli-palestinian-conflict.

16. See "AIPAC Policy Conference 2020 Highlights," http://www.policy conference.org/article/transcripts/cruz-2016.asp.

17. Hillary Clinton speech to AIPAC, transcript published in *Time*, 21 March 2016, https://time.com/4265947/hillary-clinton-aipac-speech-transcript.

18. See "Dean and Pelosi: Carter's Wrong on Israel," *Forward*, 23 October 2006.

19. Richard Cohen, "Israel Has Its Faults, but Apartheid Isn't One of Them," *Washington Post*, 2 March 2010.

20. Alan M. Dershowitz, "Countering Challenges to Israel's Legitimacy," Jerusalem Center for Public Affairs, http://jcpa.org/wp-content/uploads/2012/02/Kiyum-Dershowitz.pdf.

21. Peter Beaumont, "Israel Risks Becoming Apartheid State If Peace Talks Fail, Says John Kerry," *Guardian*, 28 April 2014, https://www.theguardian.com/world/2014/apr/28/israel-apartheid-state-peace-talks-john-kerry.

22. "GOP Slams Kerry 'Apartheid' Line," *Politico*, 28 April 2014.

23. Barbara Boxer, Twitter, 28 April 2014, 2:52 p.m., quoted in Sarah Muller, "Kerry Pushes Back as Israel 'Apartheid' Controversy Builds," *MSNBC*, 28 April 2014, https://www.msnbc.com/the-last-word/kerry-defends-israel-apartheid-controversy-msna317456.

24. Beaumont, "John Kerry Apologises for 'Apartheid' Remarks."

25. "Community Guide," Nefesh B'Nefesh, accessed 14 July 2021, http://www.nbn.org.il/aliyahpedia/community-housing-aliyahpedia/community-profiles/eshchar.

26. "Background," Eshchar, accessed 14 July 2021, http://www.eshchar.co.il/objDoc.asp?PID=38594&OID=52802.

27. Wolfe, *Traces of History*, 266.

28. See "Suggested Items to UN Committee on Elimination of Racial Discrimination (CERD) for the List of Themes for the State of Israel," Adalah, 8 December 2011, http://www2.ohchr.org/english/bodies/cerd/docs/ngos/Adalah_Israel_CERD80.pdf.

29. "High Court Upholds Residential Screening Laws, Enabling Jewish Villages to Keep Arabs Out," *Ha'aretz*, 18 September 2014.

30. In 2000, the Israeli High Court ruled that a Palestinian family, the Ka'adans, who had been denied entry into the Jewish Israeli town of Katzir by its admissions committee, had the right to live there, for which they had applied in 1995. It took the Ka'adans another seven years of petitions, complaints, and court filings (for a total of twelve years) to even be able to start building their house. This solitary case is sometimes proclaimed with great fanfare by Zionist apologists to demonstrate that Palestinians do not suffer from discrimination in terms of access to land and housing. Either way, the 2011 law (see "High Court Upholds Residential Screening Laws") superseded the Ka'adan case, allowing formal discrimination to flourish. For more on the Ka'adan case, see Mazen Masri, *The Dynamics of Exclusionary Constitutionalism: Israel as a Jewish and Democratic State* (Portland, OR: Hart Studies in Comparative Public Law, 2017), 69–70.

31. "Examples of this," writes Tawfiq Zayyad, include that "Nazareth was deprived of most of its land, while its population tripled (from 15,000 to 45,000). Umm al-Fahim, the largest Arab [Palestinian] village, used to own 140,000 dunums [1 dunum is a quarter acre] in 1948 while its population was only 4,000; today this same village owns 12,000 dunums while its population has

increased to 17,000 (i.e., 128,000 dunums confiscated). Another Arab [Palestin-
ian] village, Taybih, lost 23,000 dunums, Tyrah also lost 23,000—and so on with
the other Arab [Palestinian] villages." Zayyad, "The Fate of the Arabs in Israel,"
Journal of Palestine Studies 6, no. 1 (Autumn 1976): 96. As the Israeli-Palestinian human rights organization Adalah points out, the result of land confiscations and the state's refusal to allow Palestinians to develop new towns has led to
severe overcrowding: Palestinians constitute a fifth of the population inside
Israel, but Palestinian municipalities exercise jurisdiction over only 2.5% of the
land inside the state. See Adalah, *The Inequality Report: The Palestinian Arab
Minority in Israel* (Haifa, Israel, March 2011), https://www.adalah.org/uploads
/oldfiles/upfiles/2011/Adalah_The_Inequality_Report_March_2011.pdf.

32. Yinon Cohen and Neve Gordon, "Israel's Biospatial Politics: Territory,
Demography, and Effective Control," *Public Culture* 30, no. 2 (2018): 200. See
also Gershon Shafir and Yoav Peled, *Being Israeli: The Dynamics of Multiple
Citizenship* (Cambridge: Cambridge University Press, 2002), esp. 115–16.

33. It goes without saying that no other state on the planet goes around obsessively counting population ratios in this perverse way. "In mid-1975 the Arab
[Palestinian] population of the northern district was 250,000 while the Jewish
population was 289,000," the report notes with alarm. "A regional examination
shows that in western Galilee the Arab [Palestinian] population constitutes 67
percent of the total; in the region of Yizre'el the Arab [Palestinian] population
constitutes 48 percent of the total population. In 1974 only 759 Jews were added
to the population of the northern district while the Arab [Palestinian] population increased by 9,035. According to this rate of increase, by 1978 Arabs [Pales-
tinians] will constitute over 51 percent of the total population of that district."
See "Top Secret: Memorandum—Proposal [for] Handling the Arabs of Israel,"
translated from the Hebrew and published in *Journal of Palestine Studies* 6, no.
1 (Autumn 1976): 191, 193.

34. On the "Judaization" of Galilee, see Yiftachel, *Ethnocracy*, 64–69.

35. Jonathan Cook, "Unwanted Citizens," *al-Ahram Weekly*, 10–16 January
2002.

36. See Adalah's Discriminatory Laws Database (accessed 14 July 2021),
https://www.adalah.org/en/content/view/7771.

37. Cohen and Gordon, "Israel's Biospatial Politics," 202, 216.

38. This is not to say that all Israeli Jews adopt this blindness toward Palestinians, of course, for some of them work toward justice and coexistence, and I
count them as friends and comrades in a common cause. That position, however,
requires considerable thoughtfulness; the default mode lends itself to oblivious-
ness, which was never the case in South Africa.

39. "Under Israeli law and policy, group membership is an official category
imposed and monitored by the state, not simply a voluntary identity," notes the
Russell Tribunal on Palestine. "Israeli Jews are a group unified by law, sharing

the same legal status wherever they reside, while Palestinian Arabs are a separate group, sub-divided into citizens, occupied residents (whose residence rights
may be lost if they leave the territory in which they live), and refugees who do not
have the right to return to any part of historic Palestine." See Russell Tribunal on
Palestine, *Findings of the South African Session* (Cape Town, 2011), paragraph
5.19 (p. 14).

40. I use the term "race" here and throughout this book as expressed in the
1965 International Convention on the Elimination of All Forms of Racial
Discrimination(ICERD). This major international convention on racial identity
and attendant forms of discrimination adopted an understanding of race as
encompassing what might otherwise be distinguished from now discredited
understandings of "race" (in a narrowly biological sense) as national or ethnic origin. Thus, Article 1 of the convention states: "In this Convention, the term 'racial
discrimination' shall mean any distinction, exclusion, restriction or preference
based on race, colour, descent, or national or ethnic origin which has the purpose
or effect of nullifying or impairing the recognition, enjoyment or exercise, on an
equal footing, of human rights and fundamental freedoms in the political, economic, social, cultural or any other field of public life." International Convention
on the Elimination of All Forms of Racial Discrimination, 1965, Office of the
High Commissioner on Human Rights, accessed 14 July 2014, http://www.ohchr
.org/EN/ProfessionalInterest/Pages/CERD.aspx. As the international legal scholars John Dugard and John Reynolds note, this passage from the ICERD "provides
categories that Jewish Israelis and Arab Palestinians may be classified by, even if
not clearly discernible under the more ambiguous category of race or color" in the
"traditional sense." Thus, they conclude, "Jewish and Palestinian identities," while
not typically seen as 'races' in the old (discredited) sense of biological or skin colour categories, are constructed as groups distinguished by ancestry or descent as
well as ethnicity, nationality, and religion. As such they are distinguished from
each other in a number of forms within the parameters of racial discrimination
under international human rights law." See Dugard and Reynolds, "Apartheid,
International Law, and the Occupied Palestinian Territory," *European Journal of
International Law* 24, no. 3 (2013), 867–913, 885–86, 889.

41. Quoted in John Quigley, *Palestine and Israel: A Challenge to Justice* (Durham, NC: Duke University Press, 1990), 129. As Dugard and Reynolds point out,
this ruling "made it clear that to recognize a common Israeli nationality would
be to 'negate the very foundation upon which the State of Israel was formed.'" See
Dugard and Reynolds, "Apartheid, International Law, and the Occupied Palestinian Territory," 904.

42. Robinson, *Citizen Strangers*, 108. Cards issued more recently have aster-
isks over the field for "nationality," but the Ministry of the Interior retains the
racial-national designations for each citizen in its internal records and the population registry.

43. In her meticulous reading of the state's founding, Robinson points out that there was an extensive delay in formulating and legislating the laws regarding citizenship and nationality because the Zionist leadership—above all David Ben-Gurion—were trying to figure out how best to frame the laws to include Jews but exclude Palestinians. Hence, Robinson argues, "the juridical and social content of Israeli citizenship was determined not by an ideal vision of whom to include but rather by the stark imperative of whom to keep out." See Robinson, *Citizen Strangers*, 72, 111–12.

44. Robinson, 99.

45. Masri, *Dynamics of Exclusionary Constitutionalism*, 102–3.

46. See Robinson, *Citizen Strangers*, 108.

47. Section 2 of the law, as Robinson shows, covers "citizenship by return" and extends status "to every *oleh* [Jewish immigrant-settler] under the 1950 Law of Return," that is, to Jews only. Section 3 outlines the conditions for "citizenship by residence," and, without referring explicitly to non-Jews, devotes itself to anyone to whom Section 2 does not apply—that is, without saying it explicitly, while absolutely intending it implicitly, non-Jews. Robinson, 72.

48. Robinson, 108.

49. Cohen and Gordon, "Israel's Biospatial Politics," 203.

50. Palestinian citizens of Israel refuse the designation "Israeli Arab" and insist on their identity as Palestinians. The Haifa Declaration, issued by leading Palestinian intellectuals, scholars, and activists inside Israel, opens with the following statement:

> We, sons and daughters of the Palestinian Arab people who remained in our homeland despite the Nakba, who were forcibly made a minority in the State of Israel after its establishment in 1948 on the greater part of the Palestinian homeland; do hereby affirm in this Declaration the foundations of our identity and belonging; and put forth a vision of our collective future, one which gives voice to our concerns and aspirations and lays the foundations for a frank dialogue among ourselves and between ourselves and other peoples. Despite the setback to our national project and our relative isolation from the rest of our Palestinian people and our Arab nation since the Nakba; despite all the attempts made to keep us in ignorance of our Palestinian and Arab history; despite attempts to splinter us into sectarian groups and to truncate our identity into a misshapen 'Israeli Arab' one, we have spared no effort to preserve our Palestinian identity and national dignity and to fortify it."

See *Haifa Declaration* (Mada al-Carmel, 2007), available at https://mada-research.org/wp-content/uploads/2007/09/watheeqat-haifa-english.pdf.

51. Cohen and Gordon, "Israel's Biospatial Politics,"203.

52. To be incorporated into the Israeli state, the Arab Jews from Iraq or Yemen had to be politically and ideologically "purified," the act of stripping them of their Arabness being the flip side of the act of asserting their identities as Jews. This was sometimes done in violent and terrifying ways, by forcibly separating the children of Arab Jewish immigrants from their parents in order to

raise them separately in more "purely" Jewish foster families, thereby aligning them more fully with their Jewishness precisely at the expense of their Arabness. "In aligning Mizrahim to fellow-Jews rather than to fellow-Arabs [i.e., Palestinians], race operates in negation," Wolfe notes; "Mizrahi de-racination is a work of race." *Traces of History*, 265.

53. According to the Law of Return, "Every Jew who has immigrated into this country before the coming into force of this Law, and every Jew who was born in this country, whether before or after the coming into force of this Law, shall be deemed to be a person who has come to this country as an *oleh* [immigrant or settler] under this Law." That is, while scrupulously avoiding any mention of the indigenous non-Jewish Palestinian population, the law defines all Jews, including Palestinian Jews, as settlers. "There could hardly be a clearer example of settler colonialism's replacement of Natives by immigrants," Patrick Wolfe points out. "Under this foundational provision, the conferral of racial privilege on Palestine-born Jews was achieved by the means of the poker-faced contrivance of converting them into honorary immigrants." Thus, Wolfe notes, the divide in Israel between Jews and non-Jews is also a legal distinction "between settlers and Natives." Wolfe, *Traces of History*, 265.

54. This verbal sleight of hand is very hard to dislodge: I have had several fruitless arguments with members of the editorial board of the *Los Angeles Times* about the paper's use of the term "Israeli Arabs" to refer to Israel's Palestinian citizens.

55. Dugard and Reynolds, "Apartheid, International Law, and the Occupied Palestinian Territory," 904.

56. Dugard and Reynolds, 905.

57. For instance, Israeli military regulations governing access to certain "closed areas" in the West Bank prevent Palestinians who own the land in question from entering them while granting access to anyone "who is eligible to enter Israel in accordance with the Law of Return." So a Palestinian farmer may not be able to get to his field by order of the Israeli army, but anyone Jewish from anywhere in the world can. For a discussion of differences in rights to land, see Saree Makdisi, *Palestine Inside Out: An Everyday Occupation* (New York: W. W. Norton, 2008), 16–17.

58. See Ilan Pappe, *The Ethnic Cleansing of Palestine* (London: Oneworld, 2007); Nur Masalha, *The Politics of Denial: Israel and the Palestinian Refugee Problem* (London: Pluto Press, 2003).

59. See Yiftachel, *Ethnocracy*.

60. "Essence of Life Campaign," Jewish National Fund, accessed 28 August 2021, http://support.jnf.org/site/PageServer?pagename=Essence_of_life.

61. Gershon Shafir and Yoav Peled, *Being Israeli: The Dynamics of Multiple Citizenship* (Cambridge: Cambridge University Press, 2002), 116.

62. Jacob Landau, *The Arab Minority in Israel* (Oxford: Oxford University Press, 1993), quoted in Shafir and Peled, 120–21.

63. Shafir and Peled, 123.

64. See Shafir and Peled, 123.

65. See Parallel Report Jointly Submitted to the UN Committee on the Elimination of All Forms of Racial Discrimination, 69th Session, Geneva, July-August 2006; "The Education Gap," *Adalah Newsletter* August 2007); NGO Report: Suggested Issues for Consideration Regarding Israel's Combined 10th, 11th, 12th, and 13th Periodic Reports to the UN Committee on the Elimination of All Forms of Racial Discrimination, Adalah, 2005, available at United Nations, accessed 28 August 2021, https://www.un.org/unispal/document/auto-insert-178428/. See also Shafir and Peled, *Being Israeli,* 123.

66. See Nurit Peled-Elhanan, *Palestine in Israeli School Books: Ideology and Propaganda in Education* (London: IB Tauris, 2010).

67. For more on the racism of the occupation regime in the territories occupied in 1967, see the relevant parts of Makdisi, *Palestine Inside Out.*

68. See Palestinian Central Bureau of Statistics, "Special Statistical Bulletin on the 68th Anniversary of the Palestinian Nakba, 15 May 2016, http://www .pcbs.gov.ps/post.aspx?lang=en&ItemID=1661; "Explore All Countries—Israel," *The World Factbook* (US Central Intelligence Agency), accessed 28 August 2021, https://www.cia.gov/the-world-factbook/countries/israel/#people-and-society.

69. Economic and Social Commission for Western Asia (ESCWA), *Israeli Practices toward the Palestinian People and the Question of Apartheid* (United Nations, March 2017), 3, 6.

70. "A Regime of Jewish Supremacy from the Jordan River to the Mediterranean Sea: This Is Apartheid," *B'tselem,* January 2021, https://www.btselem.org /sites/default/files/publications/202101_this_is_apartheid_eng.pdf.

71. "Abusive Israeli Policies Constitute Crimes of Apartheid, Persecution," Human Rights Watch, 27 April 2021, https://www.hrw.org/news/2021/04/27 /abusive-israeli-policies-constitute-crimes-apartheid-persecution#.

72. International Convention on the Suppression and Punishment of the Crime of Apartheid, United Nations Treaty Collection, accessed 17 July 2021, https://treaties.un.org/doc/publication/unts/volume%201015/volume-1015-i-14861-english.pdf.

73. *Occupation, Colonialism, Apartheid? A Re-assessment of Israel's Practices in the Occupied Palestinian Territories under International Law* (Cape Town: South Africa Human Sciences Research Council, 2009), 22.

74. Dugard and Reynolds, "Apartheid, International Law, and the Occupied Palestinian Territory," 912.

75. See Russell Tribunal on Palestine, *Findings of the South African Session,* 5.45, 21.

76. See ESCWA, *Israeli Practices toward the Palestinian People*, 1.

77. See Ghassan Hage, "Recalling Anti-Racism," *Ethnic and Racial Studies* 39, no. 1 (2015), 123–33.

78. Gershon Shafir, *Land, Labor, and the Origins of the Israeli-Palestinian Conflict, 1882–1914* (Berkeley: University of California Press, 1996), 14, 60, among other pages.

79. Achille Mbembe, "Necropolitics," *Public Culture* 15, no. 1 (2003), 11–40.

80. See David Theo Goldberg, "Racisms without Racism," *PMLA* 123, no. 5 (October 2008), 1712–16.

81. See Dugard and Reynolds, "Apartheid, International Law, and the Occupied Palestinian Territory," 897.

82. Richard Goldstone, "Israel and the Apartheid Slander," *New York Times*, 31 October 2011.

83. See interview with Ruthie Blum, "It's the Demography Stupid," *Jerusalem Post*, 20 May 2004.

CHAPTER 3. DIVERSITY

1. "Tel Aviv Glams Up for the Eurovision 2019 Opening Ceremony," *Eurovision.tv*, 13 May 2019, https://eurovision.tv/story/tel-aviv-glams-for-the-official-opening-ceremony-of-eurovision-2019.

2. "Next Year in Jerusalem! In Israel, Eurovision Is Seen as a Diplomatic Victory, Too," *New York Times*, 13 May 2018.

3. Christopher Muther, "Welcome to Tel Aviv, the Gayest City on Earth," *Boston Globe*, 17 March 2016. See also Catherine Baker, "The 'Gay Olympics'? The Eurovision Song Contest and the Politics of LGBT/European Belonging," *European Journal of International Relations* 23, no. 1 (2017): 97–121.

4. On the political culture of Eurovision, see, for instance, Karen Fricker and Milija Gluhovic, eds., *Performing the "New" Europe: Identities, Feelings, and Politics in the Eurovision Song Contest* (London: Palgrave, 2013); and Shannon Jones and Jelena Subotic, "Fantasies of Power: Performing Europeanization on the European Periphery," *European Journal of Cultural Studies* 14, no. 5 (2011): 542–57. On camp, subversion, and politics, see, for example, Fabio Cleto, ed., *Camp: Queer Aesthetics and the Performing Subject—A Reader* (Ann Arbor: University of Michigan Press, 1999), notably the essays by Sontag and Britton; David Bergman, ed., *Camp Grounds: Style and Homosexuality* (Amherst: University of Massachusetts Press, 1993); Elizabeth Whitney, "Capitalizing on Camp: Greed and the Queer Marketplace," *Text and Performance Quarterly* 26, no. 1 (2006): 36–46; Pamela Robertson, *Guilty Pleasures: Feminist Camp from Mae West to Madonna* (Durham, NC: Duke University Press, 1996); and Judith Hal-

berstam, *In a Queer Time and Place: Transgender Bodies, Subcultural Lives* (New York: New York University Press, 2005).

5. "Eurovision Kicks Off in Tel Aviv as BDS Activists Protest Outside," *Ha'aretz*, 12 May 2019.

6. Eurovision Song Contest Rules, *Eurovision.tv*, accessed 15 September 2020, https://eurovision.tv/about/rules.

7. "Iceland Fined for Pro-Palestinian Protest at Eurovision Song Contest in Tel Aviv," *Times of Israel*, 21 September 2019. See also Ali Abunimah, "Don't Praise Iceland's Hatari for Violating Eurovision Boycott," *Electronic Intifada*, 20 May 2019.

8. Israeli army snipers were firing at these protestors from fortified positions and at a distance of several hundred meters; the protestors posed no threat to them. By late summer 2019, Israelis had killed 311 Palestinian protestors and injured more than 34,000. See "Humanitarian Snapshot," UN Office for the Coordination of Humanitarian Affairs in the Occupied Palestinian Territory, 31 August 2019, https://www.ochaopt.org/content/humanitarian-snapshot-casualties-context-demonstrations-and-hostilities-gaza-30-mar-2018-0.

9. "Sheikh Muwannis," in Khalidi, *All That Remains*, 259–60.

10. Hanaa Abueid, "Abu Kheel Ibraheem Looted Green House before Reconstructed 1989," *PalestineRemembered.com*, 12 November 2003, https://www.palestineremembered.com/Jaffa/al-Shaykh-Muwannis/Picture6382.html.

11. See Tommaso Milani and Erez Levon, "Sexing Diversity: Linguistic Landscapes of Homonationalism," *Language and Communication* 51 (2016): 69–86.

12. Ali Abunimah, "AP Corrects Story Falsely Claiming Homosexuality Is Illegal for Palestinians," *Electronic Intifada*, 7 July 2015, https://electronicintifada.net/blogs/ali-abunimah/ap-corrects-story-falsely-claiming-homosexuality-illegal-palestinians.

13. See Sarah Schulman, *Israel/Palestine and the Queer International* (Durham, NC: Duke University Press, 2012). See also "Views of China and India Slide While UK's Ratings Climb," Globescan, 22 May 2013, https://globescan.com/views-of-china-and-india-slide-while-uks-ratings-climb.

14. Schulman, *Israel/Palestine and the Queer International*, 181. See also the index itself, "East West Global Index 200" (2009), East West Communications, accessed 18 July 2021, http://www.eastwestcoms.com/global_annual_2009.htm.

15. "'Devastating' Survey Shows Huge Loss of Israel Support among Jewish College Students," *Times of Israel*, 21 June 2017.

16. "'Massive Drop in US Jewish College Students' Support for Israel,'" *Jerusalem Post*, 22 June 2017.

17. "'Devastating' Survey."

18. "'Devastating' Survey."

19. "'Devastating' Survey."

20. "Don't Mention the War: Israel Seeks Image Makeover," Reuters, 18 January 2007.

21. "Israel Aims to Improve Its Public Image" *Forward*, 14 October 2005.

22. "Israel Aims," *Forward*, 14 October 2005 (emphases added).

23. Bill Berkowitz, "Israel Looking for an Extreme Makeover," *Electronic Intifada*, 12 January 2007.

24. "Marketing a New Image," *NY Jewish Week*, 21 January 2005.

25. Mel Bezalel, "Gay Pride Being Used to Promote Israel Abroad," *Jerusalem Post*, 7 June 2009.

26. Schulman, *Israel/Palestine and the Queer International*, 183.

27. See, for example, "Hot Israeli Army Girls," *Maxim*, 24 May 2017.

28. Benjamin Doherty, "War Sporno: How the Israeli Army Uses Sex and Instagram to Sell Its Racism and Violence," *Electronic Intifada*, 26 December 2012.

29. "Israel to Put Its Babes Forward in Maxim-um PR Effort," *Jerusalem Post*, 22 March 2007.

30. "Israel to Put Its Babes Forward," *Jerusalem Post*, 22 March 2007.

31. Jon Dart, "'Brand Israel': Hasbara and Israeli Sport," *Sport in Society* 19, no. 10 (2016): 1409. As Dart observes, "Michel Platini's claim that 'I don't do politics, I do football' is a re-statement of the canard that 'sport and politics don't mix' and a clear echo of those governing bodies which supported the maintenance of sporting contacts with apartheid South Africa" (1411).

32. "Kicking Racism Out of Football," Union of European Football Associations, 24 October 2002, https://www.uefa.com/insideuefa/news/newsid=39661 .html.

33. Michael Brown, "NFL Players Pull Out of Israeli Propaganda Tour," *Electronic Intifada*, 11 February 2017.

34. "About," Israel21c, accessed 18 July 2021, https://www.israel21c.org /about.

35. Quoted in Nada Elia, "Gay Rights with a Side of Apartheid," *Settler Colonial Studies* 2, no. 2 (2012): 57.

36. Elia, 50.

37. "Foreign Ministry Promoting Gay Israel," *Jerusalem Post*, 26 October 2006.

38. Saranga quoted in "Foreign Ministry Promoting Gay Israel."

39. "Foreign Ministry Promoting Gay Israel."

40. Jasbir Puar, "Israel's Gay Propaganda War," *Guardian*, 1 July 2010.

41. Jasbir Puar, "To Be Gay and Racist Is No Anomaly," *Guardian*, 2 June 2010.

42. See Milani and Levon, "Sexing Diversity," 70.

43. Among the many studies of this framework, the single most authoritative account remains Edward W. Said, *Orientalism* (New York: Pantheon, 1979).

44. Edward W. Said, *The Question of Palestine* (New York: Vintage, 1992), 25.

45. Said, 28–29.

46. Said, 29.

47. Tommaso Milani and Erez Levon, "Israel as Homotopia: Language, Space, and Vicious Belonging," *Language in Society* 48, no. 4 (2019): 612.

48. Netanyahu quoted in Sarah Schulman, "Israel and 'Pinkwashing,'" *New York Times*, 22 November 2011.

49. Puar, "Israel's Gay Propaganda War."

50. Halevi quoted in Jason Ritchie, "How Do You Say 'Come out of the Closet' in Arabic?" *GLQ* 16, no. 4 (2010): 558–59.

51. Ritchie, 560.

52. James Kirchick, "Palestine and Gay Rights," *Advocate*, 11 July 2006.

53. Ali Abunimah, "AP Corrects Story Falsely Claiming Homosexuality Is Illegal for Palestinians," *Electronic Intifada*, 7 July 2015, https://electronicintifada .net/blogs/ali-abunimah/ap-corrects-story-falsely-claiming-homosexuality-illegal-palestinians.

54. Abunimah.

55. Massad quoted in Abunimah, "AP Corrects Story."

56. See, for example, Rebecca Stein, "Explosive: Scenes from Israel's Gay Occupation," *GLQ* 16, no. 4 (2010): 519–21.

57. Haneen Maikey and Jason Ritchie, "Israel, Palestine, and Queers," alQaws, 28 April 2009, http://alqaws.org/articles/Israel-Palestine-and-Queers?category_id=0.

58. See Lynn Darwich and Haneen Maikey, "The Road from Antipinkwashing Activism to the Decolonization of Palestine," *WSQ: Women's Studies Quarterly* 42, nos. 3–4 (Fall/Winter 2014): 281–85.

59. Heike Schotten and Haneen Maikey, "Queers Resisting Zionism: On Authority and Accountability beyond Homonationalism," alQaws, 10 October 2012, http://alqaws.org/articles/Queers-Resisting-Zionism-On-Authority-and-Accountability-Beyond-Homonationalism?category_id=0.

60. See Jasbir Puar, *Terrorist Assemblages: Homonationalism in Queer Times* (Durham, NC: Duke University Press, 2017).

61. Stein, "Explosive," 519.

62. Aeyal Gross, "The Politics of LGBT Rights in Israel and Beyond: Nationality, Normativity, and Queer Politics," *Columbia Human Rights Law Review* 46, no. 2 (Winter 2015): 105.

63. See, for example, Amalia Ziv, "Performative Politics in Israeli Queer Anti-occupation Activity," *GLQ* 16, no. 4 (2010): 537–56.

64. Ziv, 539.

65. Anat Lieber, quoted in Ziv, 540.

66. Gross, "Politics of LGBT Rights in Israel and Beyond," 94.

67. Milani and Levon, "Sexing Diversity," 70.

68. See Maikey's comments in Gil Hochberg et al., "No Pride in Occupation: A Roundtable Discussion," *GLQ* 16, no. 4 (2010): 604.

69. Ritchie, "How Do You Say 'Come out of the Closet' in Arabic?" 559–60.

70. Gross, "Politics of LGBT Rights in Israel and Beyond," 117.

71. Gross, 115.

72. Stein, "Explosive," 521.

73. Justice Yitzhak Amit, quoted in Gross, "Politics of LGBT Rights in Israel and Beyond," 85.

74. Gross, 85.

75. Aeyal Gross, "Israeli GLBT Politics between Queerness and Homonationalism," *Bully Bloggers*, 3 July 2010, https://bullybloggers.wordpress.com/2010/07/03/israeli-glbt-politics-between-queerness-and-homonationalism.

76. Michael Lucas, quoted in Max Cavitch, "Michael Lucas and the Pornography of Migration," *Senses of Cinema* 55 (July 2010).

77. Lucas, quoted in Elia, "Gay Rights with a Side of Apartheid," 62.

78. Lucas, quoted in Elia, 62.

79. Lucas, quoted in Cavitch, "Michael Lucas and the Pornography of Migration."

80. Lucas, quoted in Brett Remkus Britt, "Pinkwashed: Gay Rights, Colonial Cartographies, and Racial Categories in the Pornographic Film *Men of Israel*," *International Feminist Journal of Politics* 17 no. 3 (2015): 406.

81. "Michael Lucas Tells *Try State Magazine* All about *Inside Israel*," *Try State Magazine*, 25 November 2009.

82. Scenes and clips, as well as the whole film, are available on the *Men of Israel* website, https://www.lucasentertainment.com/tour/movies/view/men_of_israel.

83. I am indebted here to Cesare Casarino's reading of ex-Soviet gay porn; see his "Pornocairology: Or, the Communist Clinamen of Pornography," *Paragraph* 25, no. 2 (July 2002): 116–26, esp. 116.

84. See Britt, "Pinkwashed," 401. Britt's reading of the film goes in a somewhat different direction; according to him, Lucas's version of pinkwashing uses gay sexuality to recapitulate much older racial and colonial narratives (ibid., 400–406).

85. Max Blumenthal, "Nakba Porn Kingpin Michael Lucas Bullies LGBT Center against Anti-Apartheid Party," *Mondoweiss*, 24 February 2011, https://mondoweiss.net/2011/02/nakba-porn-kingpin-michael-lucas-bullies-lgbt-center-against-anti-apartheid-party.

86. "Michael Lucas Tells *Try State Magazine* All about *Inside Israel*."

87. See, among many other works, Masalha, *Expulsion of the Palestinians*; Masalha, *Palestine Nakba*; and Pappe, *Ethnic Cleansing of Palestine*.

88. See Wolfe, *Traces of History*; and Gershon Shafir, *Land, Labor, and the Origins of the Israeli-Palestinian Conflict*.

89. See Wolfe, *Traces of History*, 224–35.

90. Yaniv Halily, "IDF Soldiers New Attraction for Gay Tourists," Ynet News, 4 September 2010.

91. See Britt, "Pinkwashed," 402.

92. See Cavitch, "Michael Lucas and the Pornography of Migration."

93. Lucas quoted in Halily, "IDF Soldiers New Attraction for Gay Tourists."

94. Puar, *Terrorist Assemblages*, 16.

95. See "Call to Boycott World Pride in Jerusalem 2006," *Electronic Intifada*, 18 May 2006, https://electronicintifada.net/content/call-boycott-world-pride-jerusalem-2006/519.

96. "Call to Boycott World Pride in Jerusalem 2006."

97. Schulman, *Israel/Palestine and the Queer International*, 183.

98. See Milani and Levon, "Sexing Diversity," 71.

99. "Queers Against Israeli Apartheid Retiring," 26 February 2015, https://queersagainstapartheid.org/2015/02/26/queers-against-israeli-apartheid-retiring. See also Elia, "Gay Rights with a Side of Apartheid."

100. Mel Bezalel, "Gay Pride Being Used to Promote Israel Abroad," *Jerusalem Post*, 7 June 2009.

101. Quoted in Elia, "Gay Rights with a Side of Apartheid," 64.

102. Stand With Us, *LGBTQ Rights in Israel and the Middle East*, 2017.

103. Schulman, *Israel/Palestine and the Queer International*, 183.

104. "Gay Tel Aviv for Beginners," Tourist Israel: The Guide, accessed 21 July 2021, https://www.touristisrael.com/gay-tel-aviv-for-beginners/5686.

105. "Tel Aviv—A City with Pride: Celebrating 2018 Pride Week," Tel Aviv Nonstop City, 21 July 2021, https://www.tel-aviv.gov.il/en/Pages/ArticlePage.aspx?WebID=9336473c-1537-4ab6-8a69-d299b5db8bcc&ListID=b4eda22c-a69a-4bef-9479-05d5a832ad16&ItemId=99.

106. "Tel Aviv—A City with Pride."

107. "Tel Aviv Hosts Largest Gay Parade Ever Held in the Middle East," Israel Ministry of Foreign Affairs, 9 June 2017, https://mfa.gov.il/MFA/IsraelExperience/Lifestyle/Pages/Tel-Aviv-hosts-largest-ever-gay-parade-in-the-Middle-East-9-June-2017.aspx.

108. Schulman, *Israel/Palestine and the Queer International*, 181.

109. Schulman, 181. American launched flights to Tel Aviv in 2019.

110. "Tel Aviv Named 'World's Best Gay City' for 2011," *Jerusalem Post*, 12 January 2012.

111. Christopher Muther, "Welcome to Tel Aviv, the Gayest City on Earth," *Boston Globe*, 17 March 2016.

112. Debra Kamin, "36 Hours in Tel Aviv," *New York Times*, 31 December 2015.

113. See Milani and Levon, "Sexing Diversity."

114. Tel Aviv Gay Vibe, quoted in Milani and Levon, "Sexing Diversity," 76 (emphasis in original).

115. See Milani and Levon, 74.

116. Milani and Levon, 81.

117. "Why Tel Aviv Is the Ultimate LGBTQ Travel Destination," Tourist Israel: The Guide, accessed 21 July 2021, https://www.touristisrael.com/why-tel-aviv-is-the-ultimate-lgbtq-travel-destination/26062.

118. Catherine Baker, "The 'Gay Olympics'? The Eurovision Song Contest and the Politics of LGBT/European Belonging," *European Journal of International Relations* 23, no. 1 (2017): 104.

119. Baker, 100.

120. Baker, 101–2. See also Peter Rehberg, "Winning Failure: Queer Nationality at the Eurovision Song Contest," *SQS: Journal of Queer Studies in Finland* 2, no. 2 (2007): 60.

121. "Hotel Prices Fall as Eurovision Demand Disappoints," *Globes*, 28 April 2019, https://en.globes.co.il/en/article-hotel-prices-fall-as-eurovision-demand-disappoints-1001283666. See also "A Eurovision Fumble: How Israel Blew the Chance to Attract Thousands of Tourists," *Ha'aretz*, 12 May 2019.

122. "A Eurovision Fumble."

123. "A Eurovision Fumble."

124. "Eurovision Tickets Going for Free to Residents of South," *Jerusalem Post*, 9 May 2019.

125. "Boycott Eurovision in Israel and Tel Aviv Pride!" Pinkwatching Israel, 28 January 2019, http://www.pinkwatchingisrael.com/portfolio/boycott-eurovision-in-israel-and-tel-aviv-pride.

126. Riri Hylton, "LGBTQ Groups Call for Eurovision Boycott," *Electronic Intifada*, 1 February 2019.

127. Bill Berkowitz, "Israel Looking for an Extreme Makeover," *Electronic Intifada*, 12 January 2007.

128. Darwich and Maikey, "The Road from Antipinkwashing Activism," 284.

129. Darwich and Maikey, 283.

130. See Walaa al Qaisiya, "Decolonial Queering: The Politics of Being Queer in Palestine," *Journal of Palestine Studies* 47, no. 3 (Spring 2018): 29.

CHAPTER 4. TOLERANCE

Epigraph: Quoted in Steve Linde, "Hier: Jerusalem Tolerance Museum in 3 Years," *Jerusalem Post*, 6 June 2012.

1. Quoted in Samuel Freedman, "Frank Gehry's Mideast Peace Plan," *New York Times*, 1 August 2004.

2. Quoted in "Israeli Court OKs Museum of Tolerance's Controversial Branch," *Culture Monster* (blog), *Los Angeles Times*, 29 October 2008.

3. These quotations are from the 2003–11 Museum of Tolerance Jerusalem website, http://motj.com, which was taken down in 2011 and is no longer available, even via the Wayback Machine on archive.org.

4. See, for example, Macintyre, "Israel Plans to Build 'Museum of Tolerance' on Muslim Graves"; Jonathan Lis and Amiram Barkat, "Treatment of Skeletons Found at Museum Building Site Raises Storm," *Ha'aretz*, 8 February 2006.

5. "Hier: Jerusalem Tolerance Museum in 3 Years," *Jerusalem Post*, 6 June 2012.

6. Yehoshua Ben-Arieh, "The Tolerance Museum and the Mamilla Cemetery: The Plain Facts," January 2009, http://www.ipcri.org/files/yehoshua-eng.html (website taken down).

7. It has been suggested that in the 1930s the grand mufti of Jerusalem drew up plans to build a Muslim university campus on the site of Ma'man Allah, but the feasibility of those plans has been questioned, and in any case nothing came of them. Nevertheless, the mere possibility that such plans may have existed has been used by the advocates of the Museum of Tolerance as justification for their own plan, which is absurd. See the discussion of the grand mufti's plans in Daniel Monk, *An Aesthetic Occupation: The Immediacy of Architecture and the Palestine Conflict* (Durham, NC: Duke University Press, 2002).

8. Ben-Arieh points out that the Simon Wiesenthal center claims that the Palace Hotel was built on cemetery grounds; he demonstrates that this was not the case. Ben-Arieh, "The Tolerance Museum and the Mamilla Cemetery."

9. See Ben-Arieh.

10. The old city itself did not fall, and constituted the core of what would come to be called East Jerusalem after 1948, only to be captured by Israel during the 1967 war, along with the West Bank and the Gaza Strip. Although Israel claims to have annexed it, East Jerusalem actually remains militarily occupied territory to this day, according to international law.

11. Even with extensive Jewish immigration from Europe before, during, and after the Holocaust, Jews—the vast majority of them recent immigrants—constituted barely a third of the population of Palestine as late as 1948. The 1948 war began with a series of carefully scripted massacres and expulsions of Palestinians months before Israel's formal declaration of independence in May of that year, only after which did neighboring Arab states attempt to intervene. See Avi Shlaim, *The Iron Wall: Israel and the Arab World* (New York: W. W. Norton, 2001), 28–54; Simha Flapan, *The Birth of Israel* (New York: Pantheon, 1988); Morris, *Birth of the Palestinian Refugee Problem Revisited*; Masalha, *Expulsion of the Palestinians*; Pappe, *Ethnic Cleansing of Palestine*; Shafir, *Land, Labor, and the Origins of the Israeli-Palestinian Conflict*.

12. Palestinians driven from their homes have never been allowed to return, despite their moral and legal right to do so, as stipulated by United Nations

General Assembly Resolution 194 (1948), which was explicitly recalled by Resolution 273 (1949), granting Israel UN membership.

13. The question of land rights and state land in Israel is complex. The kinds of covenants that used to forbid home ownership in many American cities to "non-Caucasians," including blacks, Latinos, Asians, and in many cases Jews, remain in force in Israel to this day. Palestinian citizens of the state are barred from living on land held by "national institutions" such as the Jewish National Fund (JNF) or the Jewish Agency. They are legally excluded from residing in officially designated "Jewish community settlements" or "Jewish rural settlements" organized into rural councils that, between them, control some 80 percent of the land in Israel. In all, 93 percent of pre-1967 Israel—almost all of it the expropriated property of Palestinian refugees—is classified as state land, of which 13 percent is owned by the JNF. The Israel Lands Authority (ILA) took over the management of all state land, including JNF land, in the early 1960s; however, the ILA has to administer JNF lands according to JNF's discriminatory criteria (i.e., enabling access only for Jews). In response to a 2004 legal challenge to its discrimination against non-Jews, the JNF said that it "is not a public body which acts on behalf of all the citizens of the state. Its loyalty is to the Jewish people and its responsibility is to it [i.e., the Jewish people] alone. As the owner of JNF land, the JNF does not have to act with equality towards all citizens of the state." The JNF position was upheld by a 2007 law that passed its first reading by a comfortable majority in the Israeli parliament (64 to 16). See "Knesset Approves Bill on Preliminary Reading to Restrict Jewish National Fund Lands Exclusively to Jewish Citizens," *Adalah Newsletter*, July 2007, https:// www.adalah.org/uploads/oldfiles/newsletter/eng/jul07/jul07.html. See also Adalah's special report on JNF, http://www.adalah.org/eng/jnf.php; and, for all of Adalah's papers on the JNF, see https://www.adalah.org/en/tag/index/514.

14. Shortly after 1948, an official in the Israeli Ministry of Religious Affairs wrote that "the Mamilla Cemetery in Jerusalem is considered to be one of the most prominent Muslim cemeteries, where seventy thousand Muslim warriors from Salah al-Din al-Ayyoubi's [Saladin's] armies are interred, along with many Muslim scholars. Israel will always know how to protect and respect this site." Yaacov Yehoshua, quoted in Ben-Arieh, "The Tolerance Museum and the Mamilla Cemetery."

15. See Gershon Baskin, "Encountering Peace: A City of Tolerance, Not a Museum of Tolerance," *Jerusalem Post*, 4 November 2008.

16. See Arab Association for Human Rights, *Annual Review of Human Rights Violations of the Arab Palestinian Minority in Israel* (Cairo, 2006), 133–35.

17. Meron Benvenisti, "The Hypocrisy of Tolerance," *Ha'aretz*, 9 February 2006.

18. Benvenisti.

19. Benvenisti.

20. "Israeli Court Clears Way for Jerusalem Museum," Associated Press, 29 October 2008.

21. See Patrick Wolfe, "Settler Colonialism and the Elimination of the Native," *Journal of Genocide Research* 8 (2006): 387–410; Wolfe, "Structure and Event: Settler Colonialism, Time, and the Question of Genocide," in Dirk Moses, ed., *Empire, Colony, Genocide: Conquest, Occupation, and Subaltern Resistance in World History* (Oxford: Berghahn Books, 2008), 102–31; Gabriel Piterberg, *The Returns of Zionism: Myths, Politics, and Scholarship in Israel* (London: Verso, 2008); Lorenzo Veracini, *Israel and Settler Society* (London: Pluto Press, 2006); and the classic by Maxime Rodinson, *Israel: A Settler Colonial State?* (Atlanta: Pathfinder Press, 1973).

22. Mohammed Hamdi Bader, quoted in Martin Patience, "Row over Israeli Tolerance Museum," *BBC News,* 17 February 2006, news.bbc.co.uk/2/hi /middle_east/4721336.stm.

23. Hier, quoted in "Israeli Court OKs Museum of Tolerance's Controversial Branch," *Culture Monster* (blog), *Los Angeles Times,* 29 October 2008, https:// latimesblogs.latimes.com/culturemonster/2008/10/a-frank-gehry-d.html; and in Yaakov Lappin, "Wiesenthal Dean Rejects Museum Protests as Extremist Agitation," *Jerusalem Post,* 6 November 2008.

24. Hier, quoted in "Israeli Court OKs Museum of Tolerance's Controversial Branch."

25. Mohammad Hussein, quoted in Etgar Lefkovits, "Museum of Tolerance Construction Resumes in Jerusalem," *Jerusalem Post,* 30 October 2008.

26. Kamal Hatib, quoted in Lappin, "Wiesenthal Dean Rejects Museum Protests as Extremist Agitation."

27. "Israeli Court Clears Way for Jerusalem Museum"; Lefkovits, "Museum of Tolerance Construction Resumes in Jerusalem." The court's decision should be read, as well, in the context of a long history of Orthodox Jewish opposition to archaeological projects and to the desecration of cemeteries in particular.

28. See Makdisi, *Palestine Inside Out,* esp. 15–54.

29. See International Court of Justice, *Advisory Opinion on the Legal Consequences of the Construction of a Wall in the Occupied Palestinian Territory,* 9 July 2004, United Nations, https://www.un.org/unispal/document/auto-insert-178825/.

30. See Jeff Halper, "Dismantling the Matrix of Control," Middle East Research and Information Project, 11 September 2009, https://merip .org/2009/09/dismantling-the-matrix-of-control/; Office for the Coordination of Humanitarian Affairs (OCHA), *West Bank Movement and Access Update* (United Nations, June 2009); and OCHA, *West Bank Access Restrictions* (United Nations, October 2017). See also OCHA's map of West Bank access restrictions, June 2020, https://www.ochaopt.org/sites/default/files/westbank_a0_25_06_ 2020_final.pdf.

31. I have chosen to use this term rather than the more conventional "settle-ment," because it more accurately conveys the legal status of Jewish residential complexes established in the occupied territories in violation of international law.

32. "A Regime of Jewish Supremacy from the Jordan River to the Mediterra-nean Sea: This Is Apartheid," *B'tselem*, 12 January 2021, https://www.btselem .org/publications/fulltext/202101_this_is_apartheid.

33. Eyal Weizman, "1. Introduction to the Politics of Verticality," Open Democracy, 23 April 2002, https://www.opendemocracy.net/en/article_801jsp/; Weizman, *Hollow Land: Israel's Architecture of Occupation* (London: Verso, 2007).

34. See W. J. T. Mitchell, "Christo's Gates and Gilo's Wall," *Critical Inquiry* 32, no. 4 (Summer 2006).

35. Mattiyahu Drobles, quoted in Makdisi, *Palestine Inside Out*, 120–22.

36. See W. J. T. Mitchell, "Imperial Landscape," in W. J. T. Mitchell, ed., *Land-scape and Power* (Chicago: University of Chicago Press, 1994), 28–29.

37. Rafi Segal and Eyal Weizman, "The Mountain: Principles of Building in Heights," in Segal and Weizman, eds., *A Civilian Occupation: The Politics of Israeli Architecture* (London: Verso, 2003), 85–86.

38. Kriston Capps, "A Monument to Frank Gehry," *Guardian*, 2 April 2009.

39. Hal Foster, "Why All the Hoopla?" *London Review of Books*, 23 August 2001.

40. Ad in *LA Times*, quoted in Deborah Borda et al., *Symphony: Frank Gehry's Walt Disney Concert Hall* (Los Angeles: LA Philharmonic, n.d.), 54.

41. Foster, "Why All the Hoopla?"

42. http://www.arcspace.com/architects/gehry/gug_ny, accessed May 2010.

43. J. Fiona Ragheb, "Sites of Passage," in Ragheb, ed., *Frank Gehry, Architect* (New York: Guggenheim Museum, 2002), 345.

44. Jean-Louis Cohen, "Frankly Urban: Gehry from Billboards to Bilbao," in Ragheb, *Frank Gehry*, 335.

45. See Foster, "Why All the Hoopla?"

46. See, for example, Riccardo Bianchini, "Museum of Tolerance Jerusalem (MOTJ): History of a Controversial Project," *Inexhibit*, 2 November 2019, https://www.inexhibit.com/case-studies/jerusalem-museum-tolerance-chyutin-architects.

47. These quotations are from the 2003–11 Museum of Tolerance Jerusalem website, http://motj.com, which was taken down in 2011 and is no longer avail-able, even via the Wayback Machine on archive.org.

48. Gehry, quoted in Freedman, "Frank Gehry's Mideast Peace Plan."

49. The artist's impressions of Gehry's design have all been removed from the museum website, but some of them, including this image of the hanging wall in front of the visitor center, can be found in the article in *Critical Inquiry* that was

the precursor of this chapter. See Saree Makdisi, "The Architecture of Erasure," *Critical Inquiry* 36, no. 3 (Spring 2010): fig. 12, p. 546.

50. The illegality of Israel's colonial project in East Jerusalem has been repeatedly noted by international legal bodies. To name but one example, UN Security Council Resolution 465 (1980) reiterates that "all measures taken by Israel to change the physical character, demographic composition, institutional structure or status of the Palestinian and other Arab territories occupied since 1967, including Jerusalem, or any part thereof have no legal validity and that Israel's policy and practices of settling parts of its population and new immigrants in those territories constitute a flagrant violation of the Geneva Convention relative to the Protection of Civilian Persons in Time of War and also constitute a serious obstruction to achieving a comprehensive, just and lasting peace in the Middle East." The ICJ Advisory Opinion of 2004 makes the same point.

51. Dugard, quoted in Makdisi, *Palestine Inside Out*, 101.

52. See Makdisi, *Palestine Inside Out*, 94–125.

53. Kimchi, quoted in Makdisi, *Palestine Inside Out*, 103.

54. Cheshin, quoted in Makdisi, *Palestine Inside Out*, 103.

55. Thus, for example, although Palestinians today constitute a third of Jerusalem's population, they have access to less than 10 percent of the land within the city limits, which were illegally expanded after 1967 by taking land from West Bank villages near Jerusalem and incorporating it within the city's expanded limits. Almost all the territory annexed to Jerusalem after 1967 is today off-limits to Palestinian development because the land is either already built on by Jewish colonies or is being held in reserve for their future expansion. Since 1967, more than 100,000 housing units have been built for Jewish colonists in East Jerusalem, with active Israeli government sponsorship. Over the same period, the municipality has granted only 9,000 permits for housing units for Palestinians seeking to build in East Jerusalem. See Makdisi, *Palestine Inside Out*, 103–13.

56. See Office for the Coordination of Humanitarian Affairs, *The Planning Crisis in East Jerusalem: Understanding the Phenomenon of "Illegal" Construction* (United Nations, April 2009).

57. Figures from B'tselem. See "Statistics on Demolition of Houses as Punishment, 1987–2004," B'tselem, 1 January 2011, http://www.btselem.org/english/Planning_and_Building/East_Jerusalem_Statistics.asp.

58. See Rory McCarthy, "Israel 'Using Tourist Sites to Assert Control over East Jerusalem,'" *Guardian*, 10 May 2009.

59. See Adina Hoffman, "Archaeological Digs Stoke Conflict in Jerusalem," *Nation*, 30 July 2008.

60. Quoted in Paul Richter, "Clinton Criticizes Israeli Plan to Raze Palestinian Homes," *Los Angeles Times*, 5 March 2009.

61. Klein, *Vatican to Vegas*, 11; see also 333 (emphases in original).

62. "City of David—Tours of Biblical Jerusalem," City of David, accessed 24 July 2021, http://www.cityofdavid.org.il/en/tours/city-david/city-david-tours-biblical-jerusalem.

63. "About Us," City of David, accessed 24 July 2021, http://www.cityofdavid.org.il/en/about.

64. See, for example, Meron Rappaport, "Islamic-Era Skeletons 'Disappeared' from Elad-Sponsored Dig," *Ha'aretz*, 1 April 2005.

65. Nadia Abu El-Haj, *Facts on the Ground: Archaeological Practice and Territorial Self-Fashioning in Israeli Society* (Chicago: University of Chicago Press, 2001), 146.

66. See Jonathan Cook, "Archaeology Used Politically to Push Out Silwan's Residents," *Electronic Intifada*, 26 September 2008.

67. Mizrachi, quoted in Cook.

68. Makdisi, "Architecture of Erasure."

69. "Response to Saree Makdisi's 'The Architecture of Erasure,'" *Critical Inquiry* 36 (Spring 2010): 560–62 (emphasis added).

70. Sebastian Jordana, "Museum of Tolerance in Jerusalem/Chyutin Architects," *ArchDaily*, 11 October 2010, https://www.archdaily.com/81319/museum-of-tolerance-in-jerusalem-chyutin-architects.

71. See the images at Alison Furuto, "Museum of Tolerance Jerusalem/Bracha Chyutin, Michael Chyutin, Jacques Dahan, Ariel Noyman," *ArchDaily*, 20 December 2011, https://www.archdaily.com/193490/museum-of-tolerance-jerusalem-bracha-chyutin-michael-chyutin-jacques-dahan-ariel-noyman.

72. "Jerusalem's Museum of Tolerance Remains a Mystery," *Globes*, 12 April 2018.

73. "Jerusalem's Museum of Tolerance."

74. "Jerusalem's Museum of Tolerance."

75. All quotations in "Jerusalem's Museum of Tolerance."

76. "Hier."

77. "About the Project," Simon Wiesenthal Center, accessed July 2021, https://www.wiesenthal.com/museums/museum-of-tolerance-jerusalem/about-the-project.html.

78. https://www.wiesenthal.com/assets/pdf/motj-digital-brochure-11-2019.pdf (removed from Web).

79. Some of the criticism of the choice of site even hinges on reframing the issue in Jewish terms. "This is not a Muslim issue, it is not an Arab issue, it is not a Palestinian issue. In my view, this is a Jewish, an Israeli and a Jerusalemite issue," Gershon Baskin states; in other words, it's not so much about the Other as it is about the self, after all. "There is something profoundly disturbing about the idea of putting a Jewish Museum of Tolerance on a plot of ground where Muslims have been burying their dead for most of the last 800 years," admits Eric Joffe, president of the Union for Reform Judaism in a piece he wrote for the *Jewish*

Journal of Los Angeles. But what is the point of his critique? "If one were intent on undermining Israel's claim to Jerusalem, there would be no better way to accomplish this goal than to build a Jewish museum atop a historic Muslim cemetery in the heart of the city." It's especially telling, in fact, that Joffe says in his piece that the cemetery was in use "until at least the 1930s," which (given that he cites many of the same sources I have cited in this article which indicate that the cemetery was used until 1948) is an odd way of stepping around the formative crisis of 1948—the Nakba—and what it means for both Israelis and Palestinians. See Baskin, "Encountering Peace"; and Eric Joffe, "Is There No Other Site for a Museum of Tolerance?" *Jewish Journal,* 11 February 2009.

80. See, for example, the posts on Silverstein's blog, *Tikun Olam,* concerning the museum project (www.richardsilverstein.com).

81. "Where are the rabbis? Where are those Jerusalemites and Israelis who believe that in Jerusalem we can truly create a city of tolerance, understanding and peace between civilizations?" asks Gershon Baskin, looking around for more dissenting voices, and not finding any. See Baskin, "Encountering Peace."

82. "In a city sacred to the majority of the world's population, the bedrock test of the legitimacy of Israeli rule is the degree of respect the Jewish state accords the sacred sites of other faiths," writes Bradley Burston in *Ha'aretz,* for example. "The chosen location of a Muslim cemetery in Jewish West Jerusalem casts doubt on Israel's guardianship of holy sites. It calls into question not only Israel's moral claims to ruling all of Jerusalem, it erodes its claim to any of it." Bradley Burston, "Dividing Jerusalem, One Wall at a Time," *Ha'aretz,* 11 November 2008.

83. Thomas Paine, *Rights of Man* (1792; repr., Harmondsworth, UK: Penguin, 1985), 51.

84. William Blake, *The Marriage of Heaven and Hell* (London, 1790–93).

85. Brown, *Regulating Aversion,* 135.

86. See Brown, 136.

87. This and the following quotations (emphases added) are all from the 2003–11 website Museum of Tolerance Jerusalem, motj.org, which has since been taken down.

88. Hier, quoted in Freedman, "Frank Gehry's Mideast Peace Plan."

89. "Declaration on Principles of Tolerance," 16 November 1995, UNESCO: Legal Instruments, accessed 25 July 2021, portal.unesco.org/en/ev.php-URL_ID=13175&URL_DO=DO_TOPIC&URL_SECTION=201.html (emphasis added).

90. See David Theo Goldberg, "The Power of Tolerance," in Tony Kushner et al., eds., *Philosemitism, Antisemitism, and the Jews: Perspectives from Antiquity to the Twentieth Century* (London: Ashgate, 2004). Goldberg notes that the term is hardly innocent or neutral, being typically used by the powerful to offer a place of inclusion, exclusively on the terms of those who are powerful, to less

powerful others. See also Ghassan Hage, *White Nation: Fantasies of White Supremacy in a Multicultural Society* (New York: Routledge, 2000), 78–104; and Brown, *Regulating Aversion*.

91. Narcissistic nationalists, Ghassan Hage explains, are "totally self-obsessed with self-affirmation at the expense of being with others," particularly those others—in this case the Palestinians—who are seen to threaten the nationalists' claim to a pacified national space cleansed of the last taint of otherness, which is, in the situation Israel finds itself in, physically impossible. Indeed, "this is why colonial nationalism [including Zionism] has always been more narcissistic than metropolitan nationalism," Hage points out; "not because it was colonial as such, but because it never managed to pacify the space under its control to the same extent as in the home country." This is the logic, he adds, that "has contributed to making Israeli nationalism a particularly virulent form of narcissistic, self-obsessed self-affirmation." Ghassan Hage, *Alter-Politics: Critical Anthropology and the Radical Imagination* (Melbourne: Melbourne University Press, 2015), 157–58.

92. "Meet the Oscar-Winning Rabbi Whose Blessing Hollywood Seeks Each Awards Season," *Hollywood Reporter*, 26 February 2016.

CONCLUSION

1. See "Palestinian Civil Society Call for BDS," 9 July 2005, BDS: Freedom, Justice, Equality, https://bdsmovement.net/call.

2. I discuss BDS and the one- and two-state solutions at length in *Palestine Inside Out*.

3. David Landau, "Maximum Jews, Minimum Palestinians," *Ha'aretz*, accessed 26 July 2021, https://www.haaretz.com/1.4759973.

4. See, among other books on this question, Noam Chomsky, *The Fateful Triangle* (Boston: South End Press, 1999); Stephen Green, *Taking Sides: America's Secret Relations with a Militant Israel* (New York: William Morrow, 1984); Ussama Makdisi, *Faith Misplaced* (New York: PublicAffairs, 2010); Stephen Walt and John Mearsheimer, *The Lobby* (New York: Farrar, Straus & Giroux, 2008); Rashid Khalidi, *Brokers of Deceit: How the U.S. Has Undermined Peace in the Middle East* (Boston: Beacon Press, 2014).

5. "Security Council: Quick Links," United Nations, Dag Hammarskjöld Library, accessed 26 July 2021, http://research.un.org/en/docs/sc/quick.

6. Peter Beinart, "I No Longer Believe in a Jewish State," *New York Times*, 8 July 2020.

7. Masha Gessen, "Why an Israeli Human-Rights Organization Decided to Call Israel an Apartheid Regime," *New Yorker*, 27 January 2021. See also "A Regime of Jewish Supremacy."

8. Some of what I argue in the pages that follow I also elaborate in a piece I published as "The Nakba Is Now," in *The Nation*, 14–21 June 2021.

9. Michael Arria, "Vast Majority of Dem Voters Support McCollum Bill Promoting Palestinian Rights, but Less than 13% of House Dems Back It," *Mondoweiss*, 15 June 2021, https://mondoweiss.net/2021/06/vast-majority-of-dem-voters-support-mccollum-bill-promoting-palestinian-rights-but-less-than-13-of-house-dems-back-it.

10. "A Letter against Apartheid," accessed 27 July 2021, https://www.againstapartheid.com (emphasis added).

POSTSCRIPT

1. See the text of the resolution at MLA Members for Justice in Palestine, 27 July 2021, https://mlaboycott.wordpress.com/resolution.

2. See "2017 Delegate Assembly Resolutions," Modern Language Association, accessed 27 July 2021, https://www.mla.org/About-Us/Governance/Delegate-Assembly/Motions-and-Resolutions/2017-Delegate-Assembly-Resolutions.

3. Berman and Nelson quoted in Scott Jaschik, "MLA Votes to 'Refrain' from Backing Israel Boycott," *Inside Higher Education*, 15 June 2017.

4. Russell Berman, "The Goal of the Boycott," *Los Angeles Review of Books*, 16 March 2014. The following quotations come from this essay.

5. There is, however, plenty of evidence for the legality of discrimination, which Berman also does not address. In addition to taking a look at Adalah's database of discriminatory laws (see chapter 2), he might consider further the case of the Jewish National Fund, which he does mention in passing but without developing the extent of the relationship between that explicitly racist organization and the state that has empowered it in its role in managing state land. See chapter 1.

6. "Betsy DeVos Slammed for Calling Historically Black Colleges School Choice Pioneers," *Los Angeles Times*, 28 February 2017.

7. See Peled-Elhanan, *Palestine in Israeli School Books*.

8. Human Rights Watch, *Second Class: Discrimination Against Palestinian Arab Children in Israel's Schools* (New York, 2001), https://www.hrw.org/reports/2001/israel2/index.htm#TopOfPage. See also the report by the Israeli Association for the Advancement for Civic Equality (Sikkuy), *Representation of Arab Citizens in the Institutions of Higher Education in Israel*, ed. Nohad Ali (November 2013), https://www.sikkuy.org.il/wp-content/uploads/2013/11/English_final-2014_representation_higher_education1.pdf.

9. See, for example, "Court Allows Haifa University to Continue Contentious Dorm Policy," *Ha'aretz*, 11 April 2007; and "No Place in University Dorms for Arabs Who Didn't Serve in IDF," *Ha'aretz*, 12 August 2010.

10. See the Sikkuy, *Representation of Arab Citizens in the Institutions of Higher Education in Israel*, 20–21.

11. Discriminatory Laws Database, https://www.adalah.org/en/content /view/7771. The Admissions Committee Law of 2011, for instance, legalizes and renders de jure what had been the de facto operation of admissions committees that determine access to land and housing in towns built on state land—allowing them to reject applicants "unsuitable to the social life of the community" or "the social and cultural fabric of the town." This policy allows towns to preserve a uniquely Jewish-Zionist character by denying access to Palestinian citizens.

12. Carry Nelson Russell Berman, "Anti-Zionism and the Humanities: A Response to Saree Makdisi," *Fathom*, April 2018, n.p.

13. For the text of the law, see "Basic Law: Human Dignity and Liberty," Israel Ministry of Foreign Affairs, 17 March 1992, https://www.mfa.gov.il/mfa /mfa-archive/1992/pages/basic%20law-%20human%20dignity%20and%20liberty-.aspx.

14. Nelson and Berman, "Anti-Zionism and the Humanities." They follow this, by the way, with several paragraphs extolling via legal references Israel's extraordinary commitment to equality—not one of which has anything to do with the substance of my argument about racial discrimination—culminating in a digression on women's rights in Israel and the Equal Remuneration for Female and Male Employees Law of 1964, which, they assure us, "aims to ensure equality in employees' salaries." Therefore, they insist, Israel does legally guarantee equality after all!

15. Nelson and Berman.

16. This statement is from a 1972 decision, upheld in 2013, involving Jewish petitioners who wanted the state to recognize what they claimed was their *Israeli* rather than the *Jewish* nationality actually recorded on their identity documents issued by the state. See chapter 2 in the present volume.

17. See chapter 2, note 40.

18. "Israel: Discriminatory Land Policies Hem in Palestinians," Human Rights Watch, 12 May 2020, https://www.hrw.org/news/2020/05/12/israel-discriminatory-land-policies-hem-palestinians.

19. Oren Ziv, "Israel Steps up Campaign against Bedouin Village It Demolished 173 Times," *972 Mag*, 28 January 2020.

20. Nelson and Berman, "Anti-Zionism and the Humanities."

21. Nelson and Berman.

22. Nelson and Berman.

23. "To this day," Yinon Cohen and Neve Gordon point out, "the word *Palestinian* does not appear in Israel's statistical abstracts, while only in 1995 did the word *Arab* emerge, after decades in which Palestinians were referred to by their religion or as non-Jews." Cohen and Gordon, "Israel's Biospatial Politics," 203.

24. Haifa Declaration; see chapter 2 of the present volume.

25. Frank Giles, "Golda Meir: 'Who Can Blame Israel?,'" interview in *Sunday Times*, 15 June 1969, 12. It's worth noting that Israelis did not have a specific identity as Israelis until 1948!

26. Nelson and Berman, "Anti-Zionism and the Humanities."

27. Nelson and Nelson.

28. World Union of Jewish Students, *Hasbara Handbook: Promoting Israel on Campus* (Jerusalem, 2012), 8, www.middle-east-info.org/take/wujshasbara.pdf.

29. "About," Israel on Campus Coalition, 29 July 2021, https://israelcc.org /about-us.

30. See "'Working Definition' of Anti-Semitism," 8 February 2007, US State Department Archive, https://2001-2009.state.gov/g/drl/rls/56589.htm.

31. "'Working Definition' of Anti-Semitism."

32. "Defining Anti-Semitism," 8 June 1010, US State Department Archive, https://2009-2017.state.gov/j/drl/rls/fs/2010/122352.htm.

33. Ben White, "Israel Lobbyists Finally Concede That EU Has Ditched Anti-Semitism 'Definition,'" *Electronic Intifada*, 5 December 2013, https:// electronicintifada.net/blogs/ben-white/israel-lobbyists-finally-concede-eu-has-ditched-anti-semitism-definition. See also "EU Drops Its 'Working Definition' of Anti-Semitism," *Times of Israel*, 5 December 2013.

34. Seth Berkman, "Anti-Semitism Fight Hinges on Definition," *Forward*, 25 September 2012, https://forward.com/news/israel/163105/anti-semitism-fight-hinges-on-definition/?p=all.

35. HR35 (2011–2012), *California Legislative Information*, corrected August 29, 2012, https://leginfo.legislature.ca.gov/faces/billTextClient.xhtml?bill_id= 201120120HR35.

36. Larry Gordon, "Definition of Anti-Semitism Provokes Campus Debates," *Los Angeles Times*, 18 May 2015, https://www.latimes.com/local/education/la-me-ln-campuses-israel-20150518-story.html.

37. Saree Makdisi, "Wrongfully Treating Academic Debate as Anti-Semitism," *Los Angeles Times*, 26 May 2015, https://www.latimes.com/opinion/op-ed/la-oe-makdisi-criticism-of-israel-at-uc-not-anti-semitism-20150526-story.html.

38. Steve Gorman, "University of California Board Weighs Statement on Anti-Semitism," Reuters, 17 March 2016, https://www.reuters.com/article/us-california-discrimination-idUSKCN0WK081.

39. Hank Reichman, "CUCFA and AAUP Statement on UC Regent Blum's Remarks," *Academe* (blog), 25 September 2015, https://academeblog.org/2015 /09/25/cucfa-and-aaup-statement-on-uc-regent-blums-remarks.

40. Reichman, "CUCFA and AAUP Statement on UC Regent Blum's Remarks."

41. Saree Makdisi and Judith Butler, "Suppressing Criticism of Zionism on Campus Is Catastrophic Censorship," *Los Angeles Times*, 23 March 2016, https:// www.latimes.com/opinion/op-ed/la-oe-makdisibutler-uc-antisemitism-report-20160323-story.html.

42. Cassie Patton, "University of California Softens Anti-Semitism Statement," Reuters, 23 March 2016, https://www.reuters.com/article/us-california-discrimination/university-of-california-softens-anti-semitism-statement-idUSKCN0WQ03F.

43. See "Working Definition of Antisemitism," International Holocaust Remembrance Alliance, accessed 30 July 2021, https://www.holocaustremembrance .com/resources/working-definitions-charters/working-definition-antisemitism.

44. "Defining Anti-Semitism," US State Department, 26 May 2016, https:// www.state.gov/defining-anti-semitism.

45. "The Working Definition of Anti-Semitism: What Does It Mean, Why Is It Important, and What Should We Do With It?" United Nations Human Rights: Office of the High Commissioner, accessed 30 July 2021, https://www.ohchr .org/Documents/Issues/Religion/Submissions/JBI-Annex1.pdf.

46. Dan Sabbagh, "Labour Adopts IHRA Antisemitism Definition in Full," *Guardian*, 4 September 2018, https://www.theguardian.com/politics/2018 /sep/04/labour-adopts-ihra-antisemitism-definition-in-full.

47. Natan Sharansky, "Report Encourages College Campuses to Adopt IHRA Definition of Anti-Semitism," *Detroit Jewish News*, 31 January 2020, https:// thejewishnews.com/2020/01/31/report-encourages-college-campuses-to-adopt-ihra-definition-of-anti-semitism.

48. Saree Makdisi, "The Push to Quash Criticism of Israel Is a Push to Quash Free Speech," *Nation*, 19 December 2019, https://www.thenation.com/article /politics/executive-order-free-speech.

49. I point this out in my *Nation* piece on the Trump executive order, from which I am quoting here.

50. "Biden Administration 'Enthusiastically Embraces' IHRA Antisemitism Definition," *Middle East Eye*, 2 March 2021, https://www.middleeasteye .net/news/biden-administration-enthusiastically-embraces-ihra-antisemitism-definition.

51. See George Orwell, *1984* (New York: Signet, 1950), 4.

52. Nelson and Berman, "Anti-Zionism and the Humanities."

53. Nelson and Berman.

54. "About Us," Fathomjournal.org.

Index

tolerance: affirmation of, 140; denial of Palestinians, 44; embodiment of, 1, 2; Eshchar, 54, 56; and gay rights, 78-81; grave
desecration, 131, 136; homonationalism,
85; and inclusivity, 10; Israel, 56, 74,
136; Jewish Israeli ascribing to, 57; monument to, 6, 17; necropolitical logic of
Israeli apartheid, 68; racism, 183; in
sports, 76-77; Tel Aviv, 93-94, 95; Zionism, 15, 17, 139, 141
Trump, Donald, 47, 147-48, 149, 158,
182-83

United States: critics of Israeli policy, 176;
gay rights, 81; *hasbara* outlets, 92, 175;
indigenous people in, 43-44, 146; Israeli
apartheid and US policy, 178-79; Israeli
apartheid denied in, 159, 164, 183; and
Israeli democracy, 47-50, 53; and Israeli
rebranding, 75, 77; Museum of Tolerance
donors, 104, 133; Progressive Except Palestine (PEP), 7-8; support for Israel, 5, 9,
13, 60, 67, 74, 146-47, 149; Zionism in,
141, 182

Village under the Forest, The, 37

Warren, Elizabeth, 48
Waters, Roger, 155
Weitz, Josef, 21, 30, 33, 35
Weizman, Eyal, 22, 23, 112, 115-16, 120
Wolfe, Patrick, 20, 45, 54

Yehoshua, A. B., 29, 44
Yiftachel, Oren, 34, 41
Yisrael Beiteinu, 3

Zionism: abandoned by youthful liberals, 74;
(ab)uses of gender and sexuality, 102;
affirmation of classic liberal values, 7;
American, 141; anti-Zionism, 180, 181;
claim to Palestine, 134; conflict with Palestinians, 104, 141, 145, 151; criticism
of, 180; earlier settler, 89; ethno-religious
monoculture, 41; expulsion of Palestinians, 3; founded on denial of knowledge,
5-6; heteronormative, 88-90; and liberal
equal rights, 147; Los Angeles strand of,
118; museum of, 15; Museum of Tolerance Muslim cemetary site, 104, 134;
negating Palestinian claims to Palestine,
2; Orientalist terms, 79, 83, 102; and
Palestinians, 8-9, 11; pinkwashing, 102;
racism, 84, 139; resistance to, 82, 102,
139; structural bifurcation, 7, 8; support
for, 5, 9; supporting racial discrimination
without recognizing it, 7; support of outside implicated subjects, 11; system of
accumulation and displacement, 7; tolerance, 15, 17, 139, 141; and Trump
administration, 147; and white, Western
values, 79, 83
Zurayq, Constantine, 19

Founded in 1893,
UNIVERSITY OF CALIFORNIA PRESS
publishes bold, progressive books and journals
on topics in the arts, humanities, social sciences,
and natural sciences—with a focus on social
justice issues—that inspire thought and action
among readers worldwide.

The UC PRESS FOUNDATION
raises funds to uphold the press's vital role
as an independent, nonprofit publisher, and
receives philanthropic support from a wide
range of individuals and institutions—and from
committed readers like you. To learn more, visit
ucpress.edu/supportus.

Milton Keynes UK
Ingram Content Group UK Ltd.
UKHW040658070824
446492UK00002B/19/J